Karen Br...
TUSCANY &

San Gimignano
Tuscany

Italy Overview

— Romantic Tuscany
— Haunting Beauty of Umbria

| 0 | 100 | 200 KM |
| 0 | 100 | 200 Mi |

Contents

MAPS

    Places to Stay & Itineraries   Color Section at Front of Book

INTRODUCTION

    Tuscany & Umbria   1

    About Tuscany   2

    About Umbria   3

    About Driving Itineraries   4

    Handy Information   5

    Staying in Bed & Breakfasts   17

    Staying in Hotels   19

    Staying in Self Catering Accommodation   20

DRIVING ITINERARIES

    Romantic Tuscany   21

    The Haunting Beauty of Umbria   41

PLACES TO STAY—B&Bs, HOTELS, SELF CATERING

    Tuscany   53

    Umbria   213

INDEX   269

To Rick,
I look forward to exploring
Tuscany & Umbria together!
Love, Karen

Cover painting: San Gimignano, Tuscany

Authors: Nicole Franchini, Clare Brown, June Eveleigh Brown.

Editors: Clare Brown, Karen Brown, Debbie Tokumoto, Nicole Franchini, Kim Holmsen.

Illustrations: Elisabetta Franchini, Barbara Maclurcan Tapp.

Cover painting: Jann Pollard.

Maps: Rachael Kircher-Randolph, Andrew Harris.

Technical support: Andrew Harris.

Copyright © 2010 by Karen Brown's Guides Inc.

Distributed by National Book Network, 15200 NBN Way, Blue Ridge Summit, PA 17214, USA. Tel: 717-794-3800 or 1-800-462-6420, Fax: 1-800-338-4500, Email: custserv@nbnbooks.com

A catalog record for this book is available from the British Library.

ISSN 1557 3702

Tuscany & Umbria

Tuscany and Umbria are two of our favorite destinations. The two itineraries included in this book are among the most popular of those featured in our other guides to Italy. We thought it would be a good idea to marry all of our recommended places to stay (hotels as well as bed & breakfasts) to our selected sightseeing and driving instructions. The result is our first truly regional guidebook. We hope you will find it an invaluable companion in planning your own vacation to this wonderful part of the world with its architectural treasures, historical cities, medieval hill towns, vineyards and enchanting countryside.

About Tuscany

Tuscany has become synonymous with Italy. Travelers flock to its famous cities and well-preserved countryside not only to view the breathtaking art found here, but also to be swept away by the magic of its enchanting landscapes. Florence is a highlight with its rich display of Renaissance masterpieces all concentrated within the historical center of three square kilometers. One must also visit the Piazza del Campo in Siena, one of Italy's most stunning squares, hosting the world-famous Palio horse races in July and August. The charming medieval hill towns of Montepulciano, Montalcino, and San Gimignano are home to some of the region's finest wines. The small historic cities of Lucca, Pisa, Arezzo, and Cortona, each with its own individual architectural characteristics, are also well worth visiting. Tuscany is also home to the famous Chianti area, with its endless vineyards and monumental castles. Maremma, in the southern, lesser-known reaches of the region touching the sea, is rich in Etruscan history and dotted with numerous stone villages to explore.

About Umbria

Enchanting Umbria, bordering Tuscany, is located in the lush heart of Italy. A circular road in the center of the region touches the well-known cities of Perugia, Assisi, Spello, Spoleto, Todi, and Deruta. The two most spectacular towns outside of the loop are Gubbio and Orvieto. Highlights include the town of Perugia, a modern-day town with the stunning Palazzo Dei Priori where the majority of the finest Umbrian paintings are exhibited in the Galleria Nazionale dell'Umbria. Assisi is another highlight with its many beautiful churches, including the mystical Basilica di San Francesco. The northern reaches of Umbria offer remote countryside and unspoiled landscapes. Umbria is home to world-famous ceramic centers, first and foremost, Deruta, and then Gubbio, producing hand-painted pieces for the past 600 years. Umbria also boasts the famous Orvieto Classico wine: varieties can be tasted at enotecas in Orvieto with its monumental cathedral and astounding façade.

About Driving Itineraries

The Tuscany and Umbria itineraries can be easily tailored to fit your exact time frame and suit your own particular interests. If your time is limited, you can certainly follow just a segment of an itinerary. We have not specified the number of nights at each destination, since to do so seemed much too confining. Some travelers like to see as much as possible in a short period of time. For others, just the thought of packing and unpacking each night makes them shudder in horror and they would never stop for less than three or four nights at any destination. A third type of tourist doesn't like to travel at all—the destination is the focus and they use this guide to find the perfect place from which they never wander except for daytime excursions. So, use this guide as a reference to plan your personalized trip.

Our advice is not to rush. Part of the joy of traveling is to settle in at a place to stay that you like and use it as a hub from which to take side trips to explore the countryside. When you dash too quickly from place to place, you never have the opportunity to get to know the owners and to become friends with other guests. Read about the places to stay and decide which are most suited to your taste and budget.

Handy Information

The following pointers are given in alphabetical order, not in order of importance.

AFFILIATIONS

A number of properties recommended in our guides belong to private membership organizations. These associations impose their own criteria for selection and membership standards and have established a reputation for the particular type of property they include. History Traveller and Abitare La Storia are affiliations of hotels in Italy, while Relais & Châteaux includes luxurious hotels and restaurants worldwide. Properties that belong to these organizations have *History Traveller, Abitare la Storia* or *Relais & Châteaux* noted on their description page.

AIRFARE

Karen Brown's Guides have long recommended Auto Europe for their excellent car rental services. Their air travel division, Destination Europe, an airline broker working with major American and European carriers, offers deeply discounted coach- and business-class fares to over 200 European gateway cities. It also gives Karen Brown travelers an additional 5% discount off its already highly competitive prices (cannot be combined with any other offers or promotions). You can make reservations online via our website, *www.karenbrown.com*, or by phone at (800) 835-1555. When phoning, be sure to use the Karen Brown ID number 99006187 to secure your discount.

BANKS–CURRENCY

Normal banking hours are Monday through Friday from 8:30 am to 1:30 pm and 3 to 4 pm, with some city banks now opening on Saturday mornings. Cash machines accepting U.S. bank cash cards and credit cards are now widely distributed throughout Italy. An increasingly popular and convenient way to obtain foreign currency is simply to use your bankcard at an ATM machine. You pay a fixed fee for this but, depending on the amount you withdraw, it is usually less than the percentage-based fee charged to exchange currency or traveler's checks. *Cambio* signs outside and inside a bank indicate that it will exchange traveler's checks or give you cash from certain credit cards. Also privately run exchange offices are available in cities with more convenient hours and comparable rates. The euro is the official currency of most European Union countries, including Italy. Visit our website (*www.karenbrown.com*) for an easy-to-use online currency converter.

CAR RENTAL

An international driver's permit is not necessary for renting a car as a tourist: a foreign driver's license is valid for driving throughout Italy. Readers frequently ask our advice on car rental companies. We always use Auto Europe—a car rental broker that works with the major car rental companies to find the lowest possible price. They also offer motor homes and chauffeur services. Auto Europe's toll-free phone service, from every European country, connects you to their U.S.-based, 24-hour reservation center (ask for the Europe Phone Numbers Card to be mailed to you). Auto Europe offers our readers a 5% discount (cannot be combined with any other offers or promotions) and, occasionally, free upgrades. Be sure to use the Karen Brown ID number 99006187 to receive your discount and any special offers. You can make your own reservations online via our website, *www.karenbrown.com* (select *Auto Europe* from the home page), or by phone (800-223-5555).

CREDIT CARDS

Whether or not an establishment accepts credit cards is indicated in the list of icons at the bottom of each description by the symbol ▣ᶜᴿᴱᴰᴵᵀ. We have also specified in the accommodation description which cards are accepted as follows: AX–American Express, MC–MasterCard, VS–Visa, or simply, all major.

DISTANCES

Distances are indicated in kilometers (one kilometer equals 0.621 miles), calculated roughly into miles by cutting the kilometer distance in half. Distances between towns are also indicated in orange alongside the roads on the Touring Club Italiano maps. Italy is a compact country and distances are relatively short, yet you will be amazed at how dramatically the scenery can change in an hour's drive.

DRIVING

A car is a must for this type of travel—many places are inaccessible by any other means of transportation. Italy is not quite the "vehicular-free-for-all" you may have heard about, at least not outside major cities. Italians have a different relationship with the basic rules of the road: common maneuvers include running stop lights and stop signs, triple-parking, driving at 100 mph on the highways, passing on the right, and backing up at missed highway exits. But once out of the city, you will find it relatively easy to reach your destination. Road directions are quite good in Italy and people are very willing to help.

ENGLISH SPOKEN

At most hotels there is usually someone who speaks good English. This is not always the case with bed & breakfasts and self catering accommodation. We have indicated the degree of English spoken (fluent, good, some, very little, and none) at bed and breakfasts and self catering listings as well as other languages spoken. We would like to note, however, that this is just an indication, as the person who speaks English may or may not be there during your stay. In any case, it is helpful (not to mention rewarding) to have a few basic Italian phrases on hand. A phrase book or dictionary is indispensable. And when all else fails, the art of communicating with gestures is still very much alive in Italy!

FINDING YOUR ACCOMMODATION

At the front of the book is a key map of the whole of Italy plus maps showing each recommended place to stay's location. The pertinent regional map number is given at the right on the *top line* of each bed and breakfast's description. Directions to help you find your destination are given following the description. However, they are only guidelines, as it would be impossible to find the space to give more details, and to know from which direction the traveler is arriving. The beauty of many of these lodgings is that they are off the beaten track, but that characteristic may also make them very tricky to find. If you get lost, a common occurrence, first keep your sense of humor, then call the proprietors and/or ask locals at bars or gas stations for directions. It is important to know that addresses in the countryside often have no specific street name. *A common address consists of the farm name, sometimes a localita' (an unincorporated area, or vicinity, frequently not found on a map and outside the actual town named), and the town name followed by the province abbreviated in parentheses. (The accommodation is not necessarily **in** that town, but it serves as a post office reference.)* The *localita'* can also be the name of the road where the bed and breakfast is located, to make things more confusing. We state the *localita'* in the third line of the details and many times that name is the map reference name as well. Ask to be faxed a detailed map upon confirmation. Detailed maps for the area in which you will be traveling are essential and we recommend purchasing them in advance of your trip, both to aid in the planning of your journey and to avoid spending vacation time searching for the appropriate maps.

GASOLINE

Gas prices in Italy are the highest in Europe, and Americans often suspect a mistake when their first fill up comes to between $55 and $100 (most of it in taxes). Most stations now accept Visa credit cards, and the ERG stations accept American Express. Besides the AGIP stations on the autostrade which are almost always open, gas stations observe the same hours as merchants, closing in the afternoon from 12:30 to 4 and in the evening at 7:30. Be careful not to get caught running on empty in the afternoon! Many stations have a self-service pump that operates during the off hours (€ 10 or € 20 accepted).

HOLIDAYS

It is very important to know Italian holidays because most museums, shops, and offices are closed. National holidays are:

New Year's Day (January 1)   Assumption Day (August 15)
Epiphany (January 6)   All Saints' Day (November 1)
Easter (and the following Monday) Christmas (December 25)
Liberation Day (April 25)   Santo Stefano (December 26)
Labor Day (May 1)

ICONS

Icons allow us to provide additional information about our recommended properties. We have introduced the following icons in this guide to supplement each property's description. For easy reference, an icon key can also be found on the inside back cover flap.

❄ Air conditioning in rooms, ⊥ Beach nearby, ⬛ Breakfast included in room rate, 🐾 Children welcome, 🍲 Cooking classes offered, 🄲🅁🄴🄳🄸🅃 Credit cards accepted, 🍽 Dinner served upon request, ☎ Direct-dial telephone in room, 🐕 Dogs by special request, 🛗 Elevator, 🏃 Exercise room, @ Internet access available for guests, ⊻ Mini-refrigerator in rooms, 🚭 Some non-smoking rooms, **P** Parking available (free or paid), 🍴 Restaurant, ❀ Spa (massage etc.), 🏊 Swimming pool, 🎾 Tennis, 📺 Television with English channels in guestrooms, 💍 Wedding facilities, ♿ Wheelchair friendly, **W** Wireless available for guests, 🏌 Golf course nearby, 🥾 Hiking trails nearby, 🏇 Horseback riding nearby, ⛷ Skiing nearby, 🏄 Water sports nearby, 🍷 Wineries nearby.

INFORMATION

Italian Government Travel Offices (ENIT) can offer general information on various regions and their cultural attractions. They cannot offer specific information on restaurants and accommodations. If you have access to the Internet, visit the Italian Tourist Board's websites: *www.italiantourism.com* or *www.enit.it.* Offices are located in:

Chicago: Italian Government Travel Office, 500 N. Michigan Ave., Suite 2240, Chicago, IL 60611 USA; email: *enitch@italiantourism.com*, tel: (312) 644-0996, fax: (312) 644-3019.

Los Angeles: Italian Government Travel Office, 12400 Wilshire Blvd., Suite 550, Los Angeles, CA 90025, USA; email: *enitla@italiantourism.com*, tel: (310) 820-1898, fax: (310) 820-6357.

New York: Italian Government Travel Office, 630 5th Ave., Suite 1565, New York, NY 10111, USA; email: *enitny@italiantourism.com*, tel: (212) 245-4822, fax: (212) 586-9249.

Toronto: Italian Government Travel Office, 175 Bloor Street East, Suite 907, Toronto, Ontario M4W 3R8, Canada; email: *enit.canada@on.aibn.com*, tel: (416) 925-4882, fax: (416) 925-4799.

London: Italian State Tourist Office, 1 Princes Street, London WIB 2AY, England; email: *italy@italiantourism.co.uk*, tel: (020) 7408-1254, fax: (020) 7493-6695.

Sydney: Italian Government Travel Office, Level 4, 46 Market Street, Sydney NSW 2000, Australia; email: *italia@italiantourism.com.au*, tel: (61292) 621.666, fax: (61292) 621.677.

Rome: ENTE Nazionale Italiano per il Turismo (Italian Government Travel Office), Via Marghera, 2/6, Rome 00185, Italy; email: *sedecentrale@cert.enit.it*, tel: (06) 49711, fax: (06) 4463379.

MAPS

Detailed maps of Tuscany and Umbria are essential and we recommend purchasing them in advance of your trip, both to aid in the planning of your journey and to avoid spending vacation time searching for the appropriate maps. We like the regional Michelin maps (1 cm = 4 km) Tuscany and Umbria map 563. You might also want to consider the *Michelin Tourist and Motoring Atlas of Italy,* a book of maps with a scale of 1:300,000 (1 cm = 3 km). We sell the Michelin atlas and regional maps in our online store at *www.karenbrown.com.* Another fine choice is the Touring Club Italiano Map Central that can be purchased in Italy. Even the smallest town or, better, *localita* is listed in the extensive index.

PLACES TO STAY

To help you select the type of accommodation you are looking for, the bottom of the description gives one of the following classifications:

B&B: A private home that offers bed & breakfast.

HOTEL: A small, family-run hotel.

SELF-CATERING: Fully furnished accommodation with limited laundry and cooking facilities. No meals are included. These are typically rented by the week, but shorter stays are often available.

RESERVATIONS

Advanced reservations are strongly recommended. It is important to understand that once reservations for accommodation are confirmed, whether verbally by phone or in writing, you are under contract. This means that the proprietor is obligated to provide the accommodation that was promised and that you are obligated to pay for it. If you cannot, you are liable for a portion of the accommodation charges plus your deposit. As a courtesy to your hosts, in the case of cancellation, please advise them as soon as possible. Although some proprietors do not strictly enforce a cancellation policy, many, particularly the smaller properties in our book, simply cannot afford not to do so. Similarly, many airline tickets cannot be changed or refunded without penalty. We recommend insurance to cover these types of additional expenses arising from cancellation due to unforeseen circumstances.

When making your reservations, be sure to identify yourself as a "Karen Brown traveler." The hosts appreciate your visit, value their inclusion in our guide, and frequently tell us they take special care of our readers.

There are several ways to make a reservation:

Email: This is our preferred way of making a reservation. All hotels/bed and breakfasts featured on the Karen Brown Website that also have email addresses have those addresses listed on their web pages (this information is constantly kept updated and correct). You can often link directly to a property from its page on our website. (Always spell out the month as the Italians reverse the American month/day numbering system.)

Fax: If you have access to a fax machine, this is a very quick way to reach a bed and breakfast. If the place to stay has a fax, we have included the number in the description. (See comment above about spelling out the month.)

Reservation Service: If you want to pay for the convenience of having the reservations made for you, pre-payments made, vouchers issued, and cars rented, any of the bed and breakfasts in this guide can be booked through **Hidden Treasures of Italy**, a booking service run by one of the authors of this guide, Nicole Franchini. Further information can be found at the back this book.

Telephone: You can call the bed and breakfast directly, which is very efficient since you get an immediate response. The level of English spoken is given in each bed and breakfast description. To telephone Italy from the United States, dial 011 (the international code), then 39 (Italy's code), then the city area code (including the "0" unless it is a cellular phone number), and then the telephone number. Italy is six hours ahead of New York.

ROADS

Autostrada: a large, fast (and most direct) two- or three-lane toll highway, marked by green signs bearing an "A" followed by the autostrada number. As you enter you receive a ticket from an automatic machine by pushing a red button. Payment is made at your exit point. If you lose your card, you will have to pay the equivalent amount of the distance from the beginning of the autostrada to your exit. Speed limit: 130 kph.

Superstrada: a one- or two-lane freeway between secondary cities marked by blue signs and given a number. Speed limit: 110 kph.

Strada Statale: a small one-lane road marked with S.S. followed by the road number. Speed limit: 90 kph.

Raccordo or *Tangenziale*: a ring road around main cities, connecting to an autostrada and city centers.

ROAD SIGNS: Yellow signs are for tourists and indicate sites of interest, hotels, and restaurants. Black-and-yellow signs indicate private companies and industries.

TOLLS: Tolls on Italian autostrade are quite steep, ranging from $15 to $28 for a three-hour stretch, but offering the fastest and most direct way to travel between cities. Fortunately for the agritourist, tollways are rarely necessary. However, if it suits your needs, a *Viacard*, or magnetic reusable card for tolls, is available in all tollway gas stations for €20–€50, or even more convenient, a MasterCard or Visa card can be used in specified blue lanes (the lines for these automatic machines are notably shorter).

SAFETY

If certain precautions are taken, most unfortunate incidents can be avoided. It is extremely helpful to keep copies of passports, tickets, and contents of your wallet in your room in case you need them. Pickpocketing most commonly occurs in cities on buses, train stations, crowded streets, or from passing motorbikes. WARNING: At tollway gas stations and snack bars, **always** lock your car and beware of gypsies and vendors who try to sell you stolen merchandise. In general, **never** leave valuables or even luggage in the car. Also, **never** set down luggage even for a minute in train stations.

TELEPHONES

The Italian phone company (TELECOM) has been an object of ridicule, a source of frustration, and a subject of heated conversation since its inception. More modern systems are gradually being installed, and most areas have touch-tone phones now. Telephone numbers can have from four to eight digits, so don't be afraid of missing numbers. Cellular phones have saved the day (Italians wouldn't be caught dead without at least one) and are recognized by three-digit area codes beginning with 3. We have added cellphone numbers many of properties in the guide. Cellphones offer the B&B owner great flexibility and give guests the advantage of always finding someone "home."

It is now very easy to rent cellular phones for your stay in Italy either through car rental companies or directly at airports.

All calls to Italy need to include the "0" in the area code, whether calling from abroad, within Italy, or even within the same city, *cellphone numbers drop the "0" in all cases.*

Dial 113 for emergencies of all kinds—24-hour service nationwide.

Dial 116 for Automobile Club for urgent breakdown assistance on the road.

Dial 118 for Ambulance service.

Remember that no warning is given when the time you've paid for in a public phone is about to expire (the line just goes dead), so put in plenty of change or a phone card. There are several types of phones (in various stages of modernization) in Italy:

Bright-orange pay phones, with attached apparatus permitting insertion of a *scheda telefonica,* reusable magnetic cards worth €5–€25, or now more rarely, coins.

To call the United States from Italy, matters have been eased by the ongoing installation of the Country Direct System, whereby you can reach an American operator by dialing 800-900-5825 for AT&T. Either a collect call or a credit-card call can then be placed. If you discover this system doesn't work from some smaller towns, dial 170 to place a collect call, or, in some cities, try dialing direct (from a *scatti* phone), using the international code 001 + area code + number.

TIPPING

Hotels: Service charges are normally included in four- and five-star hotels only. It is customary to leave a token tip for staff.

Restaurants: If a service charge is included, it will be indicated on the bill, otherwise 10–15% is standard tipping procedure.

Taxis: 10%.

WHEN TO VISIT

Many places to stay are open only from Easter through November. If you are traveling outside this time, however, it is often worth a phone call to find out if they can accommodate you anyway (at very affordable rates). The best time to travel is without a doubt during the spring and fall months, when nature is in its glory. You can enjoy the flowers blossoming in May, the *vendemmia*, or grape harvest, at the end of September, the fall foliage in late October, or olive-oil production and truffle hunts in November and December. The vast majority of Italians vacation at the same time, during the month of August, Easter weekend, and Christmas, so these time periods are best avoided, if possible.

Staying in Bed & Breakfasts

All of the bed & breakfasts featured in this guide have been visited and selected solely on their merits. Our judgments are made on charm, setting, cleanliness, and, above all, warmth of welcome. The most important thing to remember is that you will be staying in the private homes of families who run their bed & breakfasts without hiring additional personnel aside from family and farmhands. Do not expect the service of a hotel. **Rooms may not necessarily always be cleaned daily**. Nevertheless, do anticipate a comfortable and enjoyable stay, because the proprietors will do everything possible to assure it. Cost will vary according to the level of service offered.

Bed & breakfast accommodation should not be thought of strictly in terms of the British or American definitions of bed and breakfasts, as in Italy they vary greatly according to each proprietor's interpretation of the concept. The bed and breakfasts in this guide have been described in terms of the criteria used in their selection—warmth of hospitality, historic character, charm of the home, scenery, proximity to sites of touristic interest, and quality of cuisine. Obviously, all of these attributes are not always found in each one. Most of them have an average of six rooms situated either within the family's home or in a separate guesthouse. Unless otherwise indicated in the bottom description details, all bedrooms have private bathrooms. Furthermore, we have tried to include only those with en suite bathrooms. Having another bed or two added to a room at an extra charge for families with small children is usually not a problem. According to laws of the European Community, all new or renovated establishments must now offer facilities for the handicapped. It is best to enquire about the individual bed and breakfast's facilities when making reservations to see if they have accommodation that is suitable for you.

Bed and breakfasts often serve only a continental breakfast of coffee, tea, fresh breads, and jams. However, many prepare a buffet breakfast plus other meals and offer (sometimes require) half- or full-board plans. Half board means that breakfast and dinner are both included in the daily per-person room rate. Full board includes the room and all three meals and is less common, since most guests are out and about during the day, or prefer one lighter meal. Dinner is a hearty three-course meal, often shared at a common table with the host family, and normally does not include wine and other beverages. Menus might be set daily, according to the availability of fresh produce, or a limited choice may be given. Some farms have a full-fledged restaurant serving non-guests as well. Travelers who are not guests at a particular bed and breakfast may take advantage of this opportunity to sample other fare (it is advisable to reserve in advance). When a listing offers dinner by arrangement we indicate this with the icon 🔺. If a property has a restaurant, we use the icon 🍴.

A highlight of the bed and breakfast experience is without a doubt the food. Most travelers would agree that a bad meal is hard to find in Italy, a country world-famous for its culinary skills. In the countryside you'll be sampling the traditional regional recipes from which Italian cuisine originates. Since, whenever possible, all of the ingredients come directly from the farms where you'll be staying and are for the most part organically grown (watch for the certificate), you'll discover the flavorful difference freshness can make. Even the olive oil has a special certificate of quality (DOP) similar to that of wines (DOC). A peek into the farm kitchen is likely to reveal pasta being rolled and cut the old-fashioned way—by hand. Many country cooks prefer to prepare food using traditional methods, and not rely on machines to speed up the process. Guests are usually welcomed into the kitchen for a look around and cooking lessons are becoming very popular.

Staying in Bed & Breakfasts

Staying in Hotels

We visit hundreds of hotels and choose only those we think are special. It might be a splendid villa or a gorgeous palace but there is a common denominator—they all have charm. Each listing is very different and occasionally the owners have their eccentricities, which all adds to the allure of these special hotels. We have tried to be candid and honest in our appraisals and attempted to convey each hotel's special flavor, so that you know what to expect and will not be disappointed. All hotels are places that we have inspected, or stayed in—places that we enjoy. It is difficult to find hotels in Italy furnished in a simple style. Italian hotels frequently reflect a rather formal opulence and tend toward a fussy style of decor. There are some exceptions. In a few instances (which we note in the hotel's description) the hotels are decorated with a more rustic ambiance using country antiques, but this is not the norm. When antiques are used, they are very often the fancy, gilded variety.

Staying in Self Catering Accommodation

Since more and more travelers are learning that it is much more advantageous to stay for longer periods in one place (distances are so short between towns within a specific region), apartment-type accommodations with fully equipped kitchenettes are flourishing. Apartment accommodation is offered either within the farmhouse along with other units for two to six persons, or as a full house rental for six to ten persons. They are rented by the week from Saturday to Saturday throughout the country, the exception being during the low season. No meals are included unless there is a bed and breakfast on the premises which also has a restaurant or makes special arrangements for breakfast or dinner. Rates include use of all facilities, linens, and often utilities. There is usually an extra charge for heating and once-a-week cleaning. Average apartments for four persons run approximately $800 weekly, a rate hotels cannot beat.

Romantic Tuscany

Romantic Tuscany

Florence, Ponte Vecchio

Nothing can surpass the exquisite beauty of the countryside of Tuscany—it is breathtaking. If you meander into the hill towns any time of the year, all your senses are rewarded with the splendors that this enchanting area of Italy has to offer. Almost every hillock is crowned with a picture-perfect walled town; fields are brilliant with vibrant red poppies; vineyards in all their glory and promise lace the fields; olive trees dress the hillsides in a frock of dusky gray-green; pine forests unexpectedly appear to highlight the landscape. As if these attributes were not enough, tucked into the colorful villages is a treasure-trove of some of the finest small hotels, B&Bs and rental accommodation in Italy. If this is still not sufficient to tempt you away from the normal tourist route, remember that the food and wines are unsurpassed.

Pacing: To explore the hill towns of Tuscany you need at least a week (in addition to the time you allocate to Florence). We recommend a minimum of four nights in the heart of Tuscany's Classico Wine Region, which stretches from Florence south to Siena. This will give the minimum time needed to enjoy the tranquil beauty of the hill towns and to sample the delicious Chianti wines. The second suggested stop is southern Tuscany where we suggest three nights to explore the stunning small towns that dot the hillsides, visit breathtaking monasteries, and taste more of Italy's superb wines: Vino Nobile, grown near Montepulciano, and Brunello, grown near Montacino.

Tuscany is laced with narrow roads that twist through the picturesque countryside. Take a detailed map so that if you get lost, you can find your way home, but part of the joy of Tuscany is to be unstructured. Enjoy the freedom to discover your own perfect village, your own charming restaurant, and your own favorite wine. Although in your wanderings you are sure to find some very special places that we have missed, we share below some of the towns we find irresistible and vineyards that are especially fun to visit.

A convenient place to begin your journey is in **Florence**, Tuscany's jewel. Magnificent art is not confined to the city limits of Florence and you will see impressive cathedrals and museums hosting spellbinding works of art throughout Tuscany. Be generous with your time and do not rush Florence—there is too much to see. You must, of course, pay a visit to Michelangelo's fabulous **David** in the **Galleria dell'Accademia** located just off the **Piazza San Marco**.

During your explorations of Florence, you will cross many times through the **Piazza della Signoria**, located in the heart of the old city. Facing this characterful medieval square is the 13th-century **Palazzo Vecchio**, a stern stone structure topped by a crenellated gallery and dominated by a tall bell tower. It was here that the *signoria* (Florence's powerful aristocratic ruling administrators) met for two months each year while attending to government business. During this period they were forbidden to leave the palace (except for funerals) so that there could not be a hint of suspicion of intrigue or bribery. Of course, you cannot miss one of Florence's landmarks, the **Ponte Vecchio**.

Spanning the Arno in the heart of Florence, this colorful bridge is lined with quaint shops just as it has been since the 14th century.

Palazzo Vecchio, Piazza della Signora, Florence

Don't miss the fantastic museums and cathedrals—the world will probably never again see a city that has produced such artistic genius. Florence's Duomo is one of the largest in the world. The cathedral's incredible dome (over 100 meters high) was designed by Brunelleschi. Climb the 464 steps to the top of the dome for a superb view of Florence. The **Baptistry** has beautiful mosaics and its bronze doors by Ghiberti were said by Michelangelo to be worthy of serving as the gates to paradise. The main door shows scenes from the life of John the Baptist, the north door shows the life of Jesus, and the east door shows stories from the prophets of the Old Testament. The **Uffizi Museum** (housed in a 16th-century palace) is undoubtedly one of the finest museums in the world. You can make advance reservations at the Uffizi Museum but you must prepay for the tickets by postal wire in euros (tel: 055 29 48 83) or call Hidden Treasures (888) 419-6700. Also, do not miss the **Pitti**

Palace with its fabulous art collection, including paintings by Titian and Raphael. NOTE: In addition to regular hours, museums stay open during June, July, August, and September until 11 pm. Be sure to buy a guidebook and city map at one of the many magazine stalls and study what you want to see. We just touch on the many highlights. Florence is best appreciated by wandering the historic ancient streets: poke into small boutiques; stop in churches that catch your eye—they all abound with masterpieces; sit and enjoy a cappuccino in one of the little sidewalk cafés and people watch; stroll through the piazzas and watch the artists at their craft—many of them incredibly clever— as they paint portraits and do sculptures for a small fee. End your day by finding the perfect small restaurant for delicious pasta made by mama in the back kitchen.

Monteriggioni

Romantic Tuscany

CHIANTI CLASSICO WINE REGION

This idyllic area lives up to every dream of Tuscany—hills crowned by picture-perfect villages, medieval walled towns, straight rows of towering cypresses, romantic villas, ancient stone farmhouses, vast fields of brilliant poppies, forests of pine trees, vineyards stretching to the horizon. Instead of moving about, packing and unpacking, choose a place to stay anywhere within the area and use it us your hub for exploring this utterly beguiling region of Italy. Below we give suggestions for towns to visit and some of our favorite wineries.

SUGGESTED SIGHTSEEING: TOWNS TO VISIT

Monteriggioni: If you are looking for a town that is truly storybook-perfect, none can surpass the tiny, magical hamlet of Monteriggioni. It is such a gem that it is hard to believe it is real and not a creation by Disney! You can spot it from afar, nestled on the top of a small hill, with 14 towers punctuating the perfectly preserved enclosing walls. No cars are allowed here, so you have to park in the designated area below the walls before walking up to the town, which is composed almost entirely of a main square with small streets radiating from it. On the square you find a Romanesque church, restaurants, boutiques, and shops selling olive oil, cheeses, and wine. It takes only a few minutes to stroll from one end of the town to the other but I assure you, you will be enchanted. As a bonus, Monteriggioni produces its own fine wine, Castello di Monteriggioni.

Passignano in Chianti: Passignano in Chianti is rarely on a tourist route, but we can't help mentioning this tiny hamlet that exudes such a tranquil beauty. For sightseeing, there really isn't much to see except the **Badia a Passignano Abbey**, founded by Benedictine monks in the 11th century. The abbey is set in a pocket of lush landscape and dominates the village, which is no more than a cluster of houses and a restaurant. However, as you drive into the valley, approaching from the west, the abbey with its towering ring of cypresses has such an idyllic setting that it is one of our favorites—a photographer's delight. The abbey can be visited on Sundays at 3 pm; tours leave from the church. (Please check to verify the abbey is open the Sunday you want to visit).

Fine wines, produced by the abbey's vineyards, can be purchased at the Osteria, tel: (055) 80 71 278.

Radda: Located in the very heart of the Chianti wine region, Radda makes a good base of operations. However, not only is the town very conveniently located for sightseeing, it is also extremely quaint and some of its walls are still intact. It was in Radda in 1924 that 33 producers gathered to create a consortium to protect a very special blend of wine that was known as **Chianti Classico**. Only vintners who maintain the standards of the consortium are allowed to proudly display its symbol of the black rooster.

San Gimignano

San Gimignano: During your exploration of Tuscany, one town you must not miss is San Gimignano. What is so dramatic about San Gimignano is that at one time the walls of the town were punctuated by 72 towers. During the Middle Ages it was a status symbol for noble families to build their own personal towers for their protection—the higher the tower, the greater the image of wealth and importance. It is amazing that 14 of the original towers are still standing. They make a striking silhouette, soaring like skyscrapers, and on a clear day you can see them on the horizon from far away. San Gimignano is truly a jewel—plan to spend at least a day here. There are many shops and marvelous restaurants tucked along the maze of streets. On Fridays there are walking tours with English-speaking guides that leave from the Porta San Giovanni at 11 am (best check with the tourist office to be sure the time and day haven't changed). One of our favorite restaurants in San Gimignano is the delightful **Ristorante Dorando,** which has great food served in cozy rooms with coved ceilings that create the ambiance of an old wine cellar. Located on Vicolo del Oro 2, a small side street just off Piazza Duomo, tel: (0577) 94 18 62. Another favorite, **Ristorante Il Pino**, offers mouthwatering homemade pastas—some of the best we have ever eaten. Located on Via Collolese, 8–10, just down the street from L'Antico Pozzo, tel: (0577) 94 04 15.

Siena: This is an entrancing walled hill town that deserves many hours to savor its rich delights—you should allow yourself at least one full day here. The ramparts are perfectly preserved with a series of massive gates guarding a meticulously maintained medieval stronghold. Drive as close as you can to the main square, park your car, and set out to explore on foot. You cannot drive into the center of the city, but there are designated parking areas (marked by "P") near each of the gates. One of the most convenient is the parking at the Porta Romana. Once you leave your car, strike off for the giant **Piazza del Campo**. This central piazza is immense and, instead of being square, is fan-shaped and slopes downward like a bowl. Eleven streets surrounding the square converge into it like spokes of a massive wheel. Like the Spanish Steps in Rome, the Piazza del Campo is a favorite for tourists who linger here just enjoying the medieval ambiance. It is in this gigantic piazza that the colorful **Palio delle Contrade** (dating back to the 11th century) takes place twice a year, on July 2 and August 16. The horse race is only a part of a colorful spectacle of medieval costumes, impressive banners, and parades, and the festivities extend beyond the actual date of the races. Monopolizing one side of the Piazza del Campo is the 13th-century Gothic **Palazzo Pubblico** (Town Hall) whose graceful arches are embellished with Siena's coat of arms. The Palazzo Pubblico is open as a museum where you can stroll through the governor's living quarters.

Although Siena looks like a large city, it is easily negotiable on foot and most of the museums are in one small area. After visiting the Piazza del Campo, most of the other major places of interest are just a few minutes' walk away, clustered about the Piazza del Duomo. There are excellent tourist signs that will guide you along the maze of narrow streets to all the museums.

You absolutely must not miss Siena's 12th-century **Duomo**, facing the Piazza del Duomo. This is one of Italy's most astounding cathedrals. Not only is its exterior breathtaking, but once you enter, you will be overwhelmed by its dramatic black-and-white, zebra-striped marble columns. Don't miss the intricately carved, 13th-century panels depicting the life of Christ on the octagonal pulpit. Also, be sure to see the **Piccolomini Library**. You need to buy a ticket to enter, but it is well worth it. This relatively small room is totally frescoed with gorgeous murals in still-vibrant colors portraying the life of Pope Pius II. The cathedral also has 59 fabulous inlaid-marble mosaic panels on the floor depicting religious scenes. However, some of the most precious of these are covered to protect them and are on display only from the end of August to the first of October.

After visiting the Duomo, the following museums are just steps away. One of our favorites is the **Ospedale di Santa Maria della Scala**, located across from the entrance to the Duomo. At first glance, it is difficult to truly appreciate its wealth of things to see. The museum goes on and on—it is enormous. Just when you think you have finished, a discreet sign will lead you ever downwards to a lower level and a stunning array of artifacts. The building, dating back to the 800s, was originally constructed as a hospital. Be sure not to miss the former infirmary with its lushly colored frescoes by the master Domenico di Bartolo depicting scenes of patients being treated by their doctors. Another nearby museum is the **Baptistry**, a small museum that, as its name implies, houses the baptismal font for the Duomo. In addition to its beautifully frescoed walls and vaulted ceiling, of prime interest is the 15th-century baptismal font, which is adorned by religious scenes cast in bronze by some of Italy's most famous Renaissance masters, including one panel by Donatello. The **Museo dell'Opera Metropolitana** is worth a visit if for no other reason that to see the sublime *Maestá* by Duccio, painted in 1311. The central scene of the Virgin Mary is truly awesome. For art lovers, the **Museo Civico** must not be missed. Here you will see stunning masterpieces by Ambrogio Lorenzetti, Spinello Aretino, and Simone Martini. It is overwhelming to ponder how Italy could have produced so many geniuses. NOTE: There is a ticket valid for three days that allows you entrance into many of Siena's sightseeing attractions—this is a bargain compared to buying individual tickets.

Volterra: Just a short drive from San Gimignano, Volterra is a delightful, non-touristy town enclosed by still-intact, 12th-century walls. Like so many of the cities founded by the Etruscans, Volterra is built upon the flat top of a steep hill. As you drive toward the city, the landscape becomes increasingly barren, since the soil is not conducive to growing grapes or olive trees. Instead, alabaster is king here and objects made of alabaster are sold in all of the shops. Not to be missed is the alabaster museum called **Museo Etrusco Guaracci**, which has a fabulous collection of works of art, including sculptures and beautiful vases, displayed with great taste in a series of interlinking rooms that show the art to perfection. There is an adjacent shop selling many alabaster items. The whole town is a jewel whose charm is best experienced by strolling through the narrow cobbled streets. Its main square, **Piazza dei Priori**, the heart of the town, is surrounded by fine examples of beautifully preserved medieval buildings and with its towers, splendid town hall (the oldest in Tuscany), and Romanesque church, it is considered by some to be one of the finest squares in Tuscany. Stroll to visit one of the main gates, the **Porta all'Arco**, the origins of which date back to the 7th century B.C. During World War II, the loyal citizens of Volterra buried the stones of the gate to keep the Nazis from blowing it up.

SUGGESTED SIGHTSEEING: WINERIES

The production of wine plays an enormous role throughout Tuscany, and between Florence and Siena (where **Chianti Classico** is produced) you are constantly reminded of this as you pass through vast rolling hills splendidly adorned with neatly tended vineyards. The Chianti Classico area covers over 172,000 acres, with Siena and Florence being the two "capitals" of the region. Included in the area are the towns of Castellina, Gaiole, Greve, Radda, and some of Barberino Val d'Elsa, Castelnuovo Berardenga, Poggibonsi, San Casciano Val di Pesa, and Tavarnelle Val di Pesa. Even if you are not a wine connoisseur, it would be a pity not to make at least one winery stop both for the fun of observing the production process and for an understanding of the industry that is so central to the soul and character of Tuscany. Many of the wineries also have gift shops and sell marvelous olive oils and cheeses in addition to wine.

As you meander through the countryside you see signs with Chianti Classico's black rooster symbol and you can buy directly from the producer where you see *Vendita Diretta*. In some cases there are also tours of the winery (these are sometimes free, but sometimes there is a charge). A *Cantina* sign means that the winery has a shop where wine is sold and can usually be sampled. One of the delights of touring the back roads of Tuscany is just to stop on whim. When you spot a *Vendita Diretta*, drive in, introduce yourself, and sample some wines. You might well discover one that will become one of your favorites.

SOME OF OUR FAVORITE WINERIES TO VISIT ARE:

Castello di Brolio: If you visit only one winery, Castello di Brolio should be it since this is not only one of the oldest wineries the world, but also where Chianti wine was "born."

Although the production of wine in Tuscany dates back to Etruscan times, the enormously wealthy Ricasoli family, owners of the Castello di Brolio since 1167, are responsible for the special blending of grapes we now consider "Chianti Classico." At one time the enormously powerful Ricasoli family owned most of the land and castles lying between Florence and Siena. The remote family castle, Castello di Brolio, had largely been abandoned when Bettino Ricasoli decided to move into it (so the story goes) after becoming jealous at a winter ball in Florence when his young bride danced a bit too closely to one of her young admirers. Thinking it best to take his wife away from temptation, he rebuilt the huge, remote, crenellated castle, replanted the vineyards, and experimented with the blending of grapes, coming up with the original formula that forms the basis of what is known today as Chianti Classico. The fortified castle tops a high, forested hill. You leave your car in the designated parking area and climb for about 20 minutes up a path or on the road through a parklike forest to the castle gates. Open daily from 9 am to noon and 3 pm to sunset. The castle is located about 10 kilometers south of Gaiole. Tel: (0577) 74 90 66.

Castello di Volpaia: The 12th-century Castello di Volpaia, located on a narrow lane about 7 kilometers north of Radda, is one of our favorite places for wine tasting. Plan to spend a day on this outing, with ample time to meander through the countryside en route, tour the winery, taste the superb wines, and enjoy a wonderful lunch at the winery's excellent restaurant, La Bottega. Although the winery is called *Castello* it really isn't located inside a castle at all, but rather in various medieval stone houses in a picture-perfect village wrapped by vineyards where you find a small church, a cluster of houses, La Bottega Ristorante, and the wine tasting room. You need to preplan this wine tour and also make reservations for lunch since both are very popular and usually booked far in advance. There is a fee for the tour based on the number of people in the group. Tel: (0577) 73 80 66, *www.volpaia.com.*

Castello d'Albola, wine tasting

Castello d'Albola: The Castello d'Albola, a spectacular property just a short drive north of Radda on a gentle hill laced with grapes, is owned by the Zonin family, who have restored the entire medieval complex beautifully. This is an intimate, extremely pretty place to taste wines and take a tour. What we particularly like about the Castello d'Albola is that it is in such a beautiful setting and offers delightfully informal, friendly, free tours. Drive up the hill to the castle, leave your car in the parking area, and walk into an inner castle courtyard, off which you find the wine tasting room and cantina. Before or after wine tasting, your hostess leads you on a short, professional tour showing you how fine wines are produced. The owner has other enormous estates as well as the Castello d'Albola and is one of the largest producers of wine in the world. Tours start at noon, 2 pm, and 5 pm daily. The cantina is open for complimentary wine tasting daily, April to October from 10 am to 6:30 pm (9 am to 5 pm November to March). Tel: (0577) 73 80 19, *www.albola.it*.

Castello di Meleto: Another favorite destination for wine tasting is the beautiful Castello di Meleto, which has an idyllic setting in the gentle hills near the town of Gaiole. Just across from the dramatic castle you find a pretty wine tasting room and gift shop where fine wines and olive oils produced on the estate can be purchased. On request, tastings of olive oil and aromatic vinegars can be arranged. What makes this a very special experience is that there is an added bonus: not only can you sample wines, but you can also visit the beautiful interior of the castle. In addition to splendidly frescoed rooms, the castle has one exceptionally intriguing feature—a whimsical private theater complete with its original stage settings. Call ahead, tel: (0577) 73 80 66, to find out the time and cost of the guided tours of the cellars and castle. The Castello features on the cover of this guide and is also a recommended place to stay.

SOUTHERN TUSCANY

The area of Tuscany that lies south/southeast of Siena is famous for its superb wines. A great bonus is that these vineyards are in one of Italy's most picturesque regions, filled with quaint villages and amazing abbeys, thus making your adventures even more enchanting. Whereas Chianti Classico wine is renowned in the area between Florence and Siena, the vineyards farther south also produce some of the mostly highly regarded wines in the world, the most famous of these being **Vino Nobile**, grown near Montepulciano, and **Brunello**, grown near Montacino. There are many wineries open to the public where wine can be tasted and purchased. Many wine tastings are free, although some wineries charge a minimal fee. As you drive through the countryside look for signs reading *Cantina* (wine shop) or *Vendita Diretta* (direct sales).

LOOP VISITING WINERIES, ABBEYS, AND QUAINT VILLAGES

We suggest a loop that covers some of our favorite wineries, medieval towns, and picturesque abbeys. It would be impossible to squeeze everything in this itinerary into one day unless you rush madly from place to place. Therefore, if your time is limited, don't stop at each place suggested but just choose a few of the sightseeing suggestions below that most appeal to you. But better yet, take several days and follow the itinerary in its entirety, covering a small section each day at a leisurely pace.

This loop begins in **Montepulciano**, a rare jewel of a walled hill town that not only oozes charm in its narrow, cobbled streets but is also center stage for the delicious Vino Nobile di Montepulciano. This wealthy town was home to many aristocrats who built magnificent palaces here. The heart of the city is the **Piazza Grande** where you find the dramatic 13th-century **Palazzo Comunale** accented by a stone tower. Also facing the square is the picturesque **Palazzo Contucci**, fronted by a charming Renaissance well decorated with the Medici coat of arms and highlighted by two stone lions. Leading off the Pizza Grande are small streets that crisscross the town, connected by staircases.

A masterpiece you absolutely must not miss when visiting Montepulciano is the **Temple of San Biagio**, a stunning church located on the west edge of town. You can walk from town, but it is a long way down the hill and then back up again, so you might want to drive, especially in hot weather. Made of creamy travertine, the church's façade is extremely picturesque and its elegant interior is equally lovely—nothing cluttered or dark but rather light and airy, with fine marble pastel-colored walls.

Within Montepulciano there are many boutiques, restaurants, and cantinas selling wine. Our favorite wine shop here is an extremely special one, the very old **Cantina del Redi**, located just down the street from the Piazza Grande with its entrance next to the Palazzo Ricco. Once you enter, an ancient staircase leads ever deeper into the hillside, passing rooms filled with huge wooden casks of wine.

When you finally reach the lowest level, you wind your way through more casks until you arrive at the cantina where you can sample and purchase wine. When finished, you discover that you have descended quite a way down the hillside and the main entrance to the winery faces onto a lower terrace.

Another of our favorite wineries, **Dei**, is just a few kilometers outside Montepulciano's city walls. What is especially fun about this winery is that it is family-owned and managed by the lovely daughter, Maria Caterina Dei, who still lives in the beautiful family villa on the property. Maria Caterina is passionate about wine and with great professionalism can explain about the production of the Dei wines, which have won many awards. Before taking over the family's vineyards, the multi-talented Maria Caterina trained in music and the theater, and sometimes she entertains the guests during wine tours. There is a fee for tours, depending upon what is requested. Lunches and wine tasting can be prearranged. Call in advance for tours: Dei, Villa Martiena, Montepulciano, tel: (0578) 71 68 78.

Leaving Montepulciano, take the S146 west toward Pienza. After driving about 3 kilometers, take a small road on the left marked to **Monticchiello**. You soon arrive at a sweet, tiny, charming walled town whose allure is its unpretentious, non-touristy ambiance. Park your car in the designated area outside the main gate. As you enter through the gate, you will see on your left **La Porta**, a charming restaurant with an outside terrace sitting on the town walls—a great place to stop for lunch. As you stroll through Monticchiello (it won't take you long), take a look inside the 13th-century church where you will see a beautiful altarpiece by Pietro Lorenzetti.

From Monticchiello, continue on the back road to **Pienza**. This is one of our favorite walled hill towns in Tuscany, a real gem that mustn't be missed. The town is perched on the top of a hill and is pedestrian-only so you need to park your car outside the walls. It is no wonder that the town is so perfect even though so tiny: it was here in the 15th century that Pope Pius II hired a famous architect, Bernardo Rossellino, to totally redesign the town where he was born, making it into a masterpiece. You will find many restaurants if you are inclined to dine.

Leaving Pienza, take S146 west to **San Quirico d'Orcia**, a very attractive small medieval town with a lovely Romanesque church. If you stop to see the town, you must not miss its lovely garden, called **Horti Leonini**. An entrance about a block from the main square leads into a tranquil Renaissance garden, originally designed as a beautiful resting place for the pilgrims who stopped here on the road to Rome. This cool oasis with clipped box hedges and shade trees makes an interesting stop. If you are hungry, the **Osteria del Leone** makes a good choice for lunch.

From San Quirico d'Orcia, head south on S2 for about 6 kilometers and watch for a small road to the right leading to **Bagno Vignoni**. This is a most unusual, very small town, known for the curative value of its hot sulphur springs. In the center of town, you find what would have been the town square made into a huge sulphur bath built by the Medicis. The pool is surrounded by picturesque medieval buildings that complete the interesting scene.

Leaving Bagno Vignoni, don't continue on the S2, but take S323 directly south for 12 kilometers and then turn right following signs to Montalcino. In a few minutes you come to **Castelnuovo dell'Abate** where, just a few minutes outside town, you will find the superb Romanesque **Abbey Sant'Antimo**, whose origins date back to the 9th century when it was founded as a Benedictine monastery. The abbey—a simple, pastel-pinkish stone church serenely set amongst fields of olive trees—makes a beautiful picture. Try to arrive at 11 am or 2:45 pm when the Benedictine monks, clad in long, pure-white robes, gather at the altar to chant their prayers in Latin. This is a haunting, beautiful experience. The singing lasts only a short time, and the times might vary from the ones we mention above, so to confirm the schedule call, tel: (0577) 83 56 59.

Leaving Castelnuovo dell'Abate, drive north on the road for Montalcino. In a few minutes you will see a sign to the **Fattoria dei Barbi**. Turn right and follow a small road up the hill to the Barbi winery, an excellent winery to visit. It is extremely pretty with many gardens and a charming cantina where you can sample the vineyard's fine wines and purchase wine and other gift items. Its restaurant serves wonderful meals made with only the freshest products, accompanied, of course, by their own wines.

Free tours of the winery are given hourly from 10 am to noon and 3 pm to 5 pm, tel: (0577) 84 82 77, *www.fattoriadeibarbi.it.*

After your visit to the Fattoria dei Barbi, continue north for 5 kilometers to **Montalcino**, which is world famous, along with Montepulciano, for its superb wine, Brunello di Montalcino. There are many places in town where wine can be tasted and purchased. In addition to wine, the town is famous for its fine honey, which can be purchased in many of the shops. Montalcino is fun for wandering—it is not large and you can in no time at all cover the area within the walls by foot. On the east edge of town is an imposing 14th-century fortress.

From Montalcino, head south on the road to Grosetto for a little over 3 kilometers to another of our favorite wineries, **Poggio Antico**. Excellent tours are offered and, of course, you can also sample the superb wines. These tours are very popular so you should reserve in advance at tel: (0577) 84 80 44. For dining, the winery's **Ristorante Poggio Antico** serves outstanding Tuscany cuisine. Reservations for the restaurant are also highly recommended—tel: (0577) 84 92 00, email: rist.poggio.antico@libero.it.

After visiting Poggio Antico, retrace your way north to Montalcino and continue on for 9 kilometers to where the road intersects with the S2. Turn left here, going north toward Siena. In 10 kilometers, turn right on S451 and continue for another 10 kilometers to the **Abbazia di Monte Oliveto Maggiore**. Founded in the early 14th century by wealthy merchants from Siena as a Benedictine retreat, this fascinating abbey is well worth a detour. Be prepared to walk since you must park your car and follow a long path through the forest to the abbey's entrance, which is through a gatehouse crowned by a beautiful della Robbia terra-cotta. Once through the gate, you continue through the woodlands to the huge brick complex. After visiting the church, it seems you could wander forever through the various hallways. Before you get too distracted, however, ask directions to the cloister because you don't want to miss this marvel. Here you find 36 frescoes depicting scenes of the life of St. Benedict, some painted by Luca Signorelli, others by Antonio Bazzi.

In the region around the abbey you will come across an entirely different type of landscape, called the *crete*. Here, tucked among the green rolling hills, you unexpectedly come across bleak, canyon-like craters, caused by erosion. These are especially out of character as the surrounding scenery is so soft and gentle.

From Abbazia di Monte Oliveto Maggiore, weave your way through the small back roads to Montepulciano. Follow signs to San Giovanni d'Asso, then Montisi, then Madongino, then **Montefollonico**. Take time to stop in Montefollonico because this is another "sleeper"—a quaint, small, medieval walled town that is fun to explore. For the gourmet, there is a superb restaurant on the edge of town called **La Chiusa.**

From Montefollonico, go south on S327. When you come to the S146, turn left to complete your loop back to Montepulciano.

Florence

Romantic Tuscany

The Haunting Beauty of Umbria

The Haunting Beauty of Umbria

Assisi

Tuscany is so popular that travelers frequently forget to visit Umbria, snuggled just "next door." Although similar in many ways to Tuscany, Umbria has its own haunting beauty and the advantage of fewer tourists. This is a region seeped in history and imbued with romantic charm. Here you find a beguiling landscape—a blend of rolling hills, craggy forests, rushing rivers, lush valleys, chestnut groves, and hillsides laced with vineyards. Adding further to Umbria's magic is that its hills and valleys radiate a soft mellow light, gleaming gently in the sun. It is not just the landscape that makes Umbria so delightful. It also has stunning medieval castles, incredible cathedrals, ancient monasteries, art treasures, fine wines, beautiful ceramics, and captivating towns perched on hilltops.

Pacing: You can conveniently follow this itinerary either before or after a tour of Tuscany. If you already have visited Tuscany on a previous trip to Italy, this itinerary stands alone. After the finishing the itinerary, you can loop back to Florence by heading north on the A1, or head south on the A1 to Rome. Whichever way you choose, in order to capture its beauty and many sightseeing possibilities, you need at least five nights in the Umbria region: We suggest three nights in the eastern part of Umbria. Choose a place to stay and in use it as a hub from which to journey out each day to explore a different sightseeing target. Next, loop south and choose a place to stay for two nights in the western part of Umbria, somewhere near Orvieto.

EASTERN UMBRIA

NOTE: This itinerary of Eastern Umbria is much too long for one day. Use it only as a framework for how the most interesting towns can be looped together. Once you choose which town you are going to use as the hub for your explorations, tailor the itinerary to visit the places mentioned in the itinerary that most appeal to you.

As you depart from Florence you are bound to run into a lot of traffic, but there are many signs to the expressway. Follow signs that lead to the A1 and take it south toward Rome.

Arezzo: About 65 kilometers after leaving Florence you come to a turnoff to **Arezzo,** located about 10 kilometers east of the highway. Arezzo is still in Tuscany, but since it is so close to Umbria and "on the way," now is the time for a visit. Arezzo has a rich history dating back to the Etruscan era, but is not as quaint as some of its smaller neighbors. It is well known as one of the largest gold centers in Europe and has many shops selling gold jewelry. Arezzo is also famous for its **Antique Fair** that is held in the Piazza Grande on the first Saturday and Sunday of every month. Here you find many unusual items such as antique coins, jewelry, furniture, stained glass remnants, paintings, light fixtures, handmade linens, pottery, trunks, etc. The fair is considered one of the most important ones in Italy and so popular that people come from far and near to browse the rich collection of antiques. Arezzo was the birthplace of Guido Monaco who around the year 1000 A.D. devised musical notes and scales.

One of Arrezo's famous inhabitants was the powerful 14th-century poet Pietro Aretino who took great glee in writing scandalous poetry about the rich and famous. Aretino's greatest skill was gentle blackmail, extorting great sums from princes and popes who paid him not to expose their indiscretions in poetry.

Cortona: From Arezzo follow S71 south to Cortona, a gem of a walled town terraced up a steep hillside covered with olive trees and vineyards. Like Arezzo, Cortona is still in Tuscany, but fits more conveniently into the itinerary for Umbria since it is on the route. Stop to enjoy the atmosphere of this medieval town: its narrow, twisting, cobbled streets, jumble of small squares, lovely boutiques, excellent restaurants, and colorful buildings are delightful. The heart of the town is the **Piazza della Repubblica**, the main square, which has many narrow streets feeding into it. If you are up for walking, climb the twisting streets to the old fortress standing guard over the town.

Lake Trasimeno: Leaving Cortona, continue driving south on S71 toward Lake Trasimeno. In about 11 kilometers you come to a four-lane expressway. Do not get on the highway, but instead continue south on S71, which traces the west shore of Lake Trasimeno, Italy's fourth largest lake, which is fed by underground channels linked to the Tiber river basin. Fascinatingly, the early Romans built these underground waterways many centuries ago. Follow the road south for 9 kilometers to **Castiglione del Lago**, the most interesting town on the lake. Built on a high rocky promontory that juts out into the water, the old walled city with its battlements and towers has lots of character. Artifacts and tombs nearby indicate it was originally an Etruscan settlement, but what you see today dates from the Middle Ages. In the 1500s it was the dukedom of the Corgna. In the church of Santa Maria Maddalena you can see a 16th-century panel with paintings of the Madonna and Child by Eusebio da San Giorgio. Also visit the Palazzo del Capitano del Popolo, the Palazzo della Cornna, and the Leone fortress.

Umbertide: Continue the loop around the lake then take the road toward Magione, which is just before the junction with the expressway heading to Perugia. In a few minutes, you see the four-lane expressway, but do not get on it. Instead, continue over the highway and follow the back roads through the countryside to Umbertide.

Stop for a short visit to this small, 10th century town that hugs the banks of the Tevere River. In addition to the castle, you might want to visit the Church of Santa Maria della Reggia, which is an intriguing octagonal, three-tiered building topped by a cupola. Another church, the Holy Cross, is famous for its lovely painting by Signorelli, called *Deposition from the Cross*.

Gubbio: Leaving Umbertide, take the road that passes over the highway E45 and continue on to Gubbio. This splendidly preserved, medieval walled town is perched high on the slopes of Monte Ingino. The setting is superb and the view from the plaza that sits like a shelf overlooking the countryside is breathtaking. The narrow, cobbled streets and walkways lacing the hillside are delightful to explore. The town is filled with architectural masterpieces, one of these, the Basilica, dominates the town. There is much to see including the Cathedral, the Consuls Palace, the Piazza Pensile, the Pretorio Palace, and the Santa Maria Nuova church where you can see Ottaviano Nelli's *Madonna del Belvedere*. Outside the city walls, nestled below the town, there are the remains of a Roman theater—another reminder of how important the city was in its prime.

Perugia: From Gubbio head south on S298 in the direction of Perugia. There is a turnoff to Perugia, which is surrounded by many modern commercial buildings. If time is short, bypass Perugia (which is not as pristine as many of Umbria's other jewels) and continue on to the junction of S75 and continue east following signs to Assisi. However, if you want to "see it all," Perguia has many delights. Perugia is a large medieval city surrounded by ramparts. An important Umbrian city since Etruscan days, the old town has at its heart the **Piazza IV Novembre**, a beautiful square with an appealing fountain, the **Fontana Maggiore**, built in the late 13th century. Although Perugia is rich in history and has a delightful medieval core, it is surrounded by modern commercial development and is not one of our favorites since it does not exude the romantic appeal and the intimacy of some of the other hill towns in Umbria.

Assisi: Coming from either Perugia or Gubbio, take S75 east following signs for Assisi, one of our favorite targets in Umbria. Built up the steep slopes of Mount Subasio, this magical city is a tribute to St. Francis. Although he was born into a family of wealth, after several visions in which Christ appeared to him, St. Francis left his privileged life. He was obviously a person with a deeply poetic soul and his tender teachings of reverence for the beauties of nature and kindness to all animals and birds still appeal to us today. To remember your visit, you might want to buy a statue of St. Francis to bring home. You will find statues in all sizes and price ranges in the many shops. Even if it were not for the lingering memory of the gentle St. Francis, Assisi would be a "must see" for it is one of the most spectacular hill towns in Umbria. Perhaps there are a few too many souvenir shops, but this is a small price to pay for the privilege of experiencing such a very special place. The town walls begin on the valley floor and completely enclose the city as it climbs the steep hillside to the enormous castle at its summit. Assisi with its maze of tiny streets is a marvelous town for walking (you must wear sturdy shoes) and it is great fun as you come across intriguing little lanes opening into small squares. When you stop to rest, there are breathtaking vistas of the lovely Umbrian fields stretching out below. Along with many other historic buildings, Assisi's most famous monument, **St. Francis' Basilica,** was severely damaged by an earthquake in September 1997. However, almost all of the repairs have now been completed and the town looks remarkably "back to normal." The basilica, which also houses a monastery, faces onto a large square bound by columns forming vaulted covered walkways. In addition to the monastery, there are two basilicas—upper and lower. Both are adorned with excellent frescoes that were unfortunately damaged by the earthquake. Also while in Assisi, visit

Santa Chiara (St. Clara's Church). Clara, a close friend of St. Francis, founded the Order of St. Clare. Go into the church to view the lovely frescoes of Santa Clara and her sisters. Part of the enjoyment of Assisi is just to stroll through its narrow, cobbled streets—the whole town is like a living museum. If you have time, hike up to the **Rocca Medioevale**, an enormous 14th-century fortress perched on the hillside overlooking the city. From here you have a magnificent bird's-eye view of Assisi and beyond to the enchanting Umbrian countryside sweeping out to the distant hills.

Collepino: From Assisi you can continue on the S75 in the direction of Foligno. However, if you feel adventuresome and enjoy getting off the beaten path, there is a narrow twisting, very scenic back road that leads through the hills making a loop from Assisi that ends up back on the S75 in Spello, about 5 kilometers before Foligno. The driving is difficult, but you can enjoy the beauty of the rugged forested mountains, an area of Umbria seldom seen by tourists. The road begins at the upper part of Assisi. Follow signs in the direction of Gualdo Tadino, but before you get there, take the road marked to Armenzano where you continue on following signs to Spello. After going through Armenzano, the road passes the adorable secluded hamlet of Collepino, which oozes charm with its winding cobbled streets and stone houses. It is so tiny that you quickly see it all. After Collepino, it is 7 kilometers on to Spello, where the road joins the S75, which you take going south.

Bevagna: Five kilometers south of Spello you come to **Foligno** where we suggest leaving the S75 and taking instead the back roads to enjoy the lovely villages and scenery. From Foligno take the S316 toward Bevagna, which you reach after about 8 kilometers. Bevagna is an enticing, intimate, charming walled village, founded by the Romans. In addition to just enjoying the allure of the town, there is much to see including a stunning 19th-century opera house, the beautiful San Michele church, well-preserved mosaics in the old Roman baths, and a paper press making paper just as it has been for centuries. If it is mealtime, there is a wonderful place for lunch, L'Orto degli Angeli.

Montefalco: From Bevagna, take the road marked to Montefalco (located 7 kilometers from Bevagna). Montefalco is a walled town that crowns a hill with sweeping views of the Umbrian countryside. The town is a maze of small, narrow streets. For sightseeing, the main attraction is **San Francisco**, a church now converted into a museum that displays some of the finest work of Benozzo Gozzoli, including the fresco *Life of St. Francis*. Also, a delicious wine, *Sagrantino*, is produced here.

Spoleto: From Montefalco, loop back to the main road, S75, and continue south following signs to Spoleto. Not only is medieval Spoleto dramatically perched atop a hill, but it also has an almost unbelievable bridge dating from Roman times. This **Ponte delle Torri**, spanning the deep ravine between Spoleto and the adjoining mountain, was built over an aqueduct existing in the 14th century. This incredible engineering wonder is 230 meters long and soars 81 meters high. It is supported by a series of ten Gothic arches and has a fort at the far end as well as a balcony in the center. The 12th-century **Cathedral** in Spoleto is also so lovely that it alone would make a stop in this charming town worth a detour. The exterior of this very old cathedral, with its beautiful rose window and intricate mosaics, is truly charming. Although a great sightseeing destination at any time of the year, Spoleto is very popular in late June and early July when it hosts the world-famous Spoleto Festival, featuring great music, dance, and theater. During the festival season rooms are usually more expensive and almost impossible to secure so should be booked far in advance.

Torgiano: Torgiano, in the center of a rich wine region, has a lovely small wine museum. You would never dream that such a tiny town could boast such a gem, but it is not a coincidence: the Lungarotti family owns the vineyards for many kilometers in every direction. Signor Lungarotti furnished the museum with artifacts pertaining to every aspect of wine production from the earliest days, creating an interesting and beautifully displayed collection worthy of a detour by anyone interested in wines. In the center of town, the Lungarotti family owns, **Le Tre Vaselle**, a charming choice for lunch.

Duomo, Orvieto

WESTERN UMBRIA

From Spoleto, a scenic route connecting the eastern part of Umbria to the western part of Umbria is to take the S418, which twists west from Spoleto for 25 kilometers through beautiful hills to the E45. Turn north on E45 for about 21 kilometers and turn west on S448, following signs to the A1 and Orvieto.

Todi: The picture-perfect village of Todi makes a great midway stop between Spoleto and Orvieto. It is located near the junction of E45 and S448 and is well signposted. This adorable small town crowning a hilltop like icing on a cake is one of our favorites. No, there isn't much to see—it is the town itself that is so picturesque. It is just fun to wander the twisting cobblestone streets, enjoy the medieval ambiance, and stop to enjoy a cappuccino in one of the sidewalk cafés. As you stroll through the small village, watch for the Cathedral, the People's Square, the intimate San Ilario Church, and the Roman/Etruscan Museum.

Leaving Todi you come to the A1, don't get onto the freeway, but instead follow signs to Orvieto. NOTE: When deciding on a town in the area to use as a hub for sightings, don't limit your choice to those in Umbria. You will also find a rich selection of places to stay very nearby in Tuscany.

The Haunting Beauty of Umbria

Orvieto: Originally founded by the Etruscans, Orvieto later became a prosperous Roman city, famous for its production of ceramics. Orvieto is spread across the top of a hill that drops down on every side in steep volcanic cliffs to the Umbrian plain 200 meters below—you wonder how the town could ever have been built! Drive as far as you can up to the town, park your car, and proceed on foot. Have a good map handy because you pass so many churches and squares that it is difficult to orient yourself—Orvieto is a maze of tiny piazzas and narrow twisting streets. Continue on to Orvieto's center where a glorious **Duomo** dominates the immense piazza. You may think you have seen sufficient stunning cathedrals to last a lifetime, but just wait—Orvieto's is truly special, one of the finest examples of Romanesque-Gothic architecture in Italy. It is brilliantly embellished with intricate mosaic designs and accented by lacy slender spires stretching gracefully into the sky. Within the Duomo, you absolutely must not miss the **Chapel of San Brizio;** here you find frescos by Fra Angelico and Luca Signorelli. Also of interest in Orvieto is **St. Patrick's Well**, hewn out of solid volcanic rock. Pope Clement VII took refuge in Orvieto in 1527 and to ensure the town's water supply in case of siege, he ordered the digging of this 62-meter-deep well. It is unique for the 70 windows that illuminate it and the two spiral staircases that wind up and down without meeting. Other sights to see include the Papal Palace, the Town Hall, and the archaeological museum.

Civita di Bagnorégio: Although **Civita di Bagnorégio** is not in Umbria, it's located just southwest of Orvieto, so it conveniently ties in with this itinerary. If you are a photographer and love picturesque walled villages, few can surpass the setting of this small town. Take the N71, which twists west from Orvieto toward **Lake Bolsena**. Stay on N71 for about 20 kilometers and then turn left heading to Bagnorégio. Go into town and follow signs to Civita, which crowns the top of a steep, circular-shaped, rocky outcrop. There is no road into the village—the only access is by walking over a long, narrow suspension bridge that joins the two sides of a deep ravine. Once you arrive, you will find a few shops, some Etruscan artifacts, a church, and a restaurant. However, the main focus is the town itself with its narrow arcaded alleyways and a dramatic 180-degree view of the desolate, rocky canyons that stretch out around the town with a haunting beauty.

Orvieto

Places to Stay in Tuscany

One of the most attractive features of Florence is that its surrounding countryside hugs the city limits, giving the possibility of staying in the tranquil foothills of Chianti. In the nearby village of Antella warm hosts Azelio and Luisa have completely restored their part of an enormous estate divided into three 14th-century villas. The downstairs area includes a large living/dining room, main kitchen, and separate kitchenette for guests' use during the day. The vaulted antique cantina below displays an enviable collection of reserve wines. Up a steep flight of stairs are the well-appointed guestrooms, all with superb views over countryside all the way to Brunelleschi's cupola. The bedrooms are double-bedded, individually decorated with country antiques and one has a hydro-jet bathtub. The real treat is the large junior suite with its high wood-beamed mansard ceilings, sitting area, and canopy bed. Originally the outdoor loggia, it retains its columns and seven windows looking out to both sides of the property. A country breakfast is served either in the small breakfast room or in the garden. *Directions:* Leave the A1 at Firenze Sud. After the toll, turn first right for Siena and after about 1.5 km turn left for Antella. In Antella the Via Montisoni starts from the square with the church on your left.

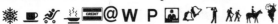

VILLA IL COLLE
Hosts: Azelio & Luisa Pierattoni
Via Montisoni 45
Antella–Florence, (FI) 50011, Italy
Tel & Fax: (055) 621822
5 Rooms, Double: €90–€130
1 Suite: €120–€150
Minimum Stay Required: 2 nights
Open: all year, Credit cards: MC, VS
B&B

The recently-restored Villa Olmi, located on the outskirts of Florence, offers three types of luxury accommodations: suites within an historic villa, standard rooms in the former farmhouse, or two fully-equipped spacious apartments. Set on a flat 15-acre property facing distant hills, the 700-year-old villa, farmhouses, barns and surrounding land once belonged to a prosperous Florentine family. The more commercial "Fattoria" building holds 38 new bedrooms with marble bathrooms, reception and lounge areas, a breakfast veranda overlooking the orchards to the pool, and the restaurant, "Il Cavaliere", where the chef creates fine Tuscan cuisine. A vaulted brick wine cellar offers wine-tasting from an extensive list. The 18th century villa however steals the spotlight—flaunting 12 luxuriously appointed suites all joined by a grand salon adorned with enormous Murano chandeliers. A laborious restoration project, under the regulations of the National Art Preservation Ministry, brought to light the splendid pastel-colored frescoes on walls and ceilings, which compliment selective antiques, canopy beds and sumptuous fabrics in the exclusive suites. Many personalized services are arranged by the courteous staff. The advantageous location of the complex allows easy touring of the Chianti area as well as Florence (complimentary shuttle service provided to and from the city center). *Directions:* Exit Firenze Sud from the A1 and follow signs for Bagno di Ripoli and the hotel.

VILLA OLMI RESORT
Host: Daniele Ronzini
Via degli Olmi 4/8
Bagno a Ripoli, (FI) 50012, Italy
Tel: (055) 63 77 10, Fax: (055) 63 77 16 00
62 Rooms, Double: €325–€1200
3 Suites: €1600–€2000
2 Apartments: €1640 daily*, €8000 weekly*
Open: all year, Credit cards: AX, MC, VS
HOTEL

Bagno Vignoni is a charming little village whose unique piazza is actually an ancient stone pool with thermal water. In medieval times the large bath was divided for men and women who came to soak in the rejuvenating waters, hoping to cure such ailments as arthritis and rheumatism. Today, tourists come to view this remarkable place and take advantage of these same curative properties in the nearby falls or modern pool facilities. With the success of their wine bar ("enoteca") here, it was only natural that the young Marinis should open a bed and breakfast for travelers. The stone building dates to the 1300's and was thoughtfully restored after having been abandoned for more than 30 years. The eight double bedrooms and large living room with loft and grand piano are very cozy and purposely old-fashioned in feeling. The beamed guestrooms and nice new bathrooms each have their own theme and corresponding soft pastel color schemes and are romantically appointed with lace curtains and pillows, antique beds and armoires, and painted stencil borders. Breakfast is served across the way in the historic enoteca, which was once part of the Capuchin friars' monastery. With its informal and warm hospitality, it is no wonder that the bar is a favorite place for artists and writers. The property also has a spa with steam room for guests. *Directions:* Bagno Vignoni is 5 km south of San Quirico. Park in the town lot and walk the short distance to the locanda.

LA LOCANDA DEL LOGGIATO
Hosts: Sabrina & Barbara Marini
Piazza del Moretto 30
Bagno Vignoni, (SI) 53023, Italy
Tel: (0577) 888925, Fax: (0577) 888370
8 Rooms, Double: €130–€160
Minimum Stay Required: 2 nights
Dinners: €30
Open: all year, Credit cards: MC, VS
B&B

After many years of traveling to Italy at any opportunity, Jennie and Alan left England to move to Tuscany and fell in love immediately with Villa Mimosa, a rustic, 18th-century home with a shady front courtyard facing the village street and the church. They have created three sweet bedrooms and one attic mansard suite for four persons, each with a different theme and lovely mountain views. A cozy sitting room and a library with grand piano are reserved upstairs for guests and decorated with the Pratts' own antiques imported from England. Jennie and Alan delight in sharing their passion for this part of the country known as Lunigiana (very near the Cinque Terre coastal area and one hour from both Parma and Lucca) and give their guests lots of personal attention, while making them feel right at home. Guests are treated to breakfast on the terrace overlooking the pretty garden and swimming pool with the Apennine Mountains as a backdrop and delight in Jennie's creative cuisine straight off the Aga, based on fresh garden vegetables and local recipes. Tea and homemade cakes are served in the shady garden. *Directions:* Leave the A15 autostrada (Parma-La Spezia) at Pontremoli from the north or Aulla from the south and take the autostrada S.S.62 to Villafranca, then Bagnone. Enter town through the yellow gateway, then over the bridge. Turn left following signs for Corlaga, and the villa is on the right 50 meters before the church.

VILLA MIMOSA
Hosts: Jennie & Alan Pratt
Localita: Corlaga
Bagnone, (MS) 54021, Italy
Tel & Fax: (0187) 427022
4 Rooms, Double: €80–€120
Dinners: €40
Open: all year, Credit cards: none
B&B

Casa Sola is just that—an ancient villa standing alone atop a hill on a gorgeous 400-acre vineyard estate in the heart of Chianti. The gracious Gambaro family produces prestigious Chianti Classico Riserva, Supertuscan-Montarsiccio, and extra-virgin olive oil of the highest quality. There are six large guest apartments on two floors of a rose-covered stone farmhouse down the road from the main villa. All the apartments consist of living room, kitchen, bedrooms, and baths, with private entrances and garden (flowers match the color scheme of each apartment!). The apartments are furnished stylishly with selected country antiques, and details such as botanical prints hung with bows, eyelet curtains, fresh flowers, and a bottle of wine are welcome touches. Number 5, for up to eight people, is the most spacious with four bedrooms, fireplace, and magnificent views over the Barberino Valley and cypress woods. Il Capanno, in the converted barn, is a delightful "nest" for honeymooners. An inviting pool overlooks the valley surrounding the main villa. Wine-cellar visits with wine tasting are organized once a week and marked hiking trails lead guests through picture-perfect landscapes. *Directions:* From the Autostrada del Sole, direction Florence, exit at Firenze Certosa joining the Firenze-Siena Superstrada. Exit S. Donato in Poggio and go beyond San Donato. Go 1 km past San Donato, look for the sign for Casa Sola on the right and follow the road for 2 km.

FATTORIA CASA SOLA
Host: Count Gambaro Family
Localita: Cortine
Barberino Val d'Elsa, (FI) 50021, Italy
Tel: (055) 8075028, Fax: (055) 8059194
4 Rooms, Double: €90–€160*, 7 Suites: €140–€440*
6 Apartments: €90–€350 daily (Sep to Jul)
Apartments: €700–€2430 weekly (Jul & Aug)
*Breakfast not included
*€15 Heating charge if needed
Open: all year, Credit cards: all major
SELF CATERING

Strategically positioned midway between Siena and Florence sits the square stone farmhouse with cupola (actually one of the bedrooms!) dating from 1700 owned by Gianni and Cristina, a couple who have dedicated their lives to the equestrian arts. The Paretaio appeals particularly to visitors with a passion for horseback riding, for the Marchis offer everything from basic riding lessons to dressage training, and day outings through the gorgeous surrounding countryside. In fact, the Paretaio is recognized as one of the top riding "schools" in Italy, with more than 30 horses. On the ground floor is a rustic living room with country antiques, comfy sofas, and piano enhanced by a vaulted brick ceiling and worn terracotta floors, off which are two bedrooms. Upstairs, the main gathering area is the dining room, which features a massive fireplace and a seemingly endless wooden table. This room gives access to more bedrooms, each decorated with touches such as dried flowers, white lace curtains, and, of course, equestrian prints. A vast collection of over 300 pieces with an equestrian theme is displayed about the home. Il Paretaio also organizes courses in Italian and is an excellent base for touring the heart of Tuscany. The swimming pool gives splendid views over olive groves and vineyards. *Directions:* Head south from Barberino on route 2 and after 2 km take the second right-hand turnoff for San Filippo. Continue on 1.5 km of dirt road to the house.

IL PARETAIO
Hosts: Cristina & Giovanni de Marchi
Localita: San Filippo
Barberino Val d'Elsa, (FI) 50021, Italy
Tel: (055) 8059218, Fax: (055) 8059231
8 Rooms, Double: €65–€105
2 Apartments: €80 daily, €490 weekly
Dinners: €35
Open: all year, Credit cards: none
B&B, SELF CATERING

The Locanda, a pale-yellow and brick house dating from 1830, sits on the border between Tuscany and Umbria and is an excellent base from which to explore this rich countryside. The villa's dining room features a vaulted ceiling in toast-colored brick, an enormous fireplace, French windows opening out to the flower garden, and antiques including a cupboard adorned with the family's blue-and-white china. The upstairs quarters are reserved primarily for guests, and contain five comfortable rooms all off one hallway and an inviting sitting room and library. The cozy bedrooms have mansard ceilings, armoires, lovely linens, and private bathrooms with showers. Additional guestrooms are located on the ground floor of the converted barn between the house and a small garden, where a swimming pool has been added. These are more spacious, private, and modern in decor. Cordial hostess Palmira assists with local itineraries. Excellent regional fare including divine vegetarian dishes with local produce is prepared by the chef who is happy to give cooking classes. Siena is only 45 kilometers away, and the quaint medieval and Renaissance villages of Pienza, Montepulciano, and Montalcino are close by. *Directions:* Exit from the Rome-Florence autostrada at Val di Chiana. Head toward Bettolle, then bear right toward Siena. Follow signs for La Bandita.

LOCANDA LA BANDITA
Host: Palmira Fiorini
Via Bandita 72
Bettolle, (SI) 53040, Italy
Tel: (0577) 624649, Fax: (0577) 622515
9 Rooms, Double: €100–€120
Dinners: €35
Open: Feb to Dec, Credit cards: all major
B&B

Luisa left her fashion business in Parma and settled in this peaceful spot 3 kilometers from the coast. The stylish, impeccable home clearly reflects the personality of the warm and yet reserved hostess who tastefully designed both the exterior and interior of this lovely accommodation. Each of the four corner bedrooms upstairs has its own large private terrace and beautiful floral-tiled bathroom. All offer beds with linen sheets and splendid views over fruit orchards and olive groves to the sea. While the hostess occupies the cupola, guests have a independent entrance to the upstairs rooms, giving utmost privacy to all. Common areas include the living room and open kitchen with large arched window and doors looking out to the surrounding garden. An ample fresh country breakfast with cakes all prepared by Luisa is served here at one long table. A separate cottage next to the main house offers a double room and beamed living room with stone fireplace and kitchen, and a second apartment is available within another cottage next door. Day trips include Elba Island, Volterra and San Gimignano, Lucca, Siena, private beaches, Etruscan itineraries, visits to the wine estates of Bolgheri, and biking in the nearby nature park. Sweet and simple. *Directions:* Exit from Aurelia on route 1 at Bibbona and turn left. Pass through La California and turn left for Bibbona. Podere Le Mezzelune is before town, well marked to the left. Pisa airport is 40 km away.

PODERE LE MEZZELUNE
Host: Luisa Chiesa Family
Via Mezzelune 126
Bibbona, (LI) 57020, Italy
Tel: (0586) 670266, Fax: (0586) 671814
4 Rooms, Double: €160–€190
2 Apartments: €180–€195 daily*
Minimum Stay Required: 2 nights
*Breakfast not included with Apartments: €13
Open: all year, Credit cards: MC, VS
B&B, SELF CATERING

The prestigious Monsignor della Casa property extending over 600 acres is a true country resort with all the trimmings in the beautiful area north of Florence called Mugello. This is the land from which such masters as Giotto, Cimabue, and Fra Angelico came and was the actual home of 16th-century writer and Vatican secretary, Giovanni della Casa, whose portrait hangs in Washington's National Gallery. The Marzi family meticulously restored a cluster of six stone farmhouses on the vast estate next to their own stately villa. The refined bi-level apartments exude pure Tuscan charm and can accommodate from two to six guests. Two individual villas, each with private swimming pool, can take a group of twelve to sixteen. The finest linens and fabrics were chosen to accent exposed stone walls, brick floors, and wood-beamed ceilings. Spend your days touring or in any of a variety of activities for every age and interest: biking, hiking, or horseback riding in the nearby woods, golf, swimming in one of two pools, tennis, volleyball, and children's playground. An elegantly rustic restaurant and wine bar serves guests a typical Tuscan menu in the evening with cordial host Alessio making sure nothing is overlooked. The "wellness center" offers sauna, steam bath, Jacuzzi, and other services. Indulge! *Directions:* From Borgo San Lorenzo follow signs for Faenza. Just after the turnoff for Scarperia turn right for Mucciano and the resort (3 km total). 27 km from Florence.

MONSIGNOR DELLA CASA
Host: Marzi Family
Via di Mucciano 16
Borgo San Lorenzo, (FI) 50032, Italy
Tel: (055) 840821, Fax: (055) 8408240
21 Rooms, Double: €160–€460
21 Apartments: €480–€3550 weekly
Minimum Stay Required: 2 to 7 nights depending on season
Dinners: €35
Closed: Jan 9 to Mar 5, Credit cards: all major
SELF CATERING

Tall cypress trees protect the cluster of ancient stone farmhouses making up the idyllic Iesolana property, situated atop 300 acres of cascading vineyards, olive groves, and sunflowers, with 360 degrees of breathtaking Tuscan views. After years of meticulous restoration of the three ochre-stained houses, eleven high-level apartments are offered, with private terraces. Apartments have from one to four bedrooms and are elegantly appointed with rustic furnishings, country fabrics, and modern kitchens and baths that harmonize beautifully with the cool stone floors and original wood-beamed ceilings. Among the many services available are individual telephones, satellite TV, barbecue facilities, and a swimming pool. The impeccable landscape is studded with terracotta pots overflowing with brightly colored geraniums. The fabulously restored barn now hosts a stylish wine bar for tastings of Iesolana's own wines, oils, and honey. Breakfast and dinners of regional cuisine are also served in the comfortable restaurant with outdoor seating as an option. A state-of-the-art meeting room is available for groups. Centrally located for day trips to Siena, Florence, and Rome, this is the perfect spot for relaxing and exploring. *Directions:* Leave the A1 at Valdarno for Montevarchi, Bucine (8 km). From town follow signs up to Iesolana, passing over a stone bridge (2 km) to the end of the road.

BORGO IESOLANA
Host: Giovanni Toscano
Localita: Iesolana
Bucine, (AR) 52021, Italy
Tel: (055) 992988, Fax: (055) 992879
11 Apartments: €140 daily, €830 weekly*
*Breakfast not included
Minimum Stay Required: 2 nights, 7 nights high season
Dinners: €25–€30
Open: all year, Credit cards: all major
SELF CATERING

La Ripolina farm is a vast 500-acre farm comprised of several different brick farmhouses. Self-catering apartments (two for up to ten people) and individual guest bedrooms are divided among five farmhouses dotting the soft hills of the property. Two very charmingly authentic apartments are found within the Pieve di Piana, a cluster of houses grouped around an ancient church with bell tower dating to the 9th century. The richly historic Pieve sits on a hill and enjoys panoramic views of vineyards and fields of grain and sunflowers extending as far as the eye can see. Hostess and owner Laura Cresti resides in the house called S. Ferdinando where there are two apartments with two bedrooms with a separate entrance. Five rooms are next door in the Ripoli house, each being individually appointed with appropriate country local antiques. Walls are painted in warm earth colors and the upstairs loggia, a typical open porch with four large arched windows, has been enclosed and transformed into the breakfast room. A full country breakfast buffet includes fresh croissants, bread, biscuits, honey, marmalade, fruit, ham and orange juice. This is strikingly beautiful countryside, chock-full of hilltowns to explore. A beautiful swimming pool and bicycles are available for guests. *Directions:* From Siena (25 km) take the S.S.2 to Buonconvento and turn right in town following signs for Bibbiano. After crossing the river, turn right at La Ripolina and drive up to the main house.

■ ✗ ☕ ▦ CREDIT ⋔ @ W P ❀ ≈ ⌂ ↑ ⋔⋔ ↟ ❦

LA RIPOLINA
Host: Laura Cresti
Pieve di Piana
Buonconvento, (SI) 53022, Italy
Tel & Fax: (0577) 282280
7 Rooms, Double: €75–€95
7 Apartments: €45–€70 daily per person
Open: all year, Credit cards: MC, VS
B&B, SELF CATERING

The beautiful Montebelli resort property, situated in Maremma, with its wild Tuscan landscapes, covers 300 acres of mountain, hills laden with vineyards and olive groves, and sunflower fields, all close to the sea. The Filotico-Tosi family divides their time and energy between their guests and production of wines and olive oil. The main guesthouse, originally a centuries-old mill, holds most of the comfortable guestrooms, while the remaining accommodation is spread out in two, one-story wings, each with individual entrance. Rooms are decorated tastefully with typical Tuscan antiques. The latest addition to Montebelli is a magnificent 4-star, 24 room country hotel perfectly integrated with the existing structure. The new hotel rooms are modern in their furnishing and amenities. The hotel also integrates into the complex spa facilities, a billiard room and spacious common areas. As a result of the new addition, the Montebelli now can offer guests a choice between a bed and breakfast and a hotel stay. The half-board requirement allows guests to sample marvelous local cuisine by candlelight within the intimate dining rooms or out on the terrace. Scenic walks or biking on marked trails, a swimming pool, tennis courts, horse riding, and courses in cooking, yoga and wine-tasting are all available. *Directions:* From the north, exit at Gavorrano Scalo from Aurelia S.S.1, following signs for Caldana. Just before Caldana, turn at the Montebelli sign and take the dirt road to the end.

MONTEBELLI
Host: Carla Filotico Tosi Family
Localita: Molinetto
Caldana, (GR) 58023, Italy
Tel: (0566) 887100, Fax: (0566) 81439
35 Rooms, Double: €210–€290*
10 Suites: €252–€320*
*Includes breakfast & dinner
Dinners: €25
Closed: Jan to Mar, Credit cards: all major
B&B

The Villa Bellaria is situated right in the picturesque village of Campagnatico with its stone streets and houses and magnificent views over the Ombrone Valley and up to Mount Amiata, it retains the authentic flavor of a noble country home from centuries past. Credit goes to gracious hostess Luisa who oversees the 900-plus-acre property, once belonging to such powerful families as the Aldobrandeschi and Medici. It was partially destroyed during World War II and completely restored by the Querci della Rovere family. Talented Luisa runs not only the hospitality activity but the entire farm as well, while her husband produces Morellino wine from another property. With its large surrounding balustraded park with cypress-lined trails and swimming pool, one forgets that it is all part of the actual town (with its many conveniences). The spacious bedrooms with family antiques and two of the apartments are situated within the main villa while the other newer but characteristic ones are spread out on three floors in the transformed olive-press building. They have either one or two bedrooms, bathroom, and sitting room with kitchenette and are appointed with the family's country furniture. This is a lovely base for exploring the area. *Directions:* From Siena (55 km) or Grosseto (20 km) exit from highway 223 at Campagnatico and continue for 4 km to the town. The villa is the second right in town—drive up to a brown gate.

VILLA BELLARIA
Host: Luisa Querci della Rovere
Campagnatico, (GR) 58042, Italy
Tel & Fax: (0564) 996626
2 Rooms, Double: €70–€80
1 Suite: €130–€150
10 Apartments: €550–€1000 weekly
Open: all year, Credit cards: all major
B&B, SELF CATERING

The Canonica a Cerreto property is truly a marvel to behold, with an extraordinary combination of features. Perfectly located in lower Chianti and equidistant from most of Tuscany's highlights, it offers not only very comfortable accommodation in a fascinating historic dwelling but also seemingly endless vistas of gorgeous countryside, and welcoming and gracious hosts. Iron gates open up to an entrance lined with gorgeous terracotta pots in the form of lions, overflowing with geraniums and oleander plants giving accents of color to the facade of the ancient stone church and attached canonica, the summer residence of the Vescovo of the Duomo of Siena. Within the walls is a complex including the family's residence, three guest apartments in the monks' former rooms, quarters for the farmhands, and a cantina. Signora Lorenzi proudly shows guests her museum-caliber art collection and magnificent home where large period paintings adorn frescoed walls and elegant antique pieces are displayed. The apartments, in an elegant country style, are tastefully appointed with antiques and include a bedroom, bathroom, and living area with kitchenette. The largest apartment has two bedrooms, each with its own bathroom. A lovely, secluded swimming pool has superb countryside views. *Directions:* From Siena follow the S.S.408 towards Gaiole and just after Pianella, take the first left (Canonica a Cerreto is marked on most maps).

CANONICA A CERRETO
Host: Egidio Lorenzi Family
Canonica a Cerreto
Castelnuovo Berardenga, (SI) 53019, Italy
Tel & Fax: (0577) 363261
3 Apartments: €735–€1250*
*Breakfast not included
Minimum Stay Required: 3 nights, 7 nights high season
Open: Apr to Oct, Credit cards: all major
SELF CATERING

The turreted medieval village of Capalbio, perched on a hilltop, has the double advantage of being close to one of the prettiest seaside spots—Argentario—plus having the beautiful countryside and villages of Maremma to explore. Monica and husband Filippo run an efficient little bed and breakfast operation, having left a long career in the restaurant business. Breakfast, composed of fresh homemade cakes, breads, and jams, is served in the stone-walled dining room or out on the patio. Ten rooms in a row, each with independent entrance from the garden, are situated next door to the main house; while five new bedrooms have been added in the adjacent converted barn. Rooms are nicely decorated in a classic style, and have such amenities as television, telephone, hairdryer, and air conditioning. This comes in handy on hot summer evenings, although there is always a cool breeze passing through and the swimming pool surrounded by a manicured lawn is wonderfully refreshing. The farm property extends over 30 acres of olive groves and fields of grain and oats. Monica and Filippo run a little restaurant in town Trattoria Al Pozzo. Guests often eat here and at Tullio's well known for its excellent food. The sculpture park of Niki de St. Phalle is 4 km away. *Directions:* From Rome on the coastal highway 1, exit before Capalbio at Pescia Fiorentina. At Pescia stay left for 3 km. Ghiaccio is 1 km after the fork for Manciano.

GHIACCIO BOSCO
Hosts: Monica Olivi & Filippo Rinaldi
Strada della Sgrilla 4
Capalbio, (GR) 58011, Italy
Tel: (0564) 896539
15 Rooms, Double: €80–€120
Minimum Stay Required
Open: Jan 3 to Oct 1, Credit cards: none
B&B

Castelfiorentino is 40 kilometers from Florence, Siena and Pisa, and although its outskirts are very commercial, it is a strategic touring base and the surrounding countryside is lovely. Continuing a long tradition of making guests feel at home—their hotel in Florence has been in the family for four generations—Massimo and Susanna opened this bed and breakfast ten years ago after major restoration of two hilltop farmhouses. The completely refurbished rooms, with many modern amenities, new bathrooms, fresh landscaping, and recently installed swimming pool and tennis court, have a very new feeling. Spacious bedrooms are appointed with authentic and reproduction antiques and have colorful Sicilian ceramic tiles above beds, with matching ones in bathrooms. The former barn was converted into a small restaurant decorated with contemporary art, a kitchen with viewing window, and a common living room/library upstairs. The preparation of delectable Tuscan fare using ancestral recipes is another strong tradition and cooking lessons are happily arranged. A buffet breakfast is served. The side terrace, overlooking soft hills, is where guests can both enjoy breakfast and watch the sunset in the evening. Olive oil and wine tasting can be arranged. *Directions:* From Castelfiorentino turn off at signs for Renai (this can be tricky to locate) and follow signs for Locanda Country Inn Le Boscarecce (5 km).

LE BOSCARECCE
Hosts: Susanna Ballerini & Massimo Ravalli
Via Renai 19
Castelfiorentino, (FI) 50051, Italy
Tel: (0571) 61280, Fax: (0571) 634008
14 Rooms, Double: €80–€150
Open: all year, Credit cards: all major
B&B

This idyllic location in the heart of Chianti, the Fattoria Tregole, five kilometers outside the charming village of Castellina, is reached by a gravel road. The ivy-covered stone farmhouse with hexagonal 18th century oratory (one of only two in Tuscany) is on the small road and opens out to the back to unspoiled hillsides covered with woods and vineyards. While husband Catello tends to the production of Chianti wine (visit the cantina with wood barrels for the reserve wines), gracious hostess Edith pays careful attention to her guests. There are five comfortable bedrooms and also two apartments complete with kitchen corner and living room, perfect for two to four guests. Particular care has been given to the décor, with peach-colored hand-stenciled walls and trim, soft colored quilts, antique pieces, painted wrought-iron beds, and dried flower arrangements all complimenting the terracotta brick floors. The breakfast room is set with white porcelain to match the white chairs and tables where Edith serves fresh cakes and breads each morning. With adequate notice an occasional dinner can also arranged. Outdoors the terrace and swimming enjoy inspiring views across the surrounding countryside. A great base for exploring Tuscany. *Directions:* From Castellina, follow south towards Siena and after 5 km turn left for Tregole and it's 1 km to Fattoria.

FATTORIA TREGOLE
Hosts: Edith Kirchlechner & Catello Conte
Località: Tregole 86
Castellina in Chianti, (SI) 53011, Italy
Tel: (0577) 740991, Fax: (0577) 741928
5 Rooms, Double: €130–€180
2 Apartments: €200–€360
Minimum Stay Required: 3 nights
Closed: Jan 15 to Mar 15, Credit cards: all major
B&B, SELF CATERING

If your dream is to discover a small luxury hotel in Tuscany that is truly "off the beaten path" look no further—the romantic Locanda Le Piazze is about as remote as you will find. Tucked in the heart of Tuscany's richest wine-growing region, the hotel crowns a gentle hill. In every direction there is nothing but a breathtaking patchwork of vineyards sweeping like the open sea across undulating hills, dotted with enchanting old farmhouses. After three years in which the buildings were totally renovated and a beautiful pool added, the hotel opened to guests in the summer of 1995. It is no wonder the design and decor are in absolutely faultless taste: the owner, Maureen Bonini, has for over 40 years been a design consultant in Florence. All of the hotel's rooms exude sophisticated country elegance. Huge bouquets of fresh flowers highlight white walls, terracotta floors, and beamed ceilings. Each of the guestrooms has its own personality, but all exude a similar comfortable, homelike ambiance. The fabrics used throughout are all from Maureen's good friend, Ralph Lauren. The stunning swimming pool, tucked in the vineyards, is reached by a path through fragrant beds of lavender. Light lunches available by request. *Directions:* From Castellina in Chianti take the road to Poggibonsi, S.S. 429. As you leave Castellina, turn left at the first road, SP130 Castagnoli, marked to Gagliole, Castellare, and Castagnoli and follow signs to the hotel—a 10-minute drive (ask for directions).

LOCANDA LE PIAZZE
Host: Maureen Bonini
Localita: Le Piazze
Castellina in Chianti, (SI) 53011, Italy
Tel: (0577) 74 31 90, Fax: (0577) 74 31 91
20 Rooms, Double: €120–€160
Dinner by reservation: €35, not Wed
Open: Apr to Oct, Credit cards: all major
HOTEL

The Tenuta di Ricavo is unique—not a hotel at all in the usual connotation, but rather a tiny, very old, Tuscan hamlet with peasants' cottages that have been transformed into delightful guestrooms. The stables are now the dining room and the barn is now the office. Unlike many of the over-renovated hotels in Tuscany where most of what you see is actually new construction, Ricavo is all real. The guestrooms have been lovingly restored to enhance their original rustic charm and are attractively furnished with country antiques. You enter the large property following a lane through a vast pine forest that leads to the cluster of weathered stone cottages, romantically embellished by climbing roses. Flowers are everywhere and in one of the gardens are two swimming pools. Before it became a hotel, the village was the summer-holiday retreat of a Swiss family who, after World War II, transformed their home into a unique, village-style hotel. However, the Tenuta di Ricavo is not for everyone. It is quiet. But it is a haven for the traveler for whom a good book, a walk through the forest, and a delicious dinner are fulfillment. Excellent English is spoken —especially by the gracious owner, Christina Lobrano, whose charming husband, Alessandro, is the talented chef. NOTE: There is a three-night minimum during high season. *Directions:* From Castellina, take the road to San Donato. A long way out of town, the hotel is on your right. Contact hotel for detailed directions.

❄ ☕ ⚙ 💳 ☎ 🍴 @ W Ⓨ P � 🍴 🚭 ≈ 🖼 ⚓ 🎿 🚶 🐎 🏌

TENUTA DI RICAVO
Hosts: Christina & Alessandro Lobrano
Località Ricavo
Castellina in Chianti, (SI) 53011, Italy
Tel: (0577) 74 02 21, Fax: (0577) 74 10 14
18 Rooms, Double: €130–€230
5 Suites: €260–€400
Minimum Stay Required: 3 nights in high season
Restaurant closed Sun, reservations required
Open: Apr to Nov, Credit cards: MC, VS
HOTEL

At Le Fontanelle it seems that wherever your eye wanders it is rewarded; from the impeccably decorated interiors, lush gardens and inviting terraced lawns looking on to picture-perfect Tuscan views. Spacious guestrooms of varying dimensions are dispersed about the large stone main building with front courtyard and annexes, all similarly appointed using crisp white linens, classic English and French fabrics, and traditional Tuscan furnishings. Most have either a private garden or terrace from which to absorb the beauty and stillness of this timeless landscape. Simple elegance characteristic of true Tuscan style prevails throughout the many common spaces and a sense of luxury is derived from the many thoughtful details, complimentary amenities, and attentive staff. Refined Tuscan cuisine is presented in the pristine dining room whose large panoramic windows replace the need for paintings and whose name, La Colonna, comes from the stone pillar conserved in the center of the room. Alternatives areas for meals are up at the swimming pool grill or the corner terrace outside the restaurant, appropriately name Belvedere for the magnificent vistas. To top it all off, a heated indoor pool, hydro-jet pool, sauna, steam room and spa treatments are all available for extra pampering. *Directions:* From the Siena-Sinalunga highway, take the 408 road. Fontanelle is 1 km after the turnoff for Pianella.

HOTEL LE FONTANELLE
Host: Marion Winski
Strada Provinciale 408
Castelnuovo Berardenga
Pianella, (SI) 53019, Italy
Tel: (0577) 35 751, Fax: (0577) 35 75 55
22 Rooms, Double: €380–€737
3 Suites: €1034–€1155
Open: Apr to Oct, Credit cards: all major
HOTEL

The Hotel Relais Borgo San Felice, located in the heart of Tuscany, is built within a feudal hamlet consisting of a cluster of stone, ivy-laced buildings linked by quaint cobbled lanes. The various buildings, including a small chapel, have been cleverly converted into reception area, guestrooms, dining rooms, lounges, conference room, and bar. The tiny village is not entirely consecrated to the hotel: local farmers still live in some of the buildings and olive oil and wine are produced. The San Felice wines, produced from grapes grown on the 2,400 surrounding acres, are some of Italy's finest. Although the hotel is secluded deep in the countryside, there is no need for guests to sacrifice any creature comforts. The Borgo San Felice, a member of the prestigious Relais & Châteaux group, is a sophisticated property offering all the amenities and services of a deluxe hotel. Although the façade is rustic, the interior exudes a gracious charm and the guestrooms, which are decorated with soft, pleasing colors, floral fabrics, and many antiques, offer every amenity. When not exploring the wealth of fascinating towns and historic sites round about, guests can relax by a large swimming pool with a view terrace, enjoy a game of tennis, or be pampered at the beauty center. *Directions:* From Florence take S2 south, until the road ends. Follow signs toward Arezzo-Monteaperti to San Felice, which is between the towns of Pianella and Villa a Sesta.

HOTEL RELAIS BORGO SAN FELICE
Host: Cinzia Fanciulli
Localita San Felice
Castelnuovo Berardenga, (SI) 53019, Italy
Tel: (0577) 39 64, Fax: (0577) 35 90 89
28 Rooms, Double: €265–€385
15 Suites: €460–€750
Open: Apr to Nov (off season by request)
Credit cards: AX, MC, VS
Relais & Châteaux
HOTEL

The family-run Relais San Pietro is an absolute dream. It offers the finest quality throughout, gorgeous views, excellent location, spectacular swimming pool, and outstanding cuisine, all at remarkably reasonable prices. This gem of a little hotel has the added benefit of superb hospitality: Luigi Protti, your host, radiates a gentle, old-fashioned, welcoming kindness. Upon retirement he and his wife, Antonietta, decided to move back to Tuscany and open a hotel. They bought a long-neglected farmhouse only a few kilometers from the town where Signora Protti had been born and a small, intimate hotel. The Protti family recently renovated the 300 year old "Canonica" (priests' house) adding four elegant and spacious suites. The interior of the hotel has a refreshing light, uncluttered appeal. All of the original architectural features such as beamed ceilings and beautiful brick archways have been meticulously preserved. Bedrooms feature beautiful wrought-iron headboards, white bedspreads, excellent lighting, doors painted with regional designs, and superb bathrooms. The romantic dining rooms occupy what were formerly the stables. Signora Protti and her daughter-in-law preside over the kitchen and the food is fabulous. *Directions:* From Cortona, go north on 71 toward Arezzo. At Castiglion Fiorentino, turn right toward Città di Castello. After 6 km, turn left at a sign to Polvano. Go up the hill. Relais San Pietro is on the left.

✽ ☕ ✗ 💳 ☎ @ W P ⑂ 🚭 ≈ 🚶 🖼 ⚓ ⑂ 👫 ⚓ ⑂

RELAIS SAN PIETRO
Host: Protti Family
Polvano
Castiglion Fiorentino, (AR) 52043, Italy
Tel: (0575) 65 01 00, Fax: (0575) 65 02 55
5 Rooms, Double: €130–€200
5 Suites: €200–€300
Meals for hotel guests
Open: Apr to Oct, Credit cards: all major
HOTEL

The lesser-known area of Tuscany south of Siena makes a delightful discovery and the variety of landscapes within an 8-kilometer drive provides one of the most fascinating excursions in the region. Besides the charming hilltowns of Montepulciano, Pienza, and Montalcino, there are the abbeys of Monte Oliveto and Sant'Antimo, plus the thermal baths of Bagno Vignoni. A perfect base in this richly historical and natural area is the fairytale castle of the Aluffi Pentini family, theirs for the past 400 years or so and practically a village in itself. The family resides in the upper reaches of the castle while guests are accommodated in several separate farmers' houses divided into a combination of apartments with one or two bedrooms, living room, and kitchenette, plus six simply and characteristically appointed bedrooms with country furniture. Rooms facing out have absolutely breathtaking views over the virgin valley (the same view that all guests enjoy from the lovely pool). Downstairs is the dining room with wood tables covered with cheery checked cloths, where breakfast and dinner are served using homegrown products. A common space for guests is the old granary, converted into a large cozy reading room with fireplace. *Directions:* The castle is well marked at 5 km from San Quirico d'Orcia. Ripa d'Orcia is marked on most maps.

CASTELLO DI RIPA D'ORCIA
Host: Aluffi Pentini Family
Localita: Ripa d'Orcia
Castiglione d'Orcia, (SI) 53023, Italy
Tel: (0577) 897376, Fax: (0577) 898038
6 Rooms, Double: €115–€170
8 Apartments: €110–€198 daily, €690–€950 weekly
Minimum Stay Required: Rooms: 2 nights, Apts: 3 nights
Open: Mar to Nov, Credit cards: MC, VS
History Traveller
B&B, SELF CATERING

La Frateria di Padre Eligio, a very special, enchanting hotel, makes an outstanding base for exploring the beauties of Tuscany and Umbria. The guestrooms of this 13th-century convent (founded by St. Francis) are the original guest quarters where the friars lodged passing pilgrims. They are simply, yet tastefully, furnished with antiques. There is nothing to interrupt the enchantment—bathrooms and telephones are the only concessions to the modern era. The silence is sweetened by the song of birds and the air by the fragrance of flowers. A centuries-old forest surrounds the hotel with beckoning paths where you can stroll in perfect stillness. The restoration of this masterpiece of history is superb, but the miracle is how it was accomplished. La Frateria di Padre Eligio, in addition to housing a deluxe hotel, is home to a commune of once-troubled young people who toiled for 12 years to restore the Convento San Francesco to its former beauty. Today these remarkable young men and women awaken at dawn to begin long days of labor. They meticulously groom the gardens, tend the vegetable garden, run the hotel, bake the fresh breads, prepare the meals (exclusively using produce from the farm), and serve in the restaurant. *Directions:* Exit the A1 at Chiusi Chianciano and follow signs to Cetona. Go through town towards Sarteano. Just after leaving Cetona, turn left at a sign "Mondo X—La Frateria di P. Eligio." Go 700 meters to the hotel.

❄ ☕ 🛎 CREDIT ☎ @ W Y P ⑪ ⚚ 🏃 🚶🚶 🐎 ⛷ 🍸

LA FRATERIA DI PADRE ELIGIO
Host: Maria Grazia Daolio
Convento San Francesco
Cetona, (SI) 53040, Italy
Tel: (0578) 23 82 61, Fax: (0578) 23 92 20
5 Rooms, Double: €240
2 Suites: €300
Open: all year, Credit cards: MC, VS
HOTEL

Il Caggio is a delightful agriturismo farm, distinguishing itself from the many others by the sincere and warm hospitality of its owners, Gabriella and Paolo, and the superb quality of the meals. Conveniently located close to the main autostrada, guests have this corner of Chianti at their fingertips, from Siena, Cortona, Chianti, to Arezzo. Two bedrooms and two apartments are in part of the main stone house and an adjacent house. All are carefully appointed in a creative, country-style with great attention to details and the comfort of guests. All accommodations have private entrances from the exterior. In the rustic main house, the ambiance really warms up around Gabriella's dinner table where a non-stop series of aperitifs, pasta specialties, and a dessert buffet are served, accompanied by good local wine. An abundant breakfast with more of Gabriella's homemade, baked cakes awaits guests in the morning. A swimming pool behind the house bordering the woods is available, as well as a six-person hot hydro-jet pool. Convinced that their guests will enjoy their stay, their brochure warns: An extended stay here generates a sense of well-being with a tendency to forget about problems, tempting one to postpone going back home! *Directions:* From A1 exit at Monte San Savino. Turn left continuing for 6.7 km to Ciggiano. Turn right and then left at abandoned farmhouse and follow up to the house.

CASALE IL CAGGIO
Hosts: Gabriella & Paolo Magini
Località: Ciggiano
Civitella in Val di Chiana, (AR) 52041, Italy
Tel & Fax: (0575) 440022
2 Rooms, Double: €100–€120
3 Apartments: €600–€1200 weekly*
*Breakfast included in rooms only; Apts by request
*Heating not included
Dinners: €30
Open: all year, Credit cards: none
B&B, SELF CATERING

Borgo Elena, located in the hills outside one of our favorite Tuscan towns, Cortona, belongs to Mario Baracchi, whose brother owns the gorgeous inn, Il Falconiere (listed in our Inns guide). In fact, you can reach Borgo Elena by passing through the Falconiere property (stop in for an exquisite meal) on a narrow, steep gravel road that ends at the cluster of stone houses bordered by dense chestnut woods. Here you are totally immersed in nature and complete silence, with hilltop Cortona to one side and the immense Chiana Valley spread out before you. Seven quaint apartments, each with independent entrance, are dispersed among the various stone houses, which were the quarters for the farmhands of the Falconiere estate a century ago. Their original rustic ambiance remains while convenient modern utilities and amenities have been incorporated. The apartments, all charmingly appointed with Tuscan country pieces, accommodate from two to six persons and are all different in layout, most being on two levels. A lovely swimming pool sits higher up and takes in even more of the expansive view. The Borgo Elena is an ideal base for independent travelers who want to settle in one place for easily touring Tuscany's highlights. *Directions:* Instead of going into the center of Cortona, follow signs for Arezzo and drive past Camucia on the outskirts of town to Tavarnelle. Turn right at San Pietro a Cegliolo and drive 2 km up to Borgo Elena.

BORGO ELENA
Host: Mario Baracchi
Localita: San Pietro a Cegliolo
Cortona, (AR) 52042, Italy
Tel & Fax: (0575) 604773
7 Apartments: per person: €40 daily, €560–€750 weekly*
*Breakfast not included
Minimum Stay Required: 3 nights
Open: all year, Credit cards: all major
SELF CATERING

The charming medieval Etruscan town of Cortona that gained international fame through Frances Mayes' bestseller, "Under the Tuscan Sun", has subsequently responded to the increased demand for tourist accommodation. The Mancini family decided to completely refurbish their lovely old farm (a village in itself on the site of an Etruscan settlement) to accommodate a variety of needs for the more demanding traveler. The 17th-century private home sits in the middle of its meticulously landscaped gardens boasting 2,500 rose plants and surrounded by ten other stone houses which are now home to the comfortable hotel, Locanda. Featuring a voluminous breakfast room, eight spacious one, two and three-bedroom apartments on two floors of the former olive oil mill and farmer's quarters, there are also two excellent restaurants, a wine bar, a stunning swimming pool with hydro-massage, and a chapel. The décor of all the rooms is in keeping with an air of elegant country ambiance. A complete country resort. *Directions:* Exit from autostrada A1 at Valdichiana, proceed towards Perugia. Exit from this highway at second exit for Cortona. Strategically located, Il Melone is well-marked on the main street leading to Arezzo, below Cortona center.

✳ ☕ ⛷ ♨ 💳 ⛽ ☎ 🏋 @ W Ⲩ P ⑪ ≈ 🖼 🐕 🚶 🐎 ⚘

BORGO IL MELONE
Host: Carlo Livraga Mancini Family
Il Sodo, Case Sparse 38
Cortona, (AR) 52042, Italy
Tel: (0575) 603330, Fax: (0575) 630001
12 Rooms, Double: €100–€220
8 Apartments: €1500–€2500 weekly
Minimum Stay Required: Apartments: 7 nights
Dinners: €25
Closed: Jan 10 to Feb 10, Credit cards: all major
B&B, SELF CATERING

If you want to find the perfect little hotel to use as a base to explore the wonders of Tuscany and Umbria, look no farther than Il Falconiere—a jewel snuggled in the countryside just a few kilometers outside Cortona. From this convenient location you can venture out each day to such beauties as Siena, Florence, Assisi, San Gimignano, Orvieto, and Pienza, all easily accessible by car. The joy is that you can return each evening to relax by the gorgeous swimming pool, enjoy some of the best food in Italy, then sleep peacefully in the hushed tranquility of the countryside. And what a value! You can stay here for much less than you would pay for a deluxe room in Florence or Rome. Il Falconiere is owned by Silvia and Riccardo Baracchi, a charming, talented young couple who have achieved amazing results from their labor of love and long years of hard work. Riccardo inherited the property from his grandmother. His wife, Silvia, is the incredibly talented chef whose superb meals have earned their restaurant a Michelin star. The guestrooms are individually decorated with great flair. Many antiques are used throughout, creating a comfortable, quietly sophisticated elegance. Il Falconiere is truly a very special place offering superb quality, charm, and genuine hospitality. Another bonus: the hotel has a wonderful wellness center and has recently restored the beautiful Baracchi estate winery just east of Cortona. *Directions:* Just north of Cortona, signposted off the road to Arezzo.

❄ ☕ ✃ ☕ 🖥 ☎ 🐕 ♿ @ 🍷 P ⚏ 🚭 ✿ 🖼 ⚒ ♿ 🎿 🚶 🐎 🍇

IL FALCONIERE RELAIS E RISTORANTE
Hosts: Silvia & Riccardo Baracchi
Localita: San Martino
Cortona, (AR) 52044, Italy
Tel: (0575) 61 26 79, Fax: (0575) 61 29 27
22 Rooms, Double: €290–€380
4 Suites: €480–€590
Closed: Jan & Feb, Credit cards: all major
Relais & Châteaux
HOTEL

The Villa di Piazzano is an enchanting inn with all the ingredients to make it very special: an historic villa, a lovely landscape, a convenient location, beautiful decor, pretty antiques, and, best of all, the heart-felt hospitality of the Wimpole family who pamper guests and welcome them like friends. As their surname suggests, your hosts are not all Italian-born. Damien Wimpole, an Australian, met his Italian wife, Adriana, in Rome. After their marriage, they traveled extensively throughout the world and, as a result, their charming daughter, Alessandra, is fluent in several languages. When searching for a perfect property to convert to a small hotel, they discovered the stunning but long-neglected Villa di Piazzano, one of the oldest villas in Umbria. The task to bring the property back to its original splendor was awesome, but well worth the effort. Today the delightful villa, set amidst romantic gardens, is a jewel—the interior decorator-perfect with handsome fabrics and many antiques. Everything has been thought of to make a stay here special, including a large swimming pool and wireless Internet access. There is a lovely restaurant specializing in fine Tuscan cuisine. The villa is officially in Umbria, but part of the property is in Tuscany, making it a great choice for those who want a base for exploring both areas. The hotel is located 5 km outside of Cortona. *Directions:* Ask for detailed driving instructions.

VILLA DI PIAZZANO
Host: Wimpole Family
Località: Piazzano
Cortona, Tuoro Sul Trasimeno, (AR) 06069, Italy
Tel: (075) 82 62 26, Fax: (075) 82 63 36
18 Rooms, Double: €160–€340
Closed: Dec to Mar, Credit cards: AX, MC, VS
HOTEL

Cortona, a picturesque walled city in Tuscany, is a favorite with tourists. On the main road that wraps around the east side of the city, the Villa Marsili has the advantages of parking facilities and of being easy to find, and is within walking distance of the center of town. A gated entrance leads into the front courtyard of this handsome yellow villa accented by dark-green shutters and beds of colorful flowers. Inside, the villa has been totally remodeled into a deluxe hotel with every modern amenity. The well-trained staff is very welcoming and gracious. The management is happy to help you plan your excursions and they even offer cooking classes. The bedrooms are all tastefully decorated and have all the comforts and appointments of a first-class hotel. Throughout the hotel a quiet, refined ambiance prevails, with soft colors enhanced by antique furniture and ceilings adorned by frescoes. Breakfast is a wonderful buffet of Tuscan specialties. There is no restaurant, but guests can enjoy a complimentary aperitif on the garden terrace with a view of the Val di Chiana valley and Lake Trasimeno before walking to a rich selection of restaurants. *Directions:* Located on the east side of Cortona on the road to Arezzo.

VILLA MARSILI
Host: Stefano Meacci
Viale C. Battisti, 13
Cortona, (AR) 52044, Italy
Tel: (0575) 60 52 52, Fax: (0575) 60 56 18
26 Rooms, Double: €120–€250
3 Suites: €230–€350
Open: all year, Credit cards: all major
Abitare La Storia
HOTEL

The Relais alla Corte del Sole has a superb location—conveniently close to Cortona and Montepulciano, yet snuggled in the tranquil countryside. This gem of a small hotel is owned by the gracious Spiganti family whose famed Tonino Restaurant in Cortona prepares such exceptional cuisine that the late Pope invited the chef to prepare his Christmas dinner. To complement their restaurant, the Spiganti family restored five 16th-century brick farmhouses into an elegantly rustic hotel that is run by their charming daughter, Ilaria, one of the most endearing, gracious hostesses you will ever meet. No two bedrooms are alike and each has been individually decorated with fine brocade fabrics and antiques that enhance the country simplicity of beams and brick floors. The bathrooms have been personalized by a local artist whose whimsical designs reflect the various room names. The restaurant, La Corte del Sole, has a wonderful outside terrace with view. A passion for flowers is evident in the surrounding garden, which leads to a large swimming pool. Bordering Umbria and Tuscany, the Relais alla Corte del Sole is the perfect spot from which to easily explore both regions. *Directions:* Exit the A1 at Val di Chiana and follow signs for Perugia. Take the second Cortona exit towards Montepulciano and drive 7 km to the turnoff for Petrignano-Pozzolo. The hotel is after Petrignano.

RELAIS ALLA CORTE DEL SOLE
Host: Ilaria Spiganti
Localita: I Giorgi
Cortona–Petrignano del Lago, (PG) 06061, Italy
Tel: (075) 96 89 008, Fax: (075) 96 89 070
18 Rooms, Double: €166–€450
2 Suites: €213–€450
Open: Apr to Oct & Christmas
Credit cards: MC, VS
HOTEL

Casa Palmira, directly north of Florence, was originally a group of rural buildings attached to an 11th-century tower guarding the road to the Mugello area of Tuscany. Stefano and Assunta, the amiable hosts, named their bed and breakfast after the old lady who lived in the house her entire life. She represents perhaps the spirit of the place, reminding everyone of the basic values of simple country living. The seven bedrooms on the top floor are decorated in a fresh, simple, country style, with hardwood floors, dried and fresh flowers, patchwork quilts, botanical prints, and local country antiques. Rooms are accessed by a large open sitting area with skylights and green plants. The hosts' naturally informal style of hospitality has guests feeling so at home that they can't resist assisting as Assunta works wonders in the open kitchen. This is part of a multi-functional space incorporating kitchen, dining room, and cozy living area with wicker chairs and large fireplace. Meals based on fresh vegetables are served either here or out in the garden under the portico. Daily cooking lessons for individuals or weekly cooking courses for small groups are arranged. Transfers from train station or airport are also offered. *Directions:* Halfway between Borgo S. Lorenzo and Florence on route 302 (Via Faentina), 2 km after Olmo coming from Florence (16 km). Casa Palmira is on the right at the sign for Ristorante Feriolo. From the north leave the A1 at Barberino del Mugello.

CASA PALMIRA
Hosts: Assunta & Stefano Mattioli
Via Faentina–Polcanto
Feriolo, (FI) 50032, Italy
Tel & Fax: (055) 8409749
7 Rooms, Double: €85–€110
1 Apartment: €130 daily, €800–€900 weekly
Minimum Stay Required: 3 nights
Open: Mar to Dec, Credit cards: none
B&B, SELF CATERING

Hotel Albergotto, situated on a corner of the elegant Via de Tornabuoni with its austere Renaissance palazzos and designer boutiques, could not be more central. It existed for the past century as a small hotel once hosting illustrious musical and literary artists like Verdi, Elliot, and Donizetti, but had been virtually forgotten in recent decades. A complete renovation has brought it back to life and it is an excellent choice in the middle price range. From the street entrance you take a red-carpeted flight of stairs to reach the elevator up to the rooms on the top three floors. Beyond the reception desk are two breakfast rooms and a comfortable living room decorated in royal-blue tones with large windows looking out to Tornabuoni. Light-wood floors throughout the hotel give the place a fresh and newer look. Very pleasant, cheerful bedrooms in mustard hues with matching floral bedspreads have amenities such as air conditioning, satellite TV, and mini-bar. The double-paned windows keep out any traffic noise from the main street. Most delightful is the large mansard suite with wood-beamed ceilings and views over the city's rooftops and bell towers. The friendly staff will help you to enjoy your stay. *Directions:* Via de Tornabuoni is three blocks north of the River Arno and two blocks west of Piazza della Repubblica.

HOTEL ALBERGOTTO
Host: Carlo Martelli
Via de Tornabuoni 13
Florence, (FI) 50123, Italy
Tel: (055) 23 96 464, Fax: (055) 23 98 108
22 Rooms, Double: €132–€335
Open: all year, Credit cards: all major
HOTEL

The latest arrival in the group of independent city bed & breakfast properties, managed by Lea, is the very charming Antica Dimora Firenze. Located in part of an ancient palazzo owned by the Pandolfini family, just 5 blocks north of the Duomo Cathedral, it has similar characteristics to the other bed & breakfasts found in the same area (Johanna I & II, Johlea) owned by the same cordial owner, but offers a great deal more. Six smartly decorated rooms are located on the second floor of the ancient, residential building. Each room is individually and tastefully appointed as in a true home, with great attention to detail and guest comfort. A cozy living/reception room with inviting sofas plus breakfast room awaits guests. Breakfast is served in this same reception room or privately in the bedrooms. It is difficult to choose a preference among the six romantic rooms, each completely different in soft pastel color schemes and a unique, additional feature. There are two lovely corner rooms and two quiet ones with small back terraces. All have antique pieces, silk or hand-woven Busatti fabrics and linens, and canopy beds. The color-coordinated bathrooms have marble or brick floors. All are delightful giving the feeling of having your own private apartment in Florence, including the key to the front door! Guests have free wireless connection, television and DVD, plus other amenities. *Directions:* 3 blocks north of San Marco church and square.

ANTICA DIMORA FIRENZE
Host: Lea Gulmanelli
Via San Gallo 72
Florence, (FI) 50129, Italy
Tel: (055) 4627296, Fax: (055) 4634450
6 Rooms, Double: €100–€150
Open: all year, Credit cards: none
B&B

In the past few years, a new breed of bed and breakfasts has developed in Italy's favorite cities, especially in Florence and Rome. A small staff is on hand which makes this an appropriate choice for the independent traveler who enjoys good value for money. It is like having your own home in Florence with keys to the front door. Hostess Lea Gulmanelli had such success with her first three bed and breakfasts (Johanna I and II, Johlea) that she opened one additional place at a superior level, Antica Dimora Johlea, in the same neighborhood. The six bedrooms with four-poster-beds are very cozily appointed in muted soft colors, with beautiful fabrics, Oriental carpets, paintings by the owner, and original tiled or parquet floors. Lea has a real flair for decorating and, as in someone's home, each well-proportioned bedroom retains its own character. There is someone on duty all day (8:30am-8pm) to assist guests with their needs. A rich breakfast is set up in the tastefully decorated breakfast room. During the summer season guests may have breakfast on the delightful flower-potted terrace which offers dreamy views over Florence's rooftops and the Cupola of the Duomo. The guests have free internet service, television, DVD plus other amenities. This property offers very tasteful accommodation and excellent quality and value. *Directions:* The B&B is located between San Marco Square and Piazza della Libertà, directly north of the Duomo, reached in 12 minutes on foot.

❄ ▬ ✄ ☎ ⛴ @ W ⵏ P 🚭 🖼

ANTICA DIMORA JOHLEA
Host: Lea Gulmanelli
Via San Gallo 80
Florence, (FI) 50129, Italy
Tel: (055) 4633292, Fax: (055) 4634552
6 Rooms, Double: €120–€170
Open: all year, Credit cards: none
B&B

In the new category of accommodation in historic residences, the Antica Torre is at the top of the list. The top floors of this ancient fortified palazzo, in the very center of Florence, has been converted into a luxurious and stunning hotel. An elevator takes guests up to the top-floor sitting/bar area and breakfast room where large windows allow heart-stopping full 360-degree views over Florence's terracotta tiled roofs, major monuments, Arno river, and distant hillside backdrop. Take a closer look by stepping out on the large rooftop terrace complete with turrets to have an eye-level peek at Brunelleschi's grand cupola. On the two floors below you find 12 upscale and extra-spacious bedrooms with many amenities, each featuring more unique views or private terraces. The classically styled rooms have been well appointed in soft hues of gold or celestial blue, many with large open windows, perfect for drinking in the marvelous cityscape, virtually identical to that of the Renaissance period. Attentive and energetic young staff definitely keep guests' every comfort in mind, and can arrange anything from special events on the terrace, to taking over the whole accommodation for family reunions or other gatherings. Magical does not even come close to describing the sensation at sunset from this special perch. *Directions:* The Antica Torre entrance is located half a block north of the Arno river on Via Tornabuoni.

❄ 🍽 ✂ 💳 ☎ ♿ @ W Y 🍴 🖼

ANTICA TORRE DI VIA TORNABUONI
Host: Jacopo Marasco
Via Tornabuoni, 1
Florence, (FI) 50123, Italy
Tel: (055) 26 58 161, Fax: (055) 21 88 41
11 Rooms, Double: €180–€325
1 Suite: €275–€375
3 Apartments: €360–€450 daily, €1200–€1600 weekly
Open: all year, Credit cards: all major
HOTEL

Another nice discovery in the category of small, renovated hotels in Florence is the Botticelli, hidden away on a narrow back street behind the Central Market. Many original features of this 16th-century building, once a private home, have been preserved including evidence of a tiny alley that divided the two now-united buildings. Guests enter into a painted, vaulted reception area appointed with large blue and gold armchairs and side sitting room. Other architectural features so typical of the Renaissance period in Florence are the austere gray stone doorways, beamed ceilings in bedrooms, and the delightful open loggia terrace on the second floor lined with terracotta vases of cascading red geraniums. The bedrooms are situated on the three upper floors, with two being up in the mansard and enjoying the best views, and are comfortably and practically decorated with clean wooden furniture and an occasional antique piece blending well with the pea-green fabrics. A full buffet breakfast is offered in the breakfast room with bar just behind the reception area. All the necessary modern amenities such as air conditioning, elevator, modern telephone system, and satellite TV were incorporated during the recent renovation. Fabrizio and his American wife, Janet, run two other hotels in Florence, one being the Hotel Athenaeum, in Via Cavour, near Michelangelo's David. Very helpful staff. *Directions:* The hotel is one block north of Piazza San Lorenzo and the Medici Chapels.

HOTEL BOTTICELLI
Hosts: Fabrizio & Janet Gheri
Via Taddea 8
Florence, (FI) 50123, Italy
Tel: (055) 290905, Fax: (055) 294322
34 Rooms, Double: €100–€240
Minimum Stay Required: 3 nights Fairs & New Year
Open: all year, Credit cards: all major
HOTEL

La Casa del Garbo is a fascinating blend of two styles of accommodation: the quality and tasteful décor of a deluxe hotel along with the warmth and charm of a bed & breakfast. This beautifully-decorated, family-owned property is in the heart of Florence, right on the spectacular Piazza Signoria. You have to look carefully to find the discreet entrance—just a small brass sign lets you know you have found the right spot. Ring the bell to announce your arrival. Once inside a nicely decorated hallway leads to a flight of stairs going up to the reception area, which is open daily from 9 am to 1 pm and 3 pm to 6 pm. Since there is no elevator in this historic 16th-century building, leave your luggage in the lower hallway and someone will pick it up for you. After being shown to your room, you are given a key to your door and another to the front entry door. From that moment on you will feel like a privileged guest in a romantic private home in Florence. You have a choice of two types of accommodation. There are four double bedrooms that include daily breakfast plus five spacious suites that accommodate from two to four guests. Since all the suites have kitchen facilities, breakfast is not included in the suite price. Everyone at La Casa del Garbo seems to have a goal to make your stay unforgettable. *Directions:* Facing the Palazzo Vecchio, in the northeast corner of Piazza della Signoria, just off Via dei Magazzini.

❄ ☕ 🛎 💳 @ W Ⓨ 🚭 🖼 🔔 🚶🚶

LA CASA DEL GARBO   **New**
Host: Simonetta Paoli
Piazza della Signoria 8
Florence, (FI) 50122, Italy
Tel: (055) 29 33 66, Fax: (055) 90 60 783
4 Rooms, Double: €110–€210
5 Suites: €150–€240*
*Breakfast not included in Suite rates
Open: all year, Credit cards: AX, MC, VS
HOTEL

In our estimation, the Hotel Helvetia and Bristol is one of the finest luxury hotels in the center of Florence. Nothing has been spared to make this showplace a true beauty—the decor is outstanding. The lounges, exquisitely decorated with an elegant, yet extremely comfortable, homelike ambiance, exude quality without flamboyance. Each of the guestrooms is also superbly decorated, and, as in a private home, no two are alike. Abundant use of exquisite padded-fabric wall coverings, with color-coordinated draperies, upholstered chairs, and bedspreads along with lovely antiques make each one special. I fell in love with all of the rooms, but my very favorites were the mini-suites: room 257 in gorgeous shades of muted green and room 363 in lovely golds, creams, and dusty pinks, with a sumptuous marble bathroom with Jacuzzi tub, heated towel racks, plus the added bonus of a tiny terrace. The "Hostaria Bibendum" restaurant and bar is a marvelous retreat —light and airy with its alfresco terrace. The restaurant serves lunch, dinner and afternoon tea and the menu features Tuscan specialties made from the freshest local ingredients. The Helvetia and Bristol is expensive, but no more so than the other luxury hotels in Florence, and for those who appreciate quality and refinement, it is unsurpassed. *Directions:*

❄ 🎿 🔳 ☎ 🛗 @ W Ⴏ P 🍽 🚭 ⊛ 🖼 ⚙ 🛇 ⚶ 🥾 🚶‍♀️ 🐎 🎿

HOTEL HELVETIA AND BRISTOL
Host: Stefano Venturi
Via dei Pescioni, 2
Florence, (FI) 50123, Italy
Tel: (055) 26 651, Fax: (055) 23 99 897
67 Rooms, Double: €350–€650*
30 Suites: €450–€1900*
*Breakfast not included: €28
Open: all year, Credit cards: all major
HOTEL

The Hotel Hermitage is a small, characteristic hotel housed in a 13th-century palazzo with breathtaking views over the city's most famous monuments. The location could not be more central—on a small street between the Uffizzi Gallery and the River Arno. The fifth-floor reception area looking out to the Ponte Vecchio bridge has a cozy living-room feeling with selected antique pieces, Oriental rugs, and corner fireplace. Across the hall is the veranda-like breakfast room dotted with crisp yellow tablecloths and topped with fresh flowers where privileged guests view the tower of Palazzo Signoria. Color-coordinated, air-conditioned rooms, some quite small, others with hydro-jet baths, have scattered antiques, framed etchings of the city, and more views. However, the highlight of a stay at the Hermitage is spending time dreaming on the intimate rooftop terrace. The view embraces not only the previously mentioned marvels of Florence, but also the famous dome of the Duomo cathedral and Giotto's tower. Guests are served a basic continental breakfast under the ivy-covered pergola and among the many flower-laden vases lining its borders. Reserve well in advance. *Directions:* Consult a detailed city map. There is a parking garage in the vicinity. Call for instructions as car traffic in this part of the city is strictly limited.

HOTEL HERMITAGE
Host: Vincenzo Scarcelli
Piazza del Pesce
Florence, (FI) 50122, Italy
Tel: (055) 287216, Fax: (055) 212208
28 Rooms, Double: €120–€220
Open: all year, Credit cards: all major
HOTEL

The Residenza D'Epoca in Piazza della Signoria is a top-quality B&B hidden away on the corner of Florence's most famous square hosting the imposing city hall, Palazzo della Signoria. Delightful hosts Sonia and Alessandro initially bought the four-story ancient building as an investment but were touched by the magic spell of this very special historic spot just up the street from the house of Dante and decided to restore it and share it with friends. The fascinating restoration project became something of an archaeological adventure, with documents discovered dating back to 1427 along with a pair of woman's shoes from that same period, and 18th-century frescoes uncovered. Up one flight from street level, Sonia, Alessandro, and occasionally their three sons, greet guests in a small reception area. The ten bedrooms, named after Renaissance masters, are spread about the two floors, with the top floor being crowned with three apartments for those able to enjoy this marvelous city for a full week. To-die-for views from this level include the piazza, Giotto's tower, and Brunelleschi's cupola. The new breakfast room with one long table has the same advantage. Impeccably styled rooms with unique personalities display lovely antique furnishings, parquet floors, and rich colors of teal, peach, and rust. None of the innovative designer bathrooms are identical. A real treat. *Directions:* On the northeast corner of the square at the beginning of Via dei Magazzini.

IN PIAZZA DELLA SIGNORIA
Hosts: Sonia & Alessandro Pini
Via dei Magazzini 2
Florence, (FI) 50122, Italy
Tel: (055) 2399546, Fax: (055) 2676616
8 Rooms, Double: €220–€290
3 Apartments: €1200–€1400 weekly
Minimum Stay Required: Apartments: 7 nights
Open: all year, Credit cards: all major
B&B

The Hotel Lungarno, one of our favorite hotels, is superbly located directly on the River Arno, a few minutes' walk from the Ponte Vecchio. Of more recent construction, the architect has cleverly incorporated into the hotel an ancient stone tower, which houses several romantic suites. The decor is superb, with fine-quality furnishings and gorgeous fabrics accented by an appealing color scheme of blues and creamy whites. The hotel has been totally refurbished with all the latest modern conveniences in smartly styled rooms that have a great appeal. In addition to classic guestrooms are six splendid two-bedroom, two-bath apartments, which are an exceptional value if you are traveling with friends or family. Throughout the hotel a gracious ambiance of understated elegance prevails, enhanced by the admirable management and warm reception. Bountiful bouquets of fresh flowers and an outstanding collection of original 20th century paintings (over 450 works) add the final touch of perfection. If you plan far in advance, you might even be lucky enough to snare a room with a large terrace overlooking the river—these are very special and well worth the extra cost. What a treat to sit on your own terrace in the evening and watch the Arno fade into gold in the setting sun. The alternative is a drink at the Lungarno's sophisticated bar or chic Borgo San Jacopo restaurant, with incomparable river views. Top class.

HOTEL LUNGARNO
Host: Mr. Sandro Alfano
Borgo San Jacopo, 14
Florence, (FI) 50125, Italy
Tel: (055) 27 26 40 00, Fax: (055) 27 26 44 44
60 Rooms, Double: €320–€640
13 Suites: €680–€1600
Restaurant closed Tue
Open: all year, Credit cards: all major
HOTEL

The hills immediately surrounding Florence, dotted with stately villas and country homes dating back to the Renaissance, offered Florentine aristocrats cool respite in summer from the higher temperatures in the city below. The gracious Bulleri family chose this alternative to the city some 30 years ago, and after a successful career in the fashion industry, Claudio and Paola transformed their splendid wooded property into a top-notch inn for discerning guests. Nine very comfortable, immaculate rooms, personally decorated by Paola, have been created in a house across from the family's villa. This includes an elegant main living and dining room with fireplace and large windows looking out over the garden. Classic-style bedrooms have parquet floors, matching fabrics for beds and drapes, and spacious sparkling-white bathrooms. Amenities include satellite TV, wireless Internet, mini-bar, safe, air conditioning, and a selection from the wine cellar. A full country breakfast is served out in the gazebo (in winter sliding glass doors keep the gazebo warm). The swimming pool has gorgeous hillside views over olive groves. The Bulleris share their personal lifestyle: charming son Lorenzo assists guests with local itineraries, guides and museum or concert ticketing, and Paola conducts cooking lessons, while Claudio accompanies guests to his nearby golf club. *Directions:* About a 15-minute drive from Florence. Ask for directions.

MARIGNOLLE RELAIS & CHARME
Host: Claudio Bulleri Family
Via di San Quirichino, 16
Florence, (FI) 50124, Italy
Tel: (055) 22 86 910, Fax: (055) 20 47 396
7 Rooms, Double: €140–€275
2 Suites: €235–€375
Lunch & dinner on request
Open: all year, Credit cards: AX, MC, VS
HOTEL

Palazzo Niccolini is one of the few hotels in Florence within a new category called Historic Residences. Dating from the 16th century, this fascinating palazzo has a prime location directly facing the Duomo Cathedral. The Niccolini family, descendants of the original owners, reside in part of the palazzo and have very meticulously restored the building, offering ten elegant, spacious bedrooms and suites for guests. Entered from the street level, the reception area is up one flight of stairs (or elevator) near the grand living room with period paintings, antiques, grand chandeliers. Breakfast is served in the elegant living room, making one feel like a private house guest. Each bedroom is elegantly decorated with antiques and all have sparkling, marble bathrooms; some with frescoed walls or ceilings. However, the "piéce de resistance" is the priceless suite upstairs that will leave guests in awe. Open the door, climb up ten steps into the glassed-in living room, and gaze right into the side of Brunelleschi's Cupola. You will never get a better view of the detailed, marble façade and roof tiles. In addition, behind the white sofa (which is located directly in front of the enormous windows) is a two-person hydro jet tub hidden among the plants. The bedroom and bathroom are accessed off to the side. *Directions:* The palazzo is on the corner of the Duomo square and Via dei Servi.

❄ 🍺 ⚙ 💳 ☎ 🐕 ♿ @ W Y P 🍴 🚭 🖼 🐾 ♿ ❦

NICCOLINI AL DUOMO
Hosts: Filippo & Ginevra Niccolini di Camugliano
Via dei Servi, 2
Florence, (FI) 50122, Italy
Tel: (055) 28 24 12, Fax: (055) 29 09 79
5 Rooms, Double: €200–€340
5 Suites: €300–€500
Open: all year, Credit cards: all major
HOTEL

Orto de'Medici was named for the Medici family's extensive gardens and orchards that once existed on the site of this hotel. Capable father-and-son team Emilio and Giacomo Bufalini recently took over the reins and took on the challenge of completely refurbishing the family's prim, centuries-old palazzo. Public areas maintain the ambiance of an elegant private home—the frescoed foyer and sitting rooms are graced with portraits, chandeliers, overstuffed armchairs, and Oriental carpets—while services and facilities in bedrooms conform to European Community standards. The spacious upper-floor guestrooms are reached by an elevator and are decorated with classic style. They have matching armoires and beds and all but ten have smart new gray-and-white-marble bathrooms. Several rooms on the top floor have a terrace or balcony with dreamy views over red Florentine rooftops. Perhaps the architectural highlight is the gracious breakfast room (breakfast is a buffet), with high ceilings, original parquet floors, and frescoed panels depicting garden scenes all around. French doors lead from this area to an outdoor terraced flower garden with wrought iron chairs and tables and a lovely view of San Marco church. Wine and cheese tastings are held here in the late afternoon. Dynamic young host Giacomo and his efficient and friendly staff ensure a perfect city sojourn. *Directions:* Four blocks north of the Duomo.

HOTEL ORTO DE'MEDICI
Host: Giacomo Bufalini Family
Via San Gallo 30
Florence, (FI) 50129, Italy
Tel: (055) 483427, Fax: (055) 461276
31 Rooms, Double: €97–€280
Open: all year, Credit cards: all major
HOTEL

The Palazzo dal Borgo–Hotel Aprile, owned by the Cantini Zucconi family for almost four decades, is located in a 15th-century Medici palace behind the Piazza Santa Maria Novella, near the train station and many fine restaurants and shops. The historical building was restored under the strict ordinance of Florence's Commission of Fine Arts. Guests are invited to three complimentary evening lectures a week on Florence's art and history by a professor of the University of Florence. The small and charming hotel is full of delightful surprises: from 16th-century paintings and a bust of the Duke of Tuscany to the frescoed breakfast room and quiet courtyard garden. The old-fashioned reception and sitting areas are invitingly furnished with Florentine Renaissance antiques, comfy, overstuffed red armchairs, and Oriental carpets worn with time. There are 34 bedrooms that vary widely in their size and decor, all with private bathrooms, telephones, mini-bars, carpeted or tile floors, and high vaulted ceilings. A recent extensive renovation has made improvements in facilities while maintaining the original overall charm. Request one of the quieter rooms at the back of the hotel, overlooking the garden. At the desk you find Roberto Gazzini and Sandra Costantini looking after guests' needs. *Directions:* Use a detailed city map to locate the hotel, three blocks north of the Duomo. There is a parking garage.

PALAZZO DAL BORGO—HOTEL APRILE
Host: Riccardo Zucconi
Via della Scala 6
Florence, (FI) 50123, Italy
Tel: (055) 216237, Fax: (055) 280947
34 Rooms, Double: €110–€310
Open: all year, Credit cards: all major
HOTEL

Palazzo Galletti, housed in an historic Florentine palazzo dating to the 1800s, comes under the category of Historic Residences—a glorified bed and breakfast. Young and enthusiastic partners, Francesca and Samuele acquired the entire upper first floor (historically referred to as the Noble floor and characterized by high ceilings and frescoed walls) with the idea of offering high quality accommodation in a more home-like ambiance. Enter from the street through ancient iron gates. Up a flight of stairs is the small reception area, from which a hallway with bedrooms extends and wraps around the center atrium. Softly styled guestrooms, each different from the next and named after the planets, are nicely appointed in beige tones contrasting with colorful abstract paintings. Elios (Sun) and Selene (Moon) are two beautiful new suites! Many rooms have original features such as the magnificent old frescoes in the two corner junior suites. A fresh buffet breakfast is served in the original kitchen with its vaulted brick ceilings, sink and oven dating to 1550. A day spa, Soul Space, offers massages and treatments. Palazzo Galletti provides all the amenities of a hotel and the hospitality and ambiance of a home. For those who seek a quiet escape, inquire about their charming farmhouse, Fattoria Bacio! *Directions:* Take the Via dell'Oriuolo from behind the Duomo to the end and turn sharp left on Via Sant'Egidio.

PALAZZO GALLETTI
Hosts: Samuele Minucci & Francesca Cascino
Via Sant'Egidio 12
Florence, (FI) 50122, Italy
Tel: (055) 3905750, Fax: (055) 3905752
7 Rooms, Double: €120–€160
4 Suites: €180–€260
Open: all year, Credit cards: all major
B&B

The stunning Palazzo Magnani Feroni, an ancient private residence of the Giannotti family, dating back to the 1500s, is on the "left bank" of the River Arno four blocks away from the Ponte Vecchio. The sensation of being in a true palace is captured immediately upon entering the grand foyer with vaulted ceilings, marble busts, statues, and precious period paintings, many from the owners' world travels. This is a unique all-suite upscale accommodation in that they have purposefully avoided adding any obvious signs of its being a hotel (a small reception room sits off the main entrance) in order to retain the aura of living in an elegant historical residence. Sumptuous bedrooms with soaring ceilings, mostly enormous suites, have retained their original architectural features and have been appointed with antique and reproduction pieces, gilded framed mirrors, Oriental carpets, brocaded gold fabrics on sofas, and tapestries. Suites on the ground floor look out onto an inner courtyard and one has two walls entirely covered with a fresco depicting a bucolic countryside scene. Breakfast is served in the suites or in the long upstairs dining room with its showcase displaying antique silk fabrics left over from the days when the palazzo was also an antique gallery. Another highlight includes a rooftop terrace with superb views over the city, where in summer the Palace Bar opens every evening. The hotel also offers complimentary in-suite dinner for late arrivals.

❄ ☕ 🛒 ⛴ 💳 ☎ 🏨 🏌 @ W ♈ P 🐾 🚶 👫 🏇 💃

PALAZZO MAGNANI FERONI
Hosts: Dr. & Sra. Alberto Giannotti
Borgo San Frediano, 5
Florence, (FI) 50124, Italy
Tel: (055) 23 99 544, Fax: (055) 26 08 908
12 Suites: €230–€900
Open: all year, Credit cards: all major
History Traveller
HOTEL

The Regency, facing out to a park in the most exclusive residential area, is one of Florence's finest luxury hotels and a welcome haven in the overcrowded tourist scene. Gracious hospitality comes naturally to owner Amedeo Ottaviani (also of the Lord Byron in Rome) and his philosophy that every guest should be treated with the best possible personal attention goes hand in hand with the intimate ambiance of the hotel, a former private home. Upon arrival guests are warmly greeted by resident manager, Lara, and invited into one of the cozy English-style sitting rooms richly appointed with fine antiques and paintings, floral-patterned carpeting, and exquisite fabrics in warm red tones. Beyond are two intimate, formal dining rooms, where the house chef is praised for his innovative creations based on Tuscan specialties incorporating the region's top-quality ingredients. The larger glassed-in dining area looks out over the exceptionally lush courtyard garden where romantic candlelit dinners are served in the summer months. Comfortable bedrooms and suites are spread among the top floors and a separate building connected to the main villa. They are uniquely appointed with white furnishings reproduced from original Tuscan antiques, patterned carpeting, and contrasting wall fabrics. Each has its own refurbished marble bathroom. The concierge is on hand to organize museum and concert reservations, and guides.

❄ ☕ 🚲 ♨ 💳 ☎ 🐕 🛏 @ W Ŧ P 🍴 🚭 🖼 🔔 🍽 🚶 🐎 🍇

HOTEL REGENCY
Host: Amedeo Ottaviani
Piazza Massimo D'Azeglio, 3
Florence, (FI) 50121, Italy
Tel: (055) 24 52 47, Fax: (055) 23 46 735
25 Rooms, Double: €275–€560
10 Suites: €740–€970
Open: all year, Credit cards: all major
HOTEL

If you are looking for a hotel in Florence that offers both a fabulous location and reasonably priced, pleasant rooms, the simple Relais Uffizi is for you. The double wood doors of the ancient building are located on the Chiasso del Buco, a quaint narrow back street accessed through an ancient arch from the Chiasso de' Baroncelli, off the Piazza della Signoria. Upstairs in the main reception lounge, the gracious owner, Elisabetta Matucci, or one of her friendly assistants will give you a warm welcome. Because there are so few rooms and the hotel is family-managed, guests are known by name and made to feel like friends. Nothing is contrived or overly sophisticated: instead there is an informal, comfortable ambiance. The heart of the hotel is the lounge where large windows look down upon the famous Piazza della Signoria with its statues and outdoor cafes. From this marvelous perch, you can relax in quiet comfort and enjoy all the drama and activity of Florence unfolding just below you. Although this is a simple hotel with remarkably low rates, no deluxe hotel in Florence can surpass this view of Florence. A maze of hallways leads to the individually decorated guestrooms. They vary in shape and size (number 3 with a canopy bed is especially spacious), but all are attractive in decor and have some antique furnishings. Best of all, they are immaculately clean and offer all the basic amenities.

RELAIS UFFIZI
Host: Elisabetta Matucci
Chiasso de' Baroncelli/Chiasso del Buco, 16
Florence, (FI) 50122, Italy
Tel: (055) 26 76 239, Fax: (055) 26 57 909
13 Rooms, Double: €160–€250
2 Suites: €220–€270
Open: all year, Credit cards: AX, MC, VS
HOTEL

The refurbished Hotel Silla is located on the left bank of the River Arno opposite Santa Croce, the famous 13th-century square and church where Michelangelo and Galileo are buried. This position offers views from some of the rooms of several of Florence's most notable architectural attractions—the Duomo, the Ponte Vecchio, and the tower of the Palazzo Vecchio. Housed on the second and third floors of a lovely 15th-century palazzo with courtyard entrance, 36 new and spotless double rooms (non-smoking upon request) with private baths are pleasantly decorated with simple dark-wood furniture and matching bedspreads and curtains. Air conditioning and an elevator were recently added necessities. The fancy, cream-colored reception area is appointed in 17th-century Venetian style, with period furniture, a chandelier, and large paintings. Breakfast is served on the splendid and spacious second-floor outdoor terrace or in the dining room overlooking the Arno. The Silla is a friendly, convenient, and quiet hotel, near the Pitti Palace, leather artisan shops, and many restaurants. It offers tourists a good value in pricey Florence. A parking garage is available. *Directions:* Refer to a detailed city map to locate the hotel.

HOTEL SILLA
Host: Gabriele Belotti
Via dei Renai 5
Florence, (FI) 50125, Italy
Tel: (055) 2342888, Fax: (055) 2341437
35 Rooms, Double: €90–€220
Open: all year, Credit cards: all major
HOTEL

The Torre di Bellosguardo is a romantic historic villa nestled on the shelf of a hill with an unsurpassed view of Florence. Below the enormous castle-like home, the tiled rooftops, steeples, towers, and domes of the city seem like a fairyland at your fingertips. It is not surprising that the setting of the Torre di Bellosguardo is so breathtaking: it was chosen by a nobleman, Guido Cavalcanti (a friend of Dante), as the most beautiful site in Florence. The villa is owned today by Amerigo Franchetti who takes great pride in his stunning home and, with a passion for perfection, is restoring the villa to its original glory. The spacious austere guestrooms with views are decorated in authentic period antiques and vary in size as they would in a private home with few frills. Other rooms include frescoed ballroom, Orangerie, and upstairs loggia terrace. The most splendid features of the hotel are its incredible setting and meticulously groomed botanical garden, which highlights a swimming pool set on a terrace overlooking Florence, Brunelleschi cupola and all. In summer lunch is served by the swimming pool, otherwise breakfast is the only meal available. For dinner, you must wind down a narrow twisting road to go to a restaurant. If you want to walk into Florence, ask about the "secret" path—a short cut down the hill to the city (15 minute walk). Down a level through an underground tunnel a small pool, sauna and steam room.

❄ ⚒ CREDIT 🏔 ☎ 🐕 ⛪ 🍸 P 🌸 🏊 🖼 ⚜ 🏃 🚶 🐎 🍇

TORRE DI BELLOSGUARDO
Host: Amerigo Franchetti
Via Roti Michelozzi, 2
Florence, (FI) 50124, Italy
Tel: (055) 22 98 145, Fax: (055) 22 90 08
8 Rooms, Double: €290*
7 Suites: €340–€390*
*Breakfast not included: €20
Poolside lunch in summer, light dinners on request
Open: all year, Credit cards: all major
HOTEL

La Torricella, just on the outskirts of Florence, offers travelers the advantage of staying in a Tuscan home in a quiet residential area, yet with the city easily accessible by public transportation. Marialisa completely restored her great-grandfather's home and converted it into a comfortable and efficient lodging. She decided to offer all the trimmings of a hotel, with amenities such as satellite TVs, mini-bars, and telephones in rooms, plus daily cleaning service. The terraced front of the pale-yellow villa is lined with terracotta vases of flowers and intoxicating wisteria vines. Upon entering the home, you pass through a small reception area with brick arches and equestrian prints into the luminous breakfast room where a buffet is served in the morning. Accommodations are scattered about the large, pristine home on various levels and are each similarly appointed in soft-green and mustard hues with sparkling new white bathrooms. Reproduction armoires and desks and wrought-iron beds harmonize well with the brick floors and high, beamed ceilings. Marialisa offers cooking classes, teaching secrets of genuine Tuscan dishes, and is a rich source of information on the area. There is a small pool at the back of the house. *Directions:* From the Certosa exit of the A1, head for the center of the city, turning right at the stoplight in Galluzzo at Piazza Acciaiuoli. Take Via Silvani for several blocks, turning right on Via Vecchia di Pozzolatico just before the fork in the road.

LA TORRICELLA
Host: Marialisa Manetti Family
Via Vecchia di Pozzolatico 25
Florence, (FI) 50125, Italy
Tel: (055) 2321818, Fax: (055) 2047402
7 Rooms, Double: €100–€130
1 Apartment: €800 weekly
Open: Mar 1 to Nov 20, Credit cards: VS
B&B, SELF CATERING

If you want to see Florence, yet be blissfully removed from its swarm of tourists and traffic congestion, the Villa La Massa makes a fabulous choice for a place to stay. Here you can enjoy the best of all worlds—the tranquil beauty of the countryside combined with the convenience of a courtesy bus to take you to and from the heart of the city (15 minutes away). This gorgeous Renaissance villa originally belonged to the rich and powerful Giraldi family—inscribed tombstones, underground tunnels, and a chapel still remain from this period of the villa's history. What makes Villa La Massa so stunning is not only the appeal of the hotel, but also its setting. This idyllic property sits on a gentle bluff that hugs the edge of the River Arno as it loops its way east from Florence. During the day guests relax by a lovely swimming pool in the central garden courtyard. The restaurant is very special, with tables set on a terrace right above the Arno, making dinner truly romantic. In 1998 Villa La Massa was bought by the owners of the Villa d'Este and totally renovated, with the hotel emerging as a shining new gem in the Florence scene. The grounds are now meticulously groomed, the gardens are splendid, and the interior lovely, reflecting the same standard of excellence as the Villa d'Este. *Directions:* Exit A1 at Firenze Sud and follow signs to Bagno a Ripoli and Candeli. At Candeli, watch for a sign on the left to the hotel.

HOTEL VILLA LA MASSA   *New*
Host: Francesca Tozzi
Via della Massa, 24
Florence, (FI) 50012, Italy
Tel: (055) 62 611, Fax: (055) 63 31 02
37 Rooms, Double: €440–€850
Open: Mar to Nov, Credit cards: all major
Relais & Châteaux
HOTEL

The pristine grey-white Villa Vedetta, originally a private home, is the only accommodation positioned right at Florence's most famous panoramic viewing point, the Piazzale Michelangelo. Brunelleschi's unmistakable dome dominates the scene and can be privately enjoyed from the hotel's garden with swimming pool and large Jacuzzi area, from the expansive terrace, and from most guestrooms. A trendy Michelin star restaurant within the villa, Onice, under the guidance of Chef Franco Del Cerria, presents artistic, innovative Tuscan-based cuisine and a vast wine list. Eight stylish guestrooms in a contemporary vein have all the trimmings expected of a luxury property and are appointed in light grays, and accented with touches of cherry red, satin peach, or celestial blues. Modern bathrooms are done in marble with mosaic trims. The main sitting areas are freshly appointed with striped sofas and modern artwork. But what guests really rave about is the attentive staff, always willing and ready to assist with warmth and knowledge. A variety of interesting theme stays involving shopping, art or Chianti wineries make your stay more complete. Complimentary shuttle service to the city center. *Directions:* From A1 autostrada, exit Firenze Sud. Turn right in Via Enrick de Nicola and continue along the river, until you reach bridge Ponte S. Niccole. At the light turn right over the bridge, and enter in Viale Michelangelo. Continue for 1km. Hotel is on the right.

❄ ✤ 🖃 ☎ P ¶ ≈ 🖼 🕴 👫 🍷

VILLA LA VEDETTA
Host: Andrea Luxoro
Via Michelangelo 78
Florence, (FI) 50125, Italy
Tel: (055) 68 16 31, Fax: (055) 65 82 544
18 Rooms, Double: €449–€1099*
*Breakfast not included: €40
Open: all year, Credit cards: all major
History Traveller
Relais & Châteaux
HOTEL

The Bencista is a real find for the traveler looking for a congenial, unpretentious, family-run hotel near Florence that has charm and yet is reasonably priced. The villa, romantically nestled in the foothills with a bird's-eye view of Florence, is owned and managed by the Simoni family who are always about, personally seeing to every need of their guests. Simone Simoni speaks excellent English, and on the day of my arrival he was patiently engrossed in conversation with one of the guests, giving him tips for sightseeing. Downstairs there is a jumble of sitting rooms, bars, and parlors, each decorated with dark Victorian furniture. Upstairs are the bedrooms, which vary in size, location, and furnishings. Some are far superior to others. Many people return year after year to their own favorite room. During the season, reservations should be made well in advance, especially for a room with a view over Florence, as the hotel is beautifully located for sightseeing in both Florence and Tuscany. (If you do not have a car, you can take the bus that runs regularly into Florence from the top of the road every 20 min.) Two meals (breakfast and a choice of lunch or dinner) are included in the price. One of the outstanding features of the pensione is its splendid terrace where guests can enjoy a sweeping panorama of Florence.

PENSIONE BENCISTA
Host: Simone Simoni
Florence–Fiesole, (FI) 50014, Italy
Tel & Fax: (055) 59 163
27 Rooms, Double: €124–€184*
3 Suites: €180–€250*
*Includes breakfast & dinner
Closed: Dec to Feb, Credit cards: MC, VS
HOTEL

Fiesole, a small town tucked in the green wooded hills above Florence, has long been a favorite of ours. Staying here gives you the best of both worlds—you can enjoy the peacefulness of the countryside while being just a short ride away from Florence. If you are looking for ultimate luxury, nothing can compete with the Villa San Michele, but the Hotel Villa Fiesole offers a delightful alternative for those on a more conservative budget. You can easily spot the Villa Fiesole, set just above the road as it loops up the wooded hillside. Originally a private mansion, the Villa Fiesole was converted into a delightful small hotel in 1995, being equipped with all the finest modern amenities but keeping the overall ambiance of an exquisite home. In this part of the hotel, the rooms vary somewhat in size because of the nature of the building. A new wing has been added and the construction was done in excellent taste so that it blends in beautifully with the original villa. Here the rooms are almost identical in size and furnishings. Each is especially spacious and decorated in a most appealing way, using tones of rich blue and whites, giving an overall ambiance of refined good taste. The hotel's restaurant, serving a combination of classic Italian cuisine and newer inovative dishes, has a stunning view over Florence from its panoramic terrace. The Florence bus #7 stops in front of the villa every 20 minutes until 6 pm.

❄ ☞ ✎ ▭ ☎ ⌂ 🏛 @ W ⅄ P ¶ ⊘ ≋ 🖼 ⚐ ⚕ 🧍 👫 🐎 ☬

HOTEL VILLA FIESOLE
Host: Simone Taddei
Via Beato Angelico, 35
Florence–Fiesole, (FI) 50014, Italy
Tel: (055) 59 72 52, Fax: (055) 59 91 33
32 Rooms, Double: €120–€430
4 Suites: €220–€460
Meals for hotel guests only
Open: all year, Credit cards: all major
HOTEL

It would be difficult to find another hotel with as many attributes as the Villa San Michele—in fact, almost impossible. How could you surpass a wooded hillside setting overlooking Florence, a stunning view, gorgeous antiques, impeccable management, gourmet dining, and, as if this were not enough, a building designed by Michelangelo. The Villa San Michele was originally a monastery dating back to the 15th century and occupied by Franciscan friars until Napoleon turned it into his headquarters. The adaptation of its rooms and public areas to today's standards has been made without affecting the ambiance of serenity and history. Most of the rooms are in the historical building and have been recently renovated and redecorated with taste and somber elegance. Eighteen junior suites are located in the Italian garden and three suites in the Limonaia, once the greenhouse for storing lemon plants during the winter. All have sweeping views of Florence and the Arno Valley. The lounges, dining rooms, terraces, and gardens are also exquisite. Meals can be enjoyed either in the elegant dining room or on a lovely veranda that stretches along the entire length of the building. A panoramic swimming pool has been built on a secluded terrace above the hotel. Now a permanent cooking school, the Villa San Michele School of Cookery offers a wide range of gastronomic courses.

❄ ☕ ✄ ♨ 💳 ☎ 🏋 @ W Y P 🍴 ≈ 🖼 🐾 🎿 🚶 🏇 💃

VILLA SAN MICHELE
Host: Luca Finardi
Via Doccia, 4
Florence–Fiesole, (FI) 50014, Italy
Tel: (055) 56 78 200, Fax: (055) 56 78 250
21 Rooms, Double: €950–€1100
25 Suites: €1300–€3200
Open: Apr to Nov, Credit cards: all major
History Traveller
HOTEL

The bed and breakfast boom of the last decade in Italy has brought about a vast variety of accommodation from classic, in-home hospitality to places with many amenities that more resemble small hotels. Il Torrino brings us back to the more traditional example, with four bedrooms offered within the hostess home. The large, old-fashioned family home of Signora Cesarina's grandparents is located in the Montechiari hills between Florence and Pisa east-west and between Volterra and Lucca north-south—a prime touring location. Here you will not find standardized rooms all decorated alike, but rather individual rooms filled with the family's personal belongings, heirloom furniture, and the authentic feeling of a Tuscan home. With her children grown and residing in various parts of the world, the very sweet hostess, Cesarina Campinotti, opened her home to travelers and welcomes guests into the downstairs living room and upstairs breakfast room where an abundant meal is served. A separate garden apartment for two persons has glass doors overlooking the small pool and countryside beyond. Here you are in the center of Tuscany. *Directions:* From Forcoli follow signs for Montechiari and Montacchita, continuing past Montacchita up to the group of houses called Montechiari (2 km). Il Torrino has the black iron gate and no sign.

VILLA IL TORRINO
Host: Cesarina Campinotti
Montechiari
Forcoli, (PI) 56030, Italy
Tel & Fax: (0587) 629181
4 Rooms, Double: €85–€90
1 Apartment: €420 weekly
Minimum Stay Required: 3 nights
Open: all year, Credit cards: all major
B&B, SELF CATERING

Forte dei Marmi, the refined Tuscan seaside between the Cinque Terre and its more popular neighbor, Viareggio, has been a favorite of the Tuscan and Milanese elite for the past century. The Hotel Byron is a classic luxury ex-private residence where one can become a part of this privileged milieu. Daily life of the summer residents includes lounging at one of the many beach clubs on the long stretch of beach directly in front of the hotel-lined with chairs, canopies, restaurants and night clubs. The scenic backdrop of the town are the towering Apuan Alps standing tall in the distance. An afternoon bike ride as the locals do is a must as is dining around the hotel's pool in the evening by candlelight at the notable La Magnolia restaurant lead by creative chef Andrea Mattei. The Madonna family from Pisa has placed the management of their three hotel properties in the very capable hands of congenial son, Salvatore, who welcomes guests to the hotel as would be in a private home. Luminous rooms and suites are either appointed in understated classic or very tasteful contemporary styles with yellow and black accents, all with marble bathrooms from local Carrara quarries, many with terraces. Several inviting sitting areas with card tables, piano and a bar lead out to a large terrace in the lush garden where an aperitif is served. Pisa, Lucca, and the Ligurian coast including the Cinque Terre are all easily reached as well as the artist's colony in Pietrasanta.

❄ ☕ 🛴 💳 ☎ 🚻 @ Υ P ⑪ 🚭 ≋ 🖼 🐾 ♿ ⚓ 🚶 🥾 👯 ❦

HOTEL BYRON   New
Host: Salvatore Madonna
Viale Morin 46
Forte dei Marmi, (LU) 55042, Italy
Tel: (0584) 78 70 52, Fax: (0584) 78 71 52
29 Rooms, Double: €250–€730
2 Suites: €600–€1330
Open: all year, Credit cards: all major
HOTEL

Borgo Argenina has all the elements of a "bestseller" bed and breakfast: the perfect location in the heart of Chianti surrounded by vineyards, very comfortable accommodation in an ancient stone farmhouse, glorious countryside views, and, above all, Elena, the Borgo Argenina's gregarious hostess. She left behind a successful fashion business in Milan and bought an entire abandoned village, restoring two of the stone houses for herself and the bed and breakfast. She chose the best artisans in the area and literally worked with them to create the house of her dreams. Everything from painting stenciled borders in rooms through restoring furniture to sewing quilted bedspreads was executed exclusively by Elena herself. The downstairs living rooms and breakfast room are beautifully done in rich cream and soft yellows that complement perfectly the brick-vaulted ceilings and terracotta floors. Elena is up at dawn baking cakes for breakfast and makes occasional dinners for the guests accompanied by classical music. Every little detail has been attended to in the pink-and-blue bedrooms adorned with white eyelet curtains, patchwork quilts, and dried flower arrangements. Across the way is a very comfortable three-bedroom, independent house. *Directions:* Follow S.S.408 from Siena for Montevarchi and after 15 km turn off to the right at Monti. Just before Monti and S. Marcellina there is a sign on the right for Borgo Argenina.

BORGO ARGENINA
Host: Elena Nappa
Localita: Argenina-Monti
Argenina
Gaiole in Chianti, (SI) 53013, Italy
Tel: (0577) 747117, Fax: (0577) 747228
5 Rooms, Double: €170–€170
2 Suites: €200–€200
3 Houses: €240 daily
Minimum Stay Required: 2 nights
Open: Mar to Nov 6, Credit cards: all major
B&B, SELF CATERING

In the heart of the beautiful Chianti wine region, a cypress-lined lane leads up to the handsome, 13th-century Castello di Meleto, set upon a gentle hill just outside Gaiole. The fairytale-perfect castle with its imposing round watchtowers and arched stone doorway embraced by fragrant roses makes an enchanting stop while exploring the back roads of Tuscany. There is a double treat in store because you can not only sample delicious wines in the attractive tasting room, but also visit the interior of this splendid castle with its walls and ceilings lavishly enhanced by superb frescoes, lovely antique furnishings, and even an adorable baroque theater dating back to the mid-1700s (call ahead for tour times). The castle also offers nine attractively decorated guestrooms with antique furnishings, five within the castle and four in the chapel house. Breakfast is served each morning in the cozy kitchen with huge open fireplace. The castle gardens stretch out to a line of lacy trees that frame a superb vista of the idyllic Tuscan countryside. There is also a stunning view from the swimming pool, which is bordered on three sides by a flagstone terrace and on the fourth flows seamlessly into the horizon. If you are traveling with friends or family and want a place for a longer stay, the castle offers 11 beautifully furnished stone cottages with well-equipped kitchens and from one to three bedrooms. Advance reservations a must. *Directions:* From Gaiole in Chianti, follow signs to the castle.

CASTELLO DI MELETO
Host: Lucia Pasquini
Gaiole in Chianti, (SI) 53013, Italy
Tel & Fax: (0577) 749129
9 Rooms, Double: €125–€148
11 Cottages: €630–€1953 weekly
Minimum Stay Required: Rooms: 2 nights, Cottages: 7 nights
Dinners: €25
Open: all year, Credit cards: all major
B&B, SELF CATERING

The Castello di Spaltenna is a charming hotel, nestled within an ancient feudal hamlet in one of the prettiest parts of Tuscany's glorious Chianti wine region. From the castle with its fortified monastery and adjacent church adorned by an 11th-century bell tower, you can look out in every direction to a blissful scene of rolling hills, valleys, and woodlands dotted with castles and medieval villages. Although deluxe in every detail, the hotel reflects its heritage with beamed ceilings, thick walls, stone floors, and watchtowers. The decor too pays tribute to the past with handsome old oil paintings, priceless tapestries, gorgeous Persian carpets, handmade wrought-iron beds, and splendid antique furniture. A wonderful feature of the hotel is its restaurant, Il Pievano, situated in the centuries old hall of the Castello di Spaltenna. The heart of the hotel is its internal courtyard. When the weather is mild, guests enjoy fine dining here in a fairy-tale setting created by softly illuminated candles, tables dressed with fine linens, fresh flowers, and for a romantic touch, a harp playing in the background. On a terrace below the castle guests can relax after a day of sightseeing and enjoy an exceptionally beautiful, large swimming pool. A final touch is an indoor pool, which is part of the resort's deluxe spa facility. *Directions:* From Gaiole in Chianti, follow signs to the castle.

❄ ☕ 🏊 💳 ☎ 🏋 @ ⅄ P ⅂⅂ ❦ ≈ 🚶 🏞 🔔 🚶🚶 🐎 🍷

CASTELLO DI SPALTENNA
Host: Guido Conti
Gaiole in Chianti, (SI) 53013, Italy
Tel: (0577) 74 94 83, Fax: (0577) 74 92 69
38 Rooms, Double: €230–€540
Closed: Feb & Mar, Credit cards: all major
HOTEL

The Castello di Tornano, a strategically situated hilltop tower dating back almost 1,000 years, has a 360-degree vista of the surrounding valley and has been of great historical significance in the seemingly endless territorial battles between Siena and Florence. The owners are the Selvolini family and it is Patrizia who welcomes guests to the expansive wine estate. Nine charming rooms are situated in the actual castle and its monumental tower. Patrizia has personally taken care of the décor of the house using many of the family's own antiques. The "piece de resistance" is the superior suite on the top floor of the tower, offering a unique architectural style and a magnificent view from eight large windows. The tower-top terrace has a 6-person hydro-jet pool, a view not easily forgotten. In the stone farmhouse, in front of the tower, 7 one- and two-bedroom apartments are offered guests, each appointed in the typical rustic style of Tuscany. The kitchen serves authentic, traditional meals as well as cooking classes. The spectacular pool was built inside the ancient moat of the castle. Trails cut across the vineyards and the surrounding woods, enjoyable for walks. It is also possible to ride the owners' horses through the scenic countryside. *Directions:* From the A1 exit at Valdarno, follow the sign to Gaiole. Take the S.S.408 towards Gaiole and pass through the village, following signs for Siena. After 6 km you see the sign for Tornano on the left.

CASTELLO DI TORNANO
Hosts: Patrizia Selvolini & Francesco Gioffreda
Gaiole in Chianti, (SI) 53013, Italy
Tel: (0577) 746067, Fax: (0577) 746094
9 Rooms, Double: €150–€325
2 Suites: €280–€520
6 Apartments: €110–€235 daily, €600–€1300 weekly*
*Breakfast not included for Apartments
Dinners: €40
Open: Mar 15 to Nov 1, Christmas & New Years
Credit cards: VS
B&B, SELF CATERING

When dreaming of Tuscany one usually envisions sweeping fields of vineyards and gentle hills dotted with olive trees. L'Ultimo Mulino has a totally different type of setting, in a heavily wooded nook by a small stream. This small hotel was originally a medieval olive mill and the antique millstone in the lounge stands testament to the hotel's colorful past, as do many architectural features, including 13 dramatic brick arches, which form a vaulted ceiling in the lounge. The primary color scheme throughout is white and blue—seen in the sofas and also in the dining room in the cushions and the table linens and china. The guestrooms all have a rustic ambiance, appropriate to the old mill, with wrought-iron headboards used throughout. The price of the rooms depends upon the size and the amenities. The least expensive rooms are fairly small but those in the upper category are large, and several have their own private terrace. The bathrooms are especially nice, and many have the added luxury of Jacuzzi tubs. All the rooms have air conditioning, direct-dial phones, mini-bars, good lighting by the beds, and satellite televisions. One of the most pleasant features of the hotel is a 20-meter swimming pool built into a terrace above the hotel. *Directions:* From Radda in Chianti, take the road for Gaiole and Siena. About 5 km from Radda, turn left at the sign to L'Ultimo Mulino. The hotel is about midway between Radda and Gaiole.

❄ ✗ ☕ 🖥 ▲ ☎ 🏠 @ W Ⴏ P ❀ ≈ 🖼 ⅙ 🏃 👫 🐎 🍇

L' ULTIMO MULINO
Host: Massimo Rossinelli
Localita: La Ripresa di Vistarenni
Gaiole in Chianti, (SI) 53013, Italy
Tel: (0577) 73 85 20, Fax: (0577) 73 86 59
12 Rooms, Double: €114–€204*
1 Suite: €212–€265*
*Breakfast not included: €9,90
Restaurant closed Mon
Closed: mid-Nov to mid-Mar, Credit cards: all major
HOTEL

On the extreme outskirts of Florence, the Fattoressa offers a location for dual exploration of both the city and the Tuscan countryside. One of the many marvelous attractions of Florence is how the countryside comes right up to the doors of the city and just behind the magnificent Certosa monastery you find the 15th-century stone farmhouse of the delightfully congenial Fusi-Borgioli family. They have transformed the farmer's quarters into guest accommodations: four sweetly simple bedrooms plus two triples, each with its own spotless bathroom. Angiolina and Amelio, who have tended to this piece of land for many years, treat their guests like family and, as a result, enjoy receiving some of them year after year. Daughters-in-law Laura and Katia, who speak English, have been a great help in assisting guests with local itineraries. Visitors take meals "en famille" at long tables in the cozy, rustic dining room with a large stone fireplace (€25-€28 for dinner). Here Angiolina proudly serves authentic Florentine specialties using ingredients from her own fruit orchard and vegetable garden. *Directions:* Entering Florence from the Certosa exit off the Siena superstrada, turn left one street after the Certosa monastery stoplight onto Volterrana. After the bridge, turn right behind the building. The house is just on the left.

LA FATTORESSA
Hosts: Angiolina Fusi & Amelio Borgioli
Via Volterrana 58
Galluzzo, (FI) 50124, Italy
Tel & Fax: (055) 2048418
6 Rooms, Double: €80
Open: all year, Credit cards: none
B&B

Casa Mezzuola is part of a small group of farmhouses atop a hill 3 kilometers outside Greve where the land was divided into separate smaller properties. Friendly hosts, Riccardo, an antiques and jewelry dealer, Nicoletta, and their two girls live in the main house while hospitality is offered within three apartments for two to four persons in the adjacent stables and fienile where the hay was once stored. The stone walls, beams, and original brick openings to allow air into the barn were all preserved in the tower-like construction housing two of the apartments. A two-story apartment has a tiled kitchen/living area on one floor and bedroom and bathroom upstairs, while the snug studio apartment crowns the top of the tower. They are all nicely furnished with colorful rugs, local country furniture, satellite TV, and fully equipped kitchens. Breakfast is served within the apartments or outside under one of the pergola terraces. Just below the apartments is a swimming pool, which enjoys the expansive vistas, and there are bikes for guests' use. This is a convenient base for travelers in the heart of Chianti. Greve has a full program of festivals, concerts, and events, especially during the summer. *Directions:* Entering Greve from the north (Florence), turn right at the Esso Petrol Station. Follow signs for Mezzuola, Cologne, not Montefioralle. After 3 km of unpaved, bumpy road, you will come across the marked property.

CASA MEZZUOLA
Host: Riccardo Franconeri Family
Via S. Cresci 30
Greve in Chianti, (FI) 50022, Italy
Tel & Fax: (055) 8544885
1 Room, Double: €80–€130
3 Apartments: €90–€150 daily, €400–€850 weekly
Minimum Stay Required: 3 nights
Open: all year, Credit cards: MC, VS
SELF CATERING

Once a 19th century hunting lodge, the charming Villa Marta property with manicured Renaissance garden and magical mountain backdrop (beyond it is Pisa) is just 10 minutes south of Lucca. Two prim houses sit side by side and contain the 15 attractive guestrooms of varying size and décor lending the sense of a private home. High beamed ceiling rooms are given a fresh, luminous and romantic air by the carefully selected array of country fabrics and furnishings with matching soft-colored bathrooms. Energetic and congenial hosts Andrea and Alessia have put their heart and soul into making guests feel part of the ambiance and actively participate in organizing and coordinating a fascinating list itineraries and activities in-house and out. A generous breakfast buffet table filled with homemade baked goods, Alessia's special talent, awaits guests each morning either out in the garden or in the intimate dining room in the main villa. The warm salmon toned restaurant, Botton d'Oro, specializes in authentic Tuscan cuisine using top quality local ingredients including the property's own olive oil. A light lunch or glass of chilled white wine at sunset can be served at the edge of the inviting swimming pool set among the olive, potted lemon and cypress trees. Truly tranquil. *Directions:* Leave autostrada A11/A12 at Lucca East, follow signs for Pisa on SS12. After 3/4 km take a left on a small, hidden street to the left, Via Guasperini and follow signs to the gated entrance.

❄ ☕ ✗ ♨ 🛎 ☎ @ ⌆ P ⍾ 🚭 ≈ 🖼 ⚓ ♦ ⚘ 🎿 ♣ 🍇

*ALBERGO VILLA MARTA   **New***
Hosts: Andrea & Alessia Martinelli
Via Del Ponte Guasperini, 873
Lucca, (LU) 55100, Italy
Tel: (0583) 37 01 01, Fax: (0583) 37 99 99
15 Rooms, Double: €100–€285
Closed: Jan & Feb, Credit cards: all major
COUNTRY HOUSE HOTEL

Lucca is decidedly one of the loveliest cities of Italy with its historical churches and circular piazzas interspersed among beautiful shops featuring original storefronts and signage. Besides the well-known summer Puccini Festival (this is his birthplace), there are antiques markets, artisan fairs, and some of the most beautiful formal gardens and villas in Italy surrounding the city. In March the villas and gardens open for a special tour when the area's famed flower, the camellia (tree size), is in bloom. Over the years we have patiently awaited the arrival of a charming place to stay within the city walls and we were eventually rewarded with the Alla Corte degli Angeli. The Bonino family, already very familiar with the hospitality business, took over a private residence in the very heart of Lucca and created ten spacious bedrooms with guests' comfort in mind. The ground-floor reception area includes a lovely dining room with fireplace where an abundant buffet breakfast is served, if not in your own room. Bedrooms on the upper two floors are reached by an elevator, and all follow a specific flower theme, with pastel-colored walls giving an overall fresh feeling. Complementing the well-put-together decor are antique dressers, parquet floors, and amenities such as air conditioning, Jacuzzi tubs, mini-bars, satellite TV, and WiFi. *Directions:* In the pedestrian-only center of Lucca near the famous Piazza Anfiteatro. Private garage parking can be arranged.

ALLA CORTE DEGLI ANGELI
Host: Pietro Bonino
Via degli Angeli 23
Lucca, (FI) 55100, Italy
Tel: (0583) 469204, Fax: (0583) 991989
10 Rooms, Double: €119–€160*
1 Suite: €150–€200*
*Breakfast not included: €10
Open: all year, Credit cards: all major
B&B

Lucca is an outstanding walled town—truly one of Italy's jewels. If you want to visit Lucca, but prefer staying in the countryside, just a ten-minute drive away sits the sumptuous Locanda L'Elisa, a pretty, deep-lavender villa with white trim peeking out from the trees. The hotel has the appearance of a private home and, happily, this intimate, homelike quality remains even after you step inside where you are warmly greeted. As you look around, it is obvious that this was previously the residence of a wealthy family. Fine antiques, splendid paintings, and luxurious fabrics combine to create a mood of refined elegance. All of the guestrooms are individually decorated, but exude a similar old-world ambiance created with dark woods and opulent materials. The walls are richly covered in damask fabrics that color-coordinate with the draperies and bedspreads. However, the mood changes dramatically in the appealing dining room, found in a glass-enclosed conservatory. During the day, sunlight streams in through the windows and guests can enjoy both excellent cuisine and a view of the trees, green lawn, and colorful, well-tended beds of flowers. In this same garden you find a refreshing swimming pool. The Locanda L'Elisa is a very special luxury hideaway with a gracious warmth of welcome. *Directions:* Take the A11 to Lucca then take N12r (not 12) toward Pisa. Soon after leaving Lucca, watch for a sign on the left for Locanda L'Elisa.

❄ ⚡ ♨ 💳 🍽 ☎ 🐕 🛗 @ W Ⅰ P ⅼⅼ 🚭 ≈ 🖼 ⚲ ⚓ 🚶 👥 🏇 🦌

LOCANDA L'ELISA
Host: Alessandro Del Grande
Via Nuova per Pisa, 1952 (S.S. 12B1S)
Massa Pisana
Lucca, (LU) 55050, Italy
Tel: (0583) 37 97 37, Fax: (0583) 37 90 19
10 Rooms, Double: €210–€390*
*Breakfast not included: €16
Closed: Jan, Credit cards: all major
HOTEL

It was welcome news to hear that a small deluxe hotel had opened in the historical center of Lucca, one of our favorite medieval walled cities. After years of meticulous restoration, the 12th-century Palazzo Alexander first opened for guests in 2000. Your gracious host and creator of this small inn is Mario Maraviglia, who welcomes guests as friends with hardly a hint of commercialism—there isn't even a hotel sign in front—and his team shares his philosophy. To the left of the marble-floored reception foyer is an ornate, intimate breakfast room and bar set with small tables and fancy, gold-embellished chairs where every morning a delicious breakfast of bacon and eggs is served. Two huge chandeliers enhance the dark, handsome, beamed ceiling. As well as the elevator, a wonderful, very old stone staircase, illuminated by a stained-glass skylight, leads up to the guestrooms, each named after a famous Italian opera. The bedrooms are furnished with antique reproduction furniture in an ornate Venetian style. All the rooms have mini-bars, hairdryers, wireless internet, air conditioning, TVs, direct-dial phones, and elegant marble bathrooms. If you want to splurge, ask for "Tosca" which has a romantic little terrace tucked in the rooftop. *Directions:* The hotel has a parking lot nearby and you can drive through the pedestrian zone to the hotel. Ask for a diagram on how to reach the hotel.

❄ ☕ 🛎 💳 ☎ ♨ @ W Ÿ P 🖼 ♿ ⛴ 🏌 🎿 🍇

PALAZZO ALEXANDER
Host: Mario Maraviglia
Via Santa Giustina, 48
Lucca, (FI) 55100, Italy
Tel: (0583) 58 35 71, Fax: (0583) 58 36 10
13 Rooms, Double: €120–€170
2 Suites: €170–€250
Open: all year, Credit cards: all major
HOTEL

La Romea is a charming and informal B&B situated in a 14th century palazzo right in the very heart of Lucca's enchanting ancient city center. Walk up to the first floor and enter the spacious apartment with its reception desk, sitting area with black leather sofas, and three breakfast tables all under one beamed ceiling. Warm and friendly hosts, Gaia and Giulio heartily welcome guests. Off the main room are the five guest rooms each decorated and named by color (yellow, red, green, ivory and blue). Individually appointed rooms, each with new bathrooms and amenities such as direct telephone line, television, mini-bar, air conditioning and internet wireless connection, are spacious and well lit with large windows and antique furnishings. Their individual color themes are carried through the wall color, bedspreads and curtains. Features include stencil painted borders, beams and parquet floors. The celestial blue room is actually a junior suite, suitable for a family of four. A number of interesting itineraries are suggested and arranged by your knowledgeable hosts, including highlights of the city, wine and villa tours in the outlying countryside. *Directions:* On the corner of the Square Sant'Andrea (12th century church) and Via Ventaglie. A two-minute walk from Lucca's most important sights, the Torre Guingi and Piazza dell'Anfiteatro, plus the lovely Via Fillungo with its many shops and original storefronts.

✳ 🍵 🚼 CREDIT ☎ 🐾 W Y P ⚲ 🏃 👫 🐴 ⛷ ⛷ 🏌

LA ROMEA
Hosts: Giulio & Gaia Calissi
Vicolo delle Ventaglie, 2
Lucca, (FI) 55100, Italy
Tel: (0583) 464175
5 Rooms, Double: €120–€170
1 Suite: €140–€170
Open: all year, Credit cards: all major
B&B

It would be difficult for anyone with a passion for the outdoors to resist the challenge offered Federico when he inherited this 1,000-plus-acre estate in the wilderness of Maremma. He and his energetic wife, Elisabetta, plunged in and in two years made this dream come true. The results are notable and very ambitious, with the complete restoration of six stone farmhouses scattered about the vast property comprised of wooded hills, olive groves, and cultivated fields of grain and sunflowers. Guests first arrive at the imposing 1850s main villa, which houses the private family quarters. Comfortable apartments and guestrooms (divided among the various farmhouses) are harmoniously furnished with country pieces old and new and can accommodate from two to ten persons. Guests have the use of five swimming pools (indoor and out), mountain bikes, sauna, exercise and game rooms, Jacuzzi, and massage therapy. They convene at Podernovo where Tuscan meals are served in the exposed-stone dining room with fireplace, or on the patio looking out over the valley and up to Massa Marittima. The Etruscan towns of Massa Marittima, Volterra, Vetulonia, and Populonia are waiting to be explored. The summer months offer a rich musical program of operas and classical concerts in the main piazza and villas. *Directions:* Drive for 2 km on the gravel road from Massa Marittima where signs indicate Il Cicalino.

TENUTA IL CICALINO
Hosts: Elisabetta & Federico Vecchioni
Localita: Cicalino
Massa Marittima, (GR) 58024, Italy
Tel: (0566) 902031, Fax: (0566) 904896
7 Rooms, Double: €80–€116*
Apartments & Houses: €518–€2070 weekly*
*Breakfast not included: €7
Minimum Stay Required: 2 nights
Open: Mar to Nov, Credit cards: MC, VS
B&B, SELF CATERING

The general trend in hotel accommodation today is to offer guests services of a wellness center whether it is simply massage or a full-fledged spa. The Grotta Giusti satisfies the latter having the advantage of thermal waters which fill one of two large swimming pools. The hotel is located next to Montecatini Terme, in what was once the private 19th-century retreat of the poet, Giuseppe Giusti, and where Giuseppe Verdi was frequently a guest. Classic-styled, very comfortable bedrooms are dispersed among the original stone home and the more recently-built wing with spacious reception, series of sitting rooms, elegant frescoed salon, cigar room and full bar. Rooms of various sizes have white marble bathrooms and deluxe and superior rooms have a direct line to the thermal waters. The spacious veranda dining room looking out to the surrounding gardens offers a regular menu featuring Tuscan specialties or tailor-made meals for those following one of the many programs. Treatments of all types are available on the long list of anti-stress therapies ranging from classic to oriental techniques. What sets this place apart from the rest is not only the historic residence with natural thermal waters but the extraordinary grotta situated below the hotel, where guests sit in total silence and benefit from the natural detoxing steam emanating from the earth. A deserved break from intense touring!

※ ☕ ⚒ ☕ 💳 ☎ 🐕 🛗 🏹 @ W ⛾ P 🍴 🚭 ✿ ≈ 🖼 ♿ 🚶 🏃 🏌

GROTTA GIUSTI NATURAL SPA RESORT
Host: Antonio Niccoli
Via Grotta Giusti, 1411
Monsummano Terme, (PT) 51015, Italy
Tel: (0572) 90 771, Fax: (0572) 90 77 200
58 Rooms, Double: €260–€456*
6 Suites: €526–€626*
*Includes breakfast & dinner
Open: all year, Credit cards: all major
HOTEL

The Castelletto di Montebenichi is an enchanting small castle in a tiny, storybook-perfect, medieval village perched on a hilltop in Tuscany, romantically facing a miniature plaza enclosed by a circle of homes built into the old tower walls. This is a sturdy, stone building with a crenellated roof, arched windows, and a row of colorful coats of armor stretching across the top. Inside, it seems as if you are truly stepping back in time—the renovation has been so carefully accomplished that you don't realize any changes have been made (until you see the modern bathrooms). All the fabulous murals have been restored and the floors and beamed ceilings reflect the rich patina of age. The furnishings, too, reflect another era with rich fabrics, beautiful light fixtures, lovely oil paintings, and many fine antiques. Your exceptionally personable hosts, Marco Gasparini and Arnaldo Soriani, want their guests to feel like friends. Everything possible is done to create this ambiance, including an open bar where guests can fix themselves refreshment whenever they want. Breakfast is served in a charming, sunny room with arched windows on three sides. There are also cozy lounges, a stunning library, a swimming pool, a gym with indoor Jacuzzi, and a sauna. This is a non-smoking hotel. No children under 14. *Directions:* Midway between Siena and Arezzo. From the A1, exit at Valdarno and follow signs for Montevarchi, Bucine, Ambra, and then Montebenichi.

CASTELLETTO DI MONTEBENICHI
Hosts: Marco Gasparini & Arnaldo Soriani
Montebenichi, (AR) 52020, Italy
Tel: (055) 99 10 110, Fax: (055) 99 10 113
9 Rooms, Double: €240–€330
Open: Apr to Nov, Credit cards: all major
History Traveller
HOTEL

Lucca, one of our favorite Italian cities, is well situated near Pisa, with the beautiful Valdera countryside to the south, the Apuane mountain range to the north, the seaside 20 kilometers away, and many splendid villas and famous gardens scattered in the vicinity. The city, however, is directly surrounded by a heavily commercial area until you get to the olive oil and wine country around the charming hilltop town of Montecarlo, 15 kilometers east of town. This medieval stone village with fortress walls has several good restaurants and cafés, its own theater where Puccini was known to put on operas, and many olive-oil-producing farms and wineries close by. Chiara with the help of her mom and her boyfriend will make your stay with them pleasant and unforgettable. All bedrooms on two upper floors but two have en suite bathrooms and are simply appointed with wrought-iron beds, eyelet curtains and floral bedspreads. A rich and tasty breakfast, made with local and homemade products, is served either out on the front patio where you can observe the daily life of the locals, or in the miniature breakfast room to the right of the reception and mini sitting area (with internet point) where a wine and coffee bar is open all day. You are left a front door key when returning in the evening. *Directions:* From the A11 autostrada, take the Altopascio exit. Head towards Pescia (3 km) and turn left for Montecarlo for another 2 km.

ANTICA CASA DEI RASSICURATI
Host: Chiara Granucci
Via della Collegiata 2
Montecarlo, (LU) 55015, Italy
Tel: (0583) 228901, Fax: (0583) 22498
8 Rooms, Double: €55–€80
Minimum Stay Required: 2 nights
Open: all year, Credit cards: MC, VS
B&B

Il Borghetto Country Inn is an absolute dream, an idyllic hideaway in one of the most enchanting areas of Tuscany. It is owned by the Cavallini family who originally bought a farmhouse in the heart of the exquisite Chianti district to use as a family weekend retreat. When the adjacent farmhouse came on the market, they bought it too, restored it to perfection, and opened a tiny hotel. What makes this small inn so special is that it is a family operation. The father, Roberto Cavallini, watches over the operation from Milan, his son, Antonio, is the on-site manager, and the charming daughter, Ilaria, ably helps out. Guests have their own intimate, beautifully decorated lounge, which also serves as the breakfast room (in warm weather breakfast is served outside on the lovely terrace). Rosie Cavallini did all the decorating and every detail is of superb quality with beautiful fabrics, original paintings, abundant displays of fresh flowers, Oriental carpets, and fine antiques. But the best I've saved for last—a sweeping vista of olive groves and vineyards that produce extra virgin olive oil, Chianti Classico and Merlot wine. Tours and wine tasting in the cellar are available, as well as on-site cooking courses which include food and art tours in Florence, Siena and the surrounding countryside. *Directions:* Leave the Florence-Siena expressway at Bargino. Exit, turning right, and then almost immediately, turn up the hill toward Montefiridolfi. 2.6 km after the exit, Il Borghetto is on your right.

IL BORGHETTO COUNTRY INN
Host: Cavallini Family
Via Collina S. Angelo, 23
Montefiridolfi, (FI) 50020, Italy
Tel: (055) 82 44 442, Fax: (055) 82 44 247
6 Rooms, Double: €100–€140
2 Suites: €200–€240
Open: Mar to Nov, Credit cards: MC, VS
HOTEL

La Loggia, built in 1427, was one of the Medici estates during the centuries of their rule. Owner Giulio Baruffaldi, weary of urban life in Milan, transplanted himself and his wife here and succeeded in reviving the wine estate's splendor while respecting its past, enhancing its architectural beauty while giving utmost attention to the preservation of the historic property. Their informal yet refined hospitality is reflected in the care given to retaining the rustic ambiance of the former farmers' homes, each containing one to three bedrooms, living room, and kitchen, some with fireplace, and adorned with country antiques and original paintings from the Baruffaldis' own art collection. In fact, many important bronze and ceramic sculptures by international artists are displayed throughout the gardens of the villa. Four double rooms have been added, some having a fireplace or hydro-massage bath and steam room. Apart from just basking in the pure romance and tranquility of this place, you can enjoy a heated seawater swimming pool, horseback riding, and nearby tennis and golf facilities. Other activities include the occasional cooking or wine-tasting lesson, and impromptu dinners in the cellar. The charming hostess Ivana personally takes care of guests' needs. *Directions:* Leave the Florence-Siena autostrada after San Casciano at Bargino. Turn right at the end of the ramp, then left for Montefiridolfi (3.5 km). La Loggia is just before town.

FATTORIA LA LOGGIA
Hosts: Giulio Baruffaldi & Cuca Roaldi
Via Collina
Montefiridolfi
San Casciano Val di Pesa, (FI) 50026, Italy
Tel: (055) 8244288, Fax: (055) 8244283
4 Rooms, Double: €100–€260
11 Apartments: €140–€570 daily
Open: all year, Credit cards: MC, VS
B&B, SELF CATERING

The Villa Sant'Andrea is a prestigious wine estate on a hilltop dominating the Pesa valley in the Chianti region of Tuscany. An impressive villa and church are its focal points. So spectacular and strategic is the location that it has been occupied since Roman times. The vast property (over 1,300 acres!) spills down the vineyard-covered terrain to the horizon and includes three typical Tuscan farmhouses, (Zobi, Perticato and Montelodoli) that can be rented weekly or daily, each with its own private swimming pool. Luckily, for those desiring accommodation with breakfast, six quaint country style rooms are also available. Situated within the hamlet and across from the proprietors' gated historic villa, they are hidden by centuries-old cypresses and a lush garden. Wrought iron beds adorned with checked bedspreads and country antiques are authentically Tuscan. Superb views are to be enjoyed from each window. Two common rooms with large open fireplaces are reserved for guests for breakfast or simply lounging. For the more active, mountain bikes are available as well as hiking trails into the scenic countryside, through olive groves, vineyards and oak trees. The office is open for check in from 3pm to 6pm. The marvels of Tuscany are at your doorstep (Siena, San Gimignano, Volterra, and everything in between). *Directions:* From the Siena-Florence highway exit at Tavarnelle and follow road for 2 km to Fabbrica and the villa entrance.

VILLA SANT'ANDREA
Host: Vicini Family
Via di Fabbrica, 63
Montefiridolfi, (FI) 50020, Italy
Tel: (055) 8544254, Fax: (055) 82442030
6 Rooms, Double: €105–€125
3 Houses: €130–€216 daily
Open: all year, Credit cards: all major
B&B, SELF CATERING

La Chiusa, nestled in the hills of Tuscany southeast of Siena, is an old stone farmhouse whose restaurant is so well known that guests come from far and wide to enjoy the meals where everything is fresh, homemade, and delicious. Dania and Umberto Lucherini are the gracious owners and Dania is the talented chef. Almost all the vegetables, olive oil, meats, wines, and cheeses come either from the inn's own farm or from those nearby. The original wood-burning oven still stands in the courtyard in front of the inn, emitting delicious aromas of freshly baking bread. The dining room is large and airy, with an uncluttered simple elegance enhanced by windows overlooking rolling hills. When the weather is balmy, meals are also served on the back terrace, which is ideally positioned to capture a sweeping view. The emphasis here is definitely on the exquisite meals, but there are also bedrooms for guests who want to spend the night. Like the dining room, the guestrooms are perfectly in keeping with the ambiance of the old farmhouse, lovely in their rustic simplicity yet with every modern convenience. In addition to the standard guestrooms, there are some deluxe suites—one even has an olive press in the bathroom! *Directions:* From the highway A1, take the "Val di Chiana" exit. Turn left and follow the signs that lead to Torrita di Siena and then Pienza. About 7 km past Torrita di Siena turn left toward Montefollonico.

LA CHIUSA
Host: Lucherini Family
Via della Madonnina, 88
Montefollonico, (SI) 53040, Italy
Tel: (0577) 66 96 68, Fax: (0577) 66 95 93
15 Rooms, Double: €230–€350
3 Suites: €500
Restaurant closed Tue
Closed: Christmas week, Credit cards: all major
HOTEL

Le Fontanelle country house sits in the heart of the Maremma area of Tuscany where, besides being pleasant and well run, it fills a need for the growing interest in this off-the-beaten-track destination. Signor Perna and his two lovely daughters, originally from Rome, searched and found this peaceful haven from the stress of city life, promptly transferring themselves and undertaking major restoration work. Looking over a soft green valley up to the nearby village of Montemerano, the stone farmhouse with its rusty-red shutters offers four comfortable rooms with spotless private bathrooms. The converted barn houses five rooms while the last room is in a separate cottage set in the woods. Sunlight pours into the front veranda-like breakfast room where coffee and cakes are taken together with other guests at one large table. The Pernas assist guests in planning local itineraries including visits to artisan workshops. With due notice, guests can find a wonderfully prepared dinner awaiting them under the ivy-covered pergola in the rose garden. The property is part of a reserve with deer, wild boar, and various types of wildlife, where Porcini mushrooms, wild asparagus, and berries are found in season. *Directions:* From Rome, take the A12 autostrada. Continue north on Aurelia route 1, turning off at Vulci after Montalto. Follow signs for Manciano then Montemerano. Turn left at the bed-and-breakfast sign before town and follow the dirt road for 1 km.

LE FONTANELLE
Hosts: Daniela & Cristina Perna
Localita: Poderi di Montemerano
Montemerano, (GR) 58050, Italy
Tel & Fax: (0564) 602762
10 Rooms, Double: €85
Open: Mar to Nov, Credit cards: MC, VS
B&B

One result of increasing interest in the singular attractions of the Maremma, or southern Tuscany, is the opening or expansion of several noteworthy places to stay. The Villa Acquaviva, once owned by nobility and a small family hotel for some years, was extensively remodeled to include seven guestrooms named for and painted in the colors of local wildflowers. The bedrooms all have private baths and are decorated with country antiques and wrought-iron beds. Breakfast of homemade cakes, breads, and jams can be eaten in the breakfast room near the enoteca. There are ten newer rooms in a stone farmhouse on the property plus eight in another, joined together by a glassed-in reception area. These are our favorites, with beautiful local antiques and colorful matching fabrics adorning beds and windows. Tennis courts and a swimming pool are attractive features of the complex. In the center of the park, in a scenic position by the swimming pool, the restaurant presents typical Maremman dishes made with fresh products from the farm. *Directions:* From Rome, take the Aurelia coastal road, exiting at Vulci. Follow signs for Manciano, then Montemerano. Acquaviva is well marked just outside the village.

❄ ☕ 🎿 CREDIT 🔒 🐾 @ W Ⴤ P 🍴 🚭 ≈ 🎿 ♿ ⚓ 🧍 👥 🐎 🍇

VILLA ACQUAVIVA
Hosts: Valentina di Virginio & Serafino d'Ascenzi
Localita: Acquaviva
Montemerano, (GR) 58050, Italy
Tel: (0564) 602890, Fax: (0564) 602895
25 Rooms, Double: €102–€240
3 Suites: €220–€240
Open: all year, Credit cards: all major
B&B

A pleasant alternative to a countryside bed and breakfast is one right in the historical center of the marvelously preserved medieval town of Montepulciano. Most famous for its prized Rosso di Montepulciano wines, its striking charm of the past rivals that of its hilltop neighbors, Pienza and Montalcino. Here Cinzia Caroti offers bed and breakfast on the first floor of a 16th-century palazzo on the main street of town, which is lined with shops and restaurants and is off limits to cars, which adds much to its medieval aura. One flight of wide stairs takes you up to L'Agnolo's reception area. There are three bedrooms off this area and another two off the frescoed dining room with wrought-iron chandelier. The spacious, high-ceilinged rooms have a subdued ambiance, with wrought-iron beds, family antiques, and new white-tiled bathrooms. Better lighting could be used to show off lovely original frescoed ceilings and painted borders. A classic breakfast of cappuccino and fresh croissants is served in the coffee shop below the home, making one feel like a true local resident. Cinzia lives two doors down and is present throughout the day to assist guests and make suggestions from the many sightseeing possibilities in this rich area of Tuscany, bordering Umbria. *Directions:* Park your car nearby (north or east lot) outside the village walls and follow Via di Gracciano running north-south to the middle. There is a small gold name plaque at the door.

L' AGNOLO
Host: Cinzia Caroti
Via di Gracciano nel Corso 63
Montepulciano, (SI) 53045, Italy
Tel: (0578) 717070, Fax: (0578) 757095
5 Rooms, Double: €90
Open: Mar 20 to Jan 10, Credit cards: MC, VS
B&B

La Dionora is a delightful hotel just outside the walled town of Montepulciano, one of Tuscany's jewels. This appealing small inn, made of tan stone and accented by brown shutters, has a stunning location, crowning a gentle hill with a 360-degree view. As far as the eye can see there are rolling hills covered with forests, fields of sunflowers, olive groves, and, in the distance, the sweet walled village of Pienza. As you approach, it is obvious that this is a well cared for, beautifully managed property. Everything is absolutely meticulous, from the perfectly tended flower beds to the lovingly decorated bedrooms. Three of the guestrooms are located upstairs in the farmhouse with windows that capture the splendid view. The other rooms, each with a private terrace, are in a similar one-story stone building just steps away. All have Tuscan-style antiques enhanced by Ferragamo fabrics and fireplaces. Breakfast is served in the garden in a most attractive stone "winter garden" with arched glass walls on four sides through which the sunlight streams in. Also in the garden is a beautiful swimming pool. Dinner is served by request during the summer season. Maria Teresa Cesarini, the friendly owner, is ably assisted by Giulio D'Antonio and they are perfect hosts who are very familiar with Tuscany and can help with planning your day. *Directions:* Take N146 from Montepulciano toward Pienza. After 3 km, turn left at the sign for La Dionora.

LA DIONORA
Host: Mrs. Maria Teresa Cesarini
Via Vicinale di Poggiano
Montepulciano, (SI) 53040, Italy
Tel: (0578) 71 74 96, Fax: (0578) 71 74 98
4 Rooms, Double: €280–€330
2 Suites: €360–€380
Closed: Dec 8 to mid-Feb, Credit cards: all major
HOTEL

Montorio makes an excellent base for exploring Tuscany and Umbria: spacious, guestrooms; glorious setting; spectacular views; cooking facilities; large modern bathrooms; and moderate prices. This 15th-century stone farmhouse is perched on a hill surrounded by olive groves, vineyards, and towering cypress trees. The views are awesome with nothing to disturb the mood of serenity except perhaps for the song of birds and the ringing of church bells. The beautiful walled town of Montepulciano is nearby and from the terrace of Montorio you can also see the charming Renaissance church of San Biagio. The inn is self-catering which means that each room has its own kitchenette and, unlike a hotel, there is not a manager on site so you need to arrive between 4–7 pm when someone is there to check you in. Some self-catering properties do not have daily maid service and charge for utilities, but the Montorio has daily maid service (except on Sunday) and includes all utilities. Each of the suites has a kitchen or kitchenette and is tastefully decorated with pleasingly simple Tuscan-style, antique furniture. Centuries-old trees and flowers cascading from terracotta pots embellish the delightful terrace. *Directions:* Just on the north edge of Montepulciano, on the road to Pienza.

MONTORIO
Host: Stefania Savini
Strada per Pienza, 2
Montepulciano, (SI) 53045, Italy
Tel: (0578) 71 74 42, Fax: (0578) 71 56 35
4 Apartments: €120–€170 daily, €650–€1500 weekly*
*Breakfast not included
Minimum Stay Required: 2 nights
Open: Feb 1 to Dec 15, Credit cards: MC, VS
HOTEL

The romantic, ochre-colored, 17th-century Villa Poggiano is truly a gem. The Savini family bought the abandoned mansion, which nestles on a wooded hillside near the charming walled city of Montepulciano, and have tenderly restored it to its original splendor. An intimate, cozy parlor with comfortable chairs grouped around an open fireplace, a sweet breakfast room, and two enormous suites are on the first floor. A wide staircase leads to four more beautiful rooms. There are also three delightful suites in a separate brick building facing a sweeping panorama of the countryside. The tasteful decor creates a warm, homelike ambiance. Throughout the villa, everything is on a grand scale with handsome fireplaces, sumptuous bathrooms, gorgeous antique furniture, exceptionally spacious rooms, and ornate chandeliers. The villa faces an idyllic Tuscan countryside with olive trees dotting the gentle hillside. Behind the villa is a thick forest with romantic paths meandering through the woodlands. There is also an enormous travertine swimming pool with a granite wall on one side embellished with a large sculpture, while on the other side, lounge chairs are set on a wide terrace outlined by very old cypress trees. The warmth of welcome by Stefania and her charming mother is so genuine you will never want to leave. *Directions:* Take the N146 from Montepulciano toward Pienza and after about 2 km, turn left at the sign for Villa Poggiano.

❄ ☕ � 💳 ☎ @ W ⅂ P 🚭 🌱 ≈ 🖼 🛏 🚶 🐎 🍇

VILLA POGGIANO
Host: Stefania Savini
Via di Poggiano, 7
Montepulciano, (SI) 53045, Italy
Tel: (0578) 75 82 92, Fax: (0578) 71 56 35
3 Rooms, Double: €185–€215
11 Suites: €210–€320
Open: Apr to Nov, Credit cards: MC, VS
Abitare La Storia
History Traveller
HOTEL

Monteriggioni is a circular medieval town with turreted fortress walls, mentioned in Dante's Inferno. To the east is an extension of unspoiled land, preserved over the centuries because it was all owned by one proprietor. Within this mix of olive groves and dense woods, in the center of a peaceful forest reserve is the Poggiarello property. The three stone farmhouses dating back to the 1700s are reached by a 2 kilometer road. The Giove family (brother and sister team) bought and restored the property creating apartments for 2-8 people, two doubles, a restaurant and swimming pool plus living quarters for both of their own families. They enjoy entertaining guests and attending to their comfort and ease, offering tasty regional meals, such as fresh pastas and country soups all made with local products and fresh produce. A casual ambiance prevails in room dècor which is basic and simple like the stone and beam houses, each with outdoor garden space or a nice wide open view. Another special feature is the Roman hot bath within its own stone house, perfect for a soak after a long day of Tuscan touring. Sights in the immediate area include Siena, San Gimignano, Volterra and Chianti. *Directions:* From the Florence-Siena highway, exit at Monteriggioni, turn right at the stop sign and after 1.4 km left for Abbadia. After 6 km turn left for Scorgiano. After 4 km turn left signed Antico Borgo Poggiarello. Go 300m, turn left and follow the road for 2 km.

ANTICO BORGO POGGIARELLO
Hosts: Roberto Giove & Paolo Ruggiero
Localita Poggiarello-Strada San Monti, 12
Monteriggioni, (SI) , Italy
Tel: (0577) 301003, Fax: (0577) 1959106
*2 Rooms, Double: €100–€140**
*7 Suites: €115–€160**
*3 Apartments: €150–€200 daily**
**Breakfast not included*
Dinners: €29
Closed: Jan 10 to end-Feb, Credit cards: all major
B&B, SELF CATERING

Tucked in the gentle Tuscan hills, Monteriggioni is a stunning sight. You will be captivated from afar at your first glimpse: the romantic town crowning the hilltop with its circular stone wall, punctuated by tall towers, still intact. If you have come just to sightsee, you must park your car below the town, but if you are one of the lucky ones who have a reservation at the Hotel Monteriggioni, drive through the portal in the wall to the hotel, which is located at the far end of the little square. It is hard to believe that this lovely small hotel, now so beautiful, used to be a stable. It took three years for the present owners to achieve the miracle you see today. Michela Cagnazzo, the owner, is responsible for the decoration and her taste is faultless. White walls, handsome antique furniture, white slipcovered sofas, and bouquets of fresh flowers create a fresh, appealing country ambiance. The guestrooms are also charming, with the same style of decor as the public rooms. Behind the hotel there is a terrace where breakfast is served, weather permitting. Just beyond is a small swimming pool tucked in the garden with a serene backdrop of the old moat, now filled with olive trees, and the stone walls of the town. The hotel has no restaurant but the Ristorante Il Pozzo next door offers authentic Tuscan cooking, and there are other restaurants nearby. It is a delightful hotel that does credit to a charming village. *Directions:* From the S2 at Monteriggioni, follow signs to the town.

❄ ☕ 🏌 💳 ☎ ♿ @ ☕ P 🚭 ♒ 🖼 🏃 👫 🏇 💃

ROMANTIK HOTEL MONTERIGGIONI
Host: Michela Gozzi Cagnazzo
Monteriggioni, (SI) 53035, Italy
Tel: (0577) 30 50 09, Fax: (0577) 30 50 11
12 Rooms, Double: €200–€240
Closed: Jan 7 to end-Feb, Credit cards: all major
Romantik Hotels
HOTEL

After years of working in a hotel in Siena, then owning a wine bar, Marcello and his wife Maria Pia decided to put their hospitality experience into practice and opened the charming Bolsinina bed and breakfast. This is a perfect location for travelers, being so close to Siena (18 km) and having easy access to the main road, which passes through the magical Crete Senesi landscapes with their low, rolling clay hills punctuated by an occasional cypress tree against the horizon, to the hilltowns of Montalcino, Pienza, and Montepulciano. The 18th-century brick house has a courtyard where meals are served in season. To one side are the apartments of varying sizes, and to the other is the large house where the beamed guestrooms are located upstairs, along with a large common living room and loggia terrace with splendid views. Downstairs is an open multi-use space rotating around the center staircase with billiard table, cozy living room with fireplace and two large brick arches, and dining room. Guests reserve in the morning for dinner accompanied by excellent local wines. The house and rooms are filled with local antique country furniture and armoires and there is an immediate at-home informal air about the place. An inviting swimming pool is an added bonus. *Directions:* From Siena on the S.R.2, follow signs to Buonconvento. Before Buonconvento turn left at Casale-Gaggiolo (km 209). Take the gravel road up to the house.

CASA BOLSININA
Hosts: Marcello & Maria Pia Mazzotta
Localita: Casale
Monteroni d'Arbia, (SI) 53014, Italy
Tel & Fax: (0577) 718477
6 Rooms, Double: €115–€135
1 Suite: €145–€165
4 Apartments: €700–€1000 weekly*
*Cleaning & heating extra for apartments
Dinners: €34
Closed: Jan 15 to Mar 31, Credit cards: all major
B&B, SELF CATERING

The island-like promontory of Argentario, facing the islands of Giglio and Giannutri, has always been a favorite seaside resort for Romans. Located on a narrow strip of land connecting Argentario to the mainland is the quaint historic town of Orbetello. Here you find the charming San Biagio Relais dating back to 1851. The Magnosi family restored the palazzo, creating the feeling of a nobleman's home, not only in the period furnishings, but also with the preservation of the original architectural features of the palazzo itself. Some of these attractive details include the high-ceilinged guestrooms with frescoed borders, each of which has a marble travertine bathroom. The family's antique pieces adorn the intimate upstairs sitting room with fireplace. The addition of 28 rooms in an adjacent connecting building, offers guests a choice of décor, with the newer rooms and bi-level suites having a more contemporary style. Common areas include a breakfast room, two lounges and a characteric double courtyard, reminiscent of the 18th century Spanish domain. This outdoor area is used in summer for a buffet breakfast with a delightful assortment of homebaked cakes, or for the aperitif hour. *Directions:* From the SS1 Aurelia N1, exit at Orbetello and continue to the historic center through arched entrance. Follow road to the right to the parking lot facing the cathedral, Via Dante is the street on its left side. Hotel is one block up.

SAN BIAGIO RELAIS
Host: Pietro Mancino
Via Dante, 40
Orbetello, (GR) 58015, Italy
Tel: (0564) 86 05 43, Fax: (0564) 86 77 87
33 Rooms, Double: €160–€300
8 Suites: €380–€450
Open: all year, Credit cards: all major
HOTEL

The Casalone farm estate, located between seaside resort Ansedonia and Orbetello Scalo, is a 700-acre property producing olive oil, wines, honey and the typical local breed of Maremman cows. It is in close proximity to the sea with a splendid view of Mount Argentario in the distance. Gracious Signora Marcella and husband, Giuseppe, live in the ivy-covered ancient stone tower and attached villa, while guests reside within seven comfortable self-catering apartments in a converted barn down the road. Spacious apartments have two bedrooms and two bathrooms, living/dining area, and kitchenette. Some apartments have the bedrooms on a second floor, while others have them split between the main floor and an open loft space. They are nicely appointed in a simple, cozy style, with fresh white walls, smart plaid cushions on built-in sofas, framed prints, wicker furniture, and wrought-iron beds. An alternative to sea bathing is a dip in the swimming pool, guarded by olive trees. For nature lovers, the area is full of marvelous expeditions on foot or bike, including the National Park of Uccellina, various forts on Mount Argentario, and the islands of Giglio and Giannutri, not to mention the Saturnia thermal spa. *Directions:* From Rome take the Aurelia Highway 1 and turn right at the sign "Piante-Vivaio" (140.5 km after the turnoff for Ansedonia). From the north you must exit at Ansedonia and return to the highway heading towards Grosseto.

IL CASALONE
Hosts: Marcella & Giuseppe Lignana
S.S. Aurelia sud km 140.5
Orbetello Scalo, (GR) 58016, Italy
Tel: (0564) 862160, Fax: (0564) 866308
7 Apartments: €600–€1390*
*Breakfast not included
Minimum Stay Required: 2 nights, 7 nights Jul & Aug
Open: all year, Credit cards: none
SELF CATERING

Elba is a beautiful small island, easily accessible in one hour by car ferry from Piombino. After exploring Tuscany, or while en route along the coast heading north from Rome, you will find that Elba makes a delightful stopover where you can happily spend several days relaxing and exploring the island's many pretty inlets and picturesque fishing villages. The Hotel Villa Ottone is idyllically nestled in a tranquil park and has its own private beach (there is also a swimming pool). The original part of the hotel is a romantic villa (which belonged to Signor Di Mario's grandfather) facing directly onto the sea. If you want to splurge, ask for one of the deluxe "Contessa" or "Colombe" rooms in the villa. Some of the guestrooms are located in an attractive building that also houses the reception area and the dining room, while more guestrooms are found in a separate wing nestled amongst the trees. The furnishings throughout are tasteful and everything is immaculately maintained. Be sure to visit the bar, which has a stunning ceiling of intricate plasterwork and lovely frescoes. In high season you need to take the modified American plan (MAP), which includes breakfast and either lunch or dinner and there is a three-night minimum. However, this is no problem as the food is very good and beautifully served. Villa Ottone is a hotel with great personality, overseen with meticulous attention to detail by the gracious Signor Di Mario.

HOTEL VILLA OTTONE
Host: Di Mario Family
Localita: Ottone
Ottone (Portoferraio), Isola di Elba, (LI) 57037, Italy
Tel: (0565) 93 30 42, Fax: (0565) 93 32 57
70 Rooms, Double: €250–€520*
10 Suites: €440–€1140*
*Includes breakfast & lunch or dinner
Open: May to Oct, Credit cards: all major
HOTEL

We look all over for bed and breakfasts that radiate a natural charm like that of Fagiolari, just outside Panzano. Cordial hostess Giulietta has seemingly unintentionally created a haven for travelers just by letting her home be a home. The unique stone farmhouse on three levels is brimming with character and has been restored with total respect for its innate simplicity using stone, terracotta brick, and chestnut-wood beams. Entering the front door into the cozy living room with large fireplace, I was impressed by the refreshingly authentic ambiance of this Tuscan home. Two bedrooms are just off this room, the larger having an en suite bathroom of stone and travertine. The main house and former barn, where you find two other good-sized bedrooms, are united by a connecting roof, left open in the middle to allow for an enormous fig tree. Bedrooms hold lovely antiques, book-lined shelves, collections of framed drawings and artwork, embroidered linens, and views of the delightful garden and cypress-lined paths. Overlooking the swimming pool, an adorable one-bedroom house on the property with a bookcase dividing the kitchen and living area is rented out weekly. Giulietta also teaches cooking classes lasting from one to four days. *Directions:* From the piazza in Panzano follow signs to centro and take the left fork for Mercatale. At a half km from the piazza turn left after a pale-green building and follow the gravel road downhill to the end.

FAGIOLARI
Host: Giulietta Giovannoni
Case Sparse 25
Panzano in Chianti, (FI) 50020, Italy
Tel & Fax: (055) 852351
5 Rooms, Double: €100–€120
1 Cottage: €120 daily, €840–€910 weekly
Minimum Stay Required: Cottage: 3 nights
Open: all year, Credit cards: all major
B&B, SELF CATERING

The Villa Le Barone was once the home of the famous Tuscan Della Robbia family, whose beautiful terracottas are still seen throughout Italy. It was restored after the First World War by Marchesa Maria Bianca Viviani Della Robbia as a wine estate and later converted into a deluxe boutique hotel by her granddaughter, Duchessa Franca Visconti. Now her cousins, Conte Corso Aloisi and his wife, are the owners. They frequently live in the villa, greet guests and ensure that the impeccable standards and taste prevail. Staying at the Villa Le Barone is very much like being the guest in a private, elegant home set in the gorgeous Tuscan hills in front of the San Leolino abbey. The lounges are especially inviting, beautifully furnished with charming, family antiques. There are 28 guestrooms, all of which vary in size with modern tiled bathrooms and are individually decorated. Rooms are in the main villa or in renovated cottages and barns. Some have their own terrace. The tennis court has a breathtaking view over the Chianti hills and there is a lovely swimming pool, romantically set on a terrace looking over the vineyards and rose garden. Wonderful little hideaways are found secluded in the park-like setting where guests can find a quiet nook to read or just to sit and soak in the beauty of the surrounding hills. Dinner is served in the restaurant, which formerly housed the winery. *Directions:* From the center of Panzano, follow signs to the hotel.

※ 🍽 🛒 💳 ☎ @ W P ≈ 🚶 🖼 🍴 🏇 💃

VILLA LE BARONE
Hosts: Count & Countess Aloisi de Larderel
Via San Leolino, 19
Panzano in Chianti, (FI) 50020, Italy
Tel: (055) 85 26 21, Fax: (055) 85 22 77
29 Rooms, Double: €230–€400*
1 Suite: €300–€400*
*Includes breakfast & dinner
Open: all year, Credit cards: all major
Abitare La Storia
HOTEL

As you wind your way up a steep road through thick woods, you will no doubt wonder as we did how Anglo-American Edward ever found the secluded 70-acre property set above the Sieve river valley to the east of Florence. Upon arrival you will be greeted and rewarded with a glass of fresh spring water from the fountain "shower" (la doccia). It is understandable that long ago the farmhouse was originally a farm for the monks of the local abbey—the views are inspirational and the positions of both the house and the swimming pool take full advantage of the expansive panorama encompassing the Rufina wine valley nature reserve. Original features remain intact after a complete restoration of the house that created a variety of high-level accommodation in the form of four bedrooms, three suites with individual kitchenettes, and two independent houses with one bedroom each for weekly stays. The perfectly charming home is filled with lovely antiques (local and imported from England), queen- or king-sized beds, and beautiful linens and tiled bathrooms. Guests can wander about the many common rooms and have a glass of wine in front of a spectacular sunset while Edward works Mediterranean wonders in the kitchen. Prepare to be pampered. *Directions:* 40 minutes from Florence, 5 km from Pelago. Detailed directions are supplied at the time of reservation.

LA DOCCIA
Host: Edward Mayhew
Localita: Paterno, Ristonchi 19/20
Pelago, (FI) 50060, Italy
Tel: 392 775 0535
3 Rooms, Double: €90
1 Suite: €70
4 Apartments: €95 daily, €600 weekly
2 Cottages: €115 daily, €750 weekly
Minimum Stay Required: 2 nights
Open: mid-Apr to end-Oct, Credit cards: all major
B&B, SELF CATERING

Nestled in the tranquil Tuscan countryside between two enchanting hilltop villages (Pienza and Monticchiello) is another jewel, L'Olmo. You cannot help instantly losing your heart to this very special little hotel. It has the warmth and intimacy of a bed and breakfast, yet the service and amenities rival those of the finest deluxe hotel. This bit of paradise is owned by the Lindo family. A few years ago they left the bustling city of Turin and bought a beautiful 16th-century stone house, which they lovingly restored to perfection, down to the smallest detail, preserving original terracotta floors and wood-beamed ceilings. With superb taste and guests' comfort in mind, four suites were created and appointed with antique chests, locally made wrought-iron beds, and pretty floral fabrics for color. Each has its own travertine marble bathroom and two have a private garden with sitting and solarium area. Francesca and her mother Loredana, your exceptionally charming hostesses, tend to guests in a warm and highly professional manner. Downstairs are two cozy sitting rooms leading out to the stone courtyard with tables and flower pots. A full buffet breakfast or gourmet candlelit dinner—upon request—is served in the luminous dining room. Lunch and dinner are also served in the romantic garden pergola. *Directions:* From Pienza drive south, after 6 km turn left to Monticchiello. Follow signs for L'Olmo on your right.

L' OLMO
Hosts: Francesca & Loredana Lindo
Monticchiello
Pienza, (SI) 53020, Italy
Tel: (0578) 75 51 33, Fax: (0578) 75 51 24
1 Room, Double: €190
4 Suites: €270–€290
1 Apartment, Double: €300
Dinner upon request
Open: Apr to Nov, Credit cards: all major
HOTEL

The Relais Il Chiostro is idyllically snuggled inside the stone walls of Pienza, a medieval hilltop village that is one of Tuscany's most perfect jewels. The hotel is built within a stunning 15th-century monastery; a heritage immediately apparent when you step through the massive arched wood doors into an exceptionally beautiful small cloister. The hushed courtyard is framed by a colonnade of marble columns linked by stone arches. The restaurant and the various lounges and sitting rooms occupy the ground floor. Upstairs there are 37 attractive, individually decorated guestrooms with splendid frescoed ceilings featured in some of the suites. The choice rooms overlook the beautiful Tuscan countryside, but views from the other rooms are also delightful—overlooking either the garden cloister or the ancient tiled rooftops of Pienza. One of the most outstanding features of the hotel is its spectacular location. Perched above the valley, the hotel takes full advantage of its position with a terrace garden (where meals are served when the weather is warm) which stretches to the edge of the wall where guests can enjoy an incredible panoramic view of Tuscany at its finest. On a terrace below, a large swimming pool nestles in another garden. *Directions:* Located one block from the main square, Piazza Pio II.

HOTEL RELAIS IL CHIOSTRO DI PIENZA
Host: Massimo Cicala
Corso Rossellino, 26
Pienza, (SI) 53026, Italy
Tel: (0578) 74 84 00, Fax: (0578) 74 84 40
37 Rooms, Double: €120–€290
Closed: Jan 7 to Mar 20, Credit cards: all major
HOTEL

The most striking images of southern Tuscany are in the Orcia Valley—enchanting landscapes with soft, rolling hills topped with rows of cypress trees silhouetted against the sky. This alternating with the area called Le Crete Senesi—barren hills made of clay and resembling moon craters—makes for fascinating scenery. Le Traverse, at 3 kilometers from Pienza, is submersed in this peaceful countryside to which your gracious hosts, Pinuccia and Enrico, retired from Milan. Their charming home has been very tastefully restored and all the right touches (such as terry bathrobes and the finest-quality bed linens) added to make guests feel right at home. The stone farmhouse with front courtyard is divided between the couple's own quarters, rooms for their visiting children, and two apartments for guests with independent entrance. The other two bedrooms are situated in the one-level converted barn nearby and are enhanced with the family's country antiques and prints. Huge terracotta vases overflowing with geraniums, trailing roses, and azalea plants dot the 50-acre property, which includes a swimming pool. Olive oil is produced as well as jams using homegrown fruit. The intimacy of the place with its four rooms makes you feel like a true house guest and the area is full of delightful day trips. *Directions:* Follow signs for Monticchiello from Pienza (circular piazza). After 3 km turn left on an unpaved road up to a group of cypress trees and the house.

LE TRAVERSE
Host: Pinuccia Barbier Meroni
Localita: Le Traverse
Pienza, (SI) 53026, Italy
Tel: (0578) 748198, Fax: (0578) 748949
4 Rooms, Double: €170–€210
Minimum Stay Required: 2 nights
Closed: Jan 22 to 30, Credit cards: all major
B&B

In a small city near the coast, not far from the charming town of Lucca and the popular town of Pisa, you will find the Albergo Pietrasanta. Although "albergo" suggests a simple hotel, this small, deluxe property does not fit that definition. Located in the center of Pietrasanta, the building dates back to the 17th century when it was the home of the prestigious and wealthy Barsanti Bonetti family. There is a sophisticated, understated elegance throughout the hotel and a mood of luxury is set as you enter the lobby. To the right of the spacious foyer are two splendid lounges which exude the ambiance of a private home, with pastel walls, soft lighting, comfortable chairs grouped around a handsome fireplace, polished terrazzo floors, beautiful paintings, and bouquets of fresh flowers. The far end of the lounge opens through arched doors into one of the hotel's most special features, a romantic garden courtyard, part of which is enclosed in glass to create a "winter garden" where a bountiful breakfast is served each morning. Forming one wall of the courtyard is a separate building, formerly the stables, which has been renovated to house additional deluxe accommodations. As would be expected, guestrooms reflect the same subdued, sophisticated good taste as the public rooms. *Directions:* From the A12, exit at Versilia-Forte dei Marmi and follow signs to Pietrasanta. In town follow signs to the hotel. The hotel is 20 km from Pisa Airport.

❄ ✚ ☕ ▭ ☎ ⌂ ♨ ☿ @ W Ⓨ P ⚐ ♿ ⚓ 🚶 👫 🏄 🏌

ALBERGO PIETRASANTA
Host: Barbara Pardini
Via Garibaldi, 35
Pietrasanta, (LU) 55045, Italy
Tel: (0584) 79 37 26, Fax: (0584) 79 37 28
18 Rooms, Double: €185–€380*
2 Suites: €550–€550*
*Breakfast not included: €20
Closed: Nov 20 to Mar 1, Credit cards: all major
HOTEL

It has not been easy to find a charming, true bed and breakfasts in Pisa, a city famous for its leaning tower and basilica, and its quaint city center and excellent restaurants. Thankfully, the Relais dell'Orologio has opened a smaller accommodation down the street. The Relais dei Fiori, a 19th-century palazzo on the main pedestrian-only street has an attractive sidewalk café lining its front with gazebo, plants and bamboo tables and chairs. Breakfast is served here or in the small bar area in front, as well as other meals throughout the day. A small reception area to the side leads up to the bedrooms by stairs or elevator on the next two floors. Twelve rooms, four to a floor, have a white base between walls and armoires, and are given each a different color theme with bedspreads and carried through in the floral-painted motifs along ceiling borders. Four different size categories have been designated doubles, with the smallest being quite tight. Hallways display collections of French porcelain and lace items. Plenty of amenities and services are arranged by the helpful staff. Pisa is strategically based near the coastline and a lesser known side of Tuscany. An international airport makes it easy coming in or leaving the country. *Directions:* Via Carducci is the main street in town, hotel is well marked.

RELAIS DEI FIORI
Host: Maria Luisa Bignardi
Via Carducci, 35/37
Pisa, (PI) 56127, Italy
Tel: (050) 556054, Fax: (050) 8311733
12 Rooms, Double: €90–€340
Open: all year, Credit cards: all major
B&B

For years there was no outstanding place to stay in Pisa, but all that changed dramatically in March 2003 when Maria Luisa Bignardi opened her deluxe, small boutique hotel (her family's home since the 1500s) within a few minutes' stroll of Pisa's stunning Piazza dei Miracoli. The Hotel Relais dell'Orologio is truly exceptional in every way—it exudes romance and offers refined comfort, staff to cater to your every whim, a perfect location, gourmet dining, fine wines, lovely decor, and, best of all, the genuine warmth of your elegant, charming hostess. It took eight years of love, imagination, and hard work to restore the long-neglected mansion to its former grandeur and now every detail exudes good taste, understated grandeur, and the highest quality. The furnishings are beautiful, with family heirlooms used in the intimate lounge and in the well-decorated guestrooms, each of which enjoys fine fabrics, excellent linens, quality mattresses, and marble bathrooms. The standard guestrooms are small, so if you prefer more space, we suggest one of the junior suites. In the evening, gourmet meals are served at the hotel's charming restaurant Lady Hallett's Bar, offering typical Tuscan food and featuring the hotel's own wines, olive oils and fresh vegetables. The Hotel Relais dell'Orologio is truly a gem. *Directions:* Take the North Pisa exit from the A12. When you get into town, follow well-marked signs to the hotel.

HOTEL RELAIS DELL'OROLOGIO
Host: Maria Luisa Bignardi
Via della Faggiola 12-14
Pisa, (PI) 56126, Italy
Tel: (050) 83 03 61, Fax: (050) 55 18 69
16 Rooms, Double: €150–€500
2 Suites: €380–€800
Open: all year, Credit cards: all major
History Traveller
HOTEL

Castello di Vicarello, an historic country residence whose origins date to the 1100's, is an enchanting resort, a peaceful spot renowned for its quality wine & oil production. After traveling and living all over the globe the Baccheschi Berti family decided to restore this lovely old home and offer top of the line guest accommodation. The castle features three suites and two adjacent stunning stone guesthouses. The smaller guesthouse, I Sassi, has one bedroom, a large bathroom, a kitchenette and a glassed-in living room taking in the sumptuous view. The other guesthouse, La Chiesina, has two spacious bedrooms, two bathrooms, a kitchen and a living room with intarsia parquet. They are sophisticatedly appointed with family antiques and colonial pieces bought around the world, as are the luxurious suites, each with bedroom, bathroom, kitchenette and large living room. The property features two swimming pools; a travertine infinity pool which hangs on the edge of the manicured garden, and a pool secluded among the olive groves. Your gracious hosts serve lunch and dinner based on organic local products and are even willing to reveal traditional family recipes and organize cookery classes for curious gourmets. *Directions:* From the Grosseto-Siena highway 223, exit at Paganico. After 3 km turn right for Sasso d'Ombrone, and right for Poggi del Sasso. In town watch for Via di Vicarello on the right and follow the road, keeping left at the fork, for 3.5 km.

CASTELLO DI VICARELLO
Hosts: Aurora & Carlo Baccheschi Berti
Via di Vicarello 1
Poggi del Sasso, (GR) 58043, Italy
Tel & Fax: (0564) 990718
2 Rooms, Double: €400–€480
5 Suites: €630–€1180
2 Houses: €780–€1400 daily
Minimum Stay Required: 2 nights
Open: all year, Credit cards: all major
Abitare La Storia, History Traveller
B&B, SELF CATERING

Thirty-five kilometers northeast of Florence, in a beautiful, hilly area of Tuscany, lies the Rufina Valley, famous for its robust red wine. Crowning a wooded slope is one of the many residences of the noble Galeotti-Ottieri family. The interior of the 15th-century main villa reveals spacious high-ceilinged halls with frescoes depicting family history. The family has also restored several stone farmhouses on the vast property, one of which is the Locanda Praticino whose upper floor contains lovely, simple double rooms with countryside views down one long hall, each named after its color scheme. Downstairs is a large rustic dining and living room with vaulted ceiling, enormous stone fireplace, worn brick floors, and casual country furniture. Full country-fresh Tuscan meals are only €18. A swimming pool and tennis courts, plus the enchanting landscape, make it difficult to tear oneself away for touring. In order to retain the characteristic flavor of farmers' quarters, the properties have an intentionally unrestored, natural air to them. Available for longer stays are three very tastefully decorated apartments. The Petrognano is a tranquil spot where guests may enjoy the gracious hospitality of this historically important Florentine family. *Directions:* From Florence head toward Pontassieve. Pass the town of Rufina and after 1.5 km turn right for Pomino. Continue for 5km on this winding road and the Locanda is signpost on the right hand side.

FATTORIA DI PETROGNANO
Host: Cecilia Galeotti-Ottieri Family
Localita: Pomino
Pomino, Rufina, (FI) 50060, Italy
Tel: (055) 8318867, Fax: (055) 8318812
8 Rooms, Double: €75–€90
3 Apartments: €400–€1000 weekly
Minimum Stay Required: 2 nights
Open: Apr to Oct, Credit cards: all major
B&B, SELF CATERING

The Il Pellicano (one of Italy's most idyllic hotels) has been cleverly designed in the traditional villa Tuscan style and, although not old, looks as though it has snuggled on its prime hillside position overlooking the Tyrrhenian sea many years. The façade is stucco, painted a typical Italian russet and set off by a tiled roof. Vines enwrap the building, further enhancing its appealing look. You enter into a spacious, attractive lobby where the sun streams through the windows enhancing the white walls, terracotta floors, and wood-beamed ceilings. The sophisticated and refined ambiance continues with comfy sofas, antique accents, and enormous displays of fresh flowers. The overall impression is one of light and color—and impeccable taste. Beyond the reception area is a spacious terrace where chef Antonio Guida (one Michelin star) prepares elaborate seafood menus, served outdoors overlooking the dramatic bay and islands. From the terrace, a lovely lawn extends down the hillside to a heated pool romantically perched at the cliff's edge and the "all'aperto" restaurant, offering informal lunches and dinners for a tradional Tuscan culinary experience. From the bluff, both steps and an elevator access a pier at the water's edge. The hotel's new "Pelliclub" offers guests a complete beauty center, fitness, Roman steam bath, coiffeur, botique, tennis court and conference room. Exquisite. *Directions:* Contact hotel for directions.

IL PELLICANO
Host: Francesca Tozzi
Localita: Sbarcatello
Porto Ercole, (GR) 58018, Italy
Tel: (0564) 85 81 11, Fax: (0564) 83 34 18
50 Rooms, Double: €470–€1602
Open: Apr to Oct, Credit cards: AX, MC, VS
Relais & Châteaux
HOTEL

Standing proudly on the cliffs overlooking Tuscany's most spectacular coastlines, Argentario, are the remains of a 13th-century Spanish watchtower. The tower has been cleverly incorporated into, and stands as the dramatic symbol for, the Hotel Torre di Cala Piccola, sharing a bay property with luxurious private villas discreetly hidden behind high walls. The first part of the hotel you see (which houses the luminous white reception area, lounge, and bar) is a sienna-toned building with red-tiled roof and green shutters, snuggled among silvery olive trees and flowering oleanders. Moderately sized, newly decorated guestrooms and suites are dispersed among the romantic stone cottages with terraces which spill down the hillside overlooking the sea far below. High cliffs drop precipitously down to the sea, forming a series of coves where the deep blue water of the Mediterranean dances in the sunlight. Also capturing this absolutely stunning vista are a lush lawn where dinner or sunset aperitifs are served and, on a lower terrace facing the island of Giglio, an infinity swimming pool, which seems to almost float high above the sea. The hotel's shuttle accompanies guests down to the cove with snack bar for a day at the sea. Attentive staff at a very special retreat.

HOTEL TORRE DI CALA PICCOLA
Host: Stefania Marconi
Cala Piccola
Porto Santo Stefano, (GR) 58019, Italy
Tel: (0564) 82 51 11
47 Rooms, Double: €195–€380
4 Suites: €295–€580
Closed: Nov to Jan, Credit cards: all major
HOTEL

From the moment you enter the grand foyer looking out over the classical Italian garden of this 16th-century country villa, all sense of time and place is lost. The Rucellai-Piqués' devotion to their estate (in the family since 1759) is apparent, as is their warm hospitality. Guests are given the run of the rambling old home, from the cozy bedrooms, varying in size and decor; antique-filled library; and spacious living room with fireplace, old comfortable sofas, and family portraits to a gracious buffet breakfast room where guests are seated at long tables. At the entrance is a duck pond, a large shady area with tables and a 15th-century swimming pool. Villa Rucellai serves as an excellent base for visiting Florence, Siena, Lucca, and Pisa. The nearby town with its many restaurant choices is conveniently just a 15–20 minute walk away. *Directions:* From Exit the A11 autostrada at Prato Est. Follow signs for centro and the railway station. Go right before the underpass onto Viale della Republica. Go straight for 2km towards the hills. After crossing the river and railway circle left onto Viale Borgo Valsugana and go 2 km keeping the river on your left. After the road bends to the right, turn right at the small roundabout (do not cross the river). After 150 meters turn left at a small piazza onto Via del Palco. Follow signs for Villa Rucellai Loc. Canneto or Trattoria La Fontana. Continue for 1.5 km after Trattoria La Fontanta on the very narrow Via di Canneto to the entry gate.

❄ ☕ 🛴 🏧 @ W P ≈ 🎿 👫 🏌

VILLA RUCELLAI DI CANNETO
Host: Rucellai Piqué Family
Via di Canneto 16
Prato, (PO) 59100, Italy
Tel: (0574) 460392, Fax: (0574) 467748
8 Rooms, Double: €100
Open: all year, Credit cards: MC, VS
B&B

Weary of life in the intense financial world of Milan, Guido and Martina packed up and headed for the hills of Chianti and the "good life" that attracts so many there. After a long search they chose the scenic property where La Locanda now stands, primarily for its magnificent position facing out to medieval Volpaia and an endless panorama filled with layers of virgin hills. The results of their meticulous restoration of three simple stone farmhouses are formidable and today fortunate guests can share in their dream. Its remote location among woods and olive groves guarantees total silence and tranquility and the comfortable, decorator-perfect common rooms and luminous colors harmonize divinely with this idyllic setting. An understated elegance permeates the six bedrooms and the suite. They are tastefully appointed with antiques and smart plaid curtains, and four have the advantage of the views. Breakfast and dinner (on request Mondays, Wednesdays & Fridays) are served out on the terrace above the swimming pool whose borderless edge disappears into the landscape. Guido and Martina, natural and gregarious hosts, exude a contagious enthusiasm for their new surroundings. *Directions:* From Radda follow signs for Florence and turn right for Volpaia. Continue on the unpaved road for another 3.8 km after Volpaia village, following signs to La Locanda/Montanino.

LA LOCANDA
Hosts: Guido & Martina Bevilacqua
Localita: Montanino
Radda in Chianti, (SI) 53017, Italy
Tel: (0577) 738833 , Fax: (0577) 739263
6 Rooms, Double: €200–€280
1 Suite: €300
Rent the entire house (3 night minimum)
Minimum Stay Required: 2 nights
Open: Apr to Oct, Credit cards: MC, VS
B&B

Podere Terreno combines idyllic location and authentic, charming ambiance with delightful hosts Sylvie and Roberto, a Franco-Italian couple, and son, Francesco. The 400-year-old rustic stone farmhouse is surrounded by terracotta flower vases, a grapevine-covered pergola, a small lake, and sweeping panoramas of the Chianti countryside. Inside are six sweet double bedrooms with small bathrooms, each decorated differently with country antiques and the family's personal possessions, which make the feeling very informal and homelike. Guests convene in the main room of the house around the massive stone fireplace on floral sofas for a glass of house wine before sitting down to a sumptuous candlelit dinner prepared by your hosts. This is a cozy, stone-walled room, filled with country antiques, brass pots, dried-flower bouquets hanging from the exposed beams, and shelves lined with bottles of the proprietors' own Chianti Classico wine. Wine tastings take place within the new cantina. The hosts are experts at suggesting local itineraries and directing guests to the many quaint villages waiting to be explored. *Directions:* From Greve follow signs to Panzano, then, on the way to Radda, pass Lucarelli. After 6 km turn left towards Volpaia and after 3 km turn right at the sign for Podere Terreno.

PODERE TERRENO
Hosts: Marie Sylvie Haniez, Roberto Melosi
*   & Pier Francesco Rapisarda-Haniez*
Via della Volpaia
Radda in Chianti, (SI) 53017, Italy
Tel: (0577) 738312
Fax: (0577) 738400
6 Rooms, Double: €190*
*Includes breakfast, dinner & wine
Closed: Christmas week, Credit cards: AX, MC, VS
B&B

Both Radda and Greve are excellent bases from which to explore the scenic Chianti wine country with its regal castles and stone villages, in addition to Siena, Florence, and San Gimignano. Radda in particular offers a myriad of possibilities for accommodation, including many private homes with rooms or apartments. The Val delle Corti is the home and vineyard property of gracious hostess Eli Bianchi and her son Roberto where they produce a high-quality Chianti Classico wine. The cozy pale-stone house with white shutters tops a hill overlooking the quaint town. The hosts, who moved here in 1974 from Milan, are extremely active in community affairs and are a superb source for area information. The guest accommodation is a lovely separate little house called il Fienile (hay barn), simply appointed with family antiques and newer pieces, which has a large open kitchen and living space looking out to the vineyards, and two bedrooms and one bathroom on the first floor. Meals can be taken at one of the excellent restaurants right in nearby Radda. *Directions:* Equidistant from Florence and Siena off the N222 Chianti road. Before entering Radda, turn right toward Lecchi-San Sano, then take the first left at Val delle Corti.

PODERE VAL DELLE CORTI
Host: Bianchi Family
Localita: La Croce
Radda in Chianti, (SI) 53017, Italy
Tel: (0577) 738215
1 Apartment: €90–€110 daily; €690 weekly*
*Breakfast not included
Minimum Stay Required: 3 nights
Open: all year, Credit cards: MC, VS
SELF CATERING

In the very heart of Chianti between Radda, Castellina, and Vagliagli sits the Pornanino farm surrounded by 90 acres of wooded hills and olive groves. Hosts Franco and Lia have carefully restored the main house for themselves plus two stone barns for guests, appointed with the same warm country style as their own home, with antique furniture enhancing beamed ceilings and terracotta floors. Il Capannino is completely refurbished and offers a large central room with open kitchen at an upper level, dining room/living room with open fireplace, and two bedrooms with two bathrooms. A large arched glass door opens onto the pergola-covered terrace for outside meals. Il Leccino is similar but has just one bedroom. Guests can also take advantage of the lovely swimming pool overlooking the olive groves. Franco and Lia are part of the increasing breed of "neo-farmers" migrating from major cities in search of a slower-paced lifestyle where the basic values of life are emphasized in everyday living. Franco has become a passionate producer of top-quality olive oil and even conducts small seminars and tastings on the subject. *Directions:* The farm is located 9 km south of Radda, 5 km from Castellina, and 4 km north of Vagliagli on route 102 but the turnoff is not marked, so it is best to call ahead. 18 km from Siena and 54 km from Florence.

PORNANINO
Hosts: Lia & Franco Lombardi
Localita: Pornanino 72
Radda in Chianti, (SI) 53017, Italy
Tel: (0577) 738658, Fax: (0577) 738794
2 Houses: €800–€1400 weekly*
*Breakfast not included
Minimum Stay Required: 4 nights
Open: all year, Credit cards: MC, VS
SELF CATERING

The Relais Vignale is a superb small hotel idyllically located in the heart of the Chianti wine region. It enjoys the enviable honor of having the best of both worlds—it feels as if you are secluded in the countryside, yet you are right in Radda, one of Tuscany's most picturesque towns. It was the manor house of a large Chianti estate, which still produces fine wines. The hotel sits on the main street, but magically, the back of the hotel opens onto a gorgeous, pristine view of rolling hills laced with vineyards and dotted with olive trees. Some of the guestrooms are in the main manor while others, which also have lovely views, are just across the street. The guestrooms and cozy lounges are tastefully decorated with antiques. Care has been taken in the restoration to preserve many of the enticing architectural features of the manor such as heavy beams, arched hallways, decorative fireplaces, and painted ceilings. Behind the hotel, meticulously kept gardens lead down the hillside to a romantic wisteria- and jasmine-covered terrace where guests enjoy breakfast, or dinner under the stars, with an incredible view. Another bonus of this fine hotel is the heated swimming pool, overlooking the vineyards. The hotel also has a wine shop with free tastings of products of the estate.

RELAIS VIGNALE
Host: Monica Bernetti
Via Pianigiani, 15
Radda in Chianti, (SI) 53017, Italy
Tel: (0577) 73 83 00, Fax: (0577) 73 85 92
34 Rooms, Double: €215–€260
5 Suites: €350–€385
Open: Mar 21 to Nov 2, Credit cards: all major
HOTEL

The new owners of La Palazzina, Eliana and Silvano Mamprin, were both international hoteliers before falling head over heels in love with this beautiful property. The stately 18th-century hilltop villa surrounded by a lush garden is located in the enchanting Orcia valley with views over wheat fields and soft green hills fringed by cypress trees. This region is part of a Unesco World Heritage preservation area. Eleven guestrooms and three apartments are appointed with country antiques, botanic prints, lace curtains and wrought iron beds set on Tuscan tiled floors. The elegant dining room looks out to a formal garden and expansive lawns. During the summer months the outdoor terrace is a special venue for enjoying Eliana's delectable Tuscan cuisine. A swimming pool hugs the side of the hill overlooking the surrounding countryside. Cooking courses and wine and olive oil tastings are offered as well as trips to the nearby hot springs and spa at San Casciano. This southeast corner of Tuscany offers a rich variety of sites to explore, including the Amiata Mountains, the Abbey of Sant'Antimo and the hilltowns of Montepulciano, Pienza, and Montalcino. *Directions:* Traveling the A1 autostrada from either the north or south, exit at Chiusi and drive towards Sarteano on route 478, turning left for Radicofani. After 14 km turn left for Celle Sul Rigo then right at the sign for Fattoria La Palazzina.

FATTORIA LA PALAZZINA
Hosts: Eliana & Silvano Mamprin
Località Le Vigne, 33
Radicofani, (SI) 53040, Italy
Tel: (0578) 55771, Fax: (0578) 283114
11 Rooms, Double: €70–€120
3 Apartments: €75–€180 daily
Dinners: €25–€35
Open: all year, Credit cards: AX, MC, VS
B&B

The Villa Rigacci is a picture-perfect example of a 15th-century Tuscan villa with its creamy-white stucco façade, thick walls, heavy red-tile roof, green-shuttered windows, and beautiful gardens. The Pierazzi family takes great care to see that all the guests receive their personal attention and are made to feel "at home." In summer, after a day of sightseeing, guests relax in the back garden where a large pool, surrounded by lounge chairs and umbrellas, stretches out on a terraced lawn. Inside, handsome family antiques adorn the sitting rooms and library. The chef specializes in traditional Tuscan cuisine, and from October to March cooking courses are organized. The dining room is especially lovely, but in summer guests usually choose to enjoy their meals outside on the terrace. Each bedroom is individually decorated with very appealing country-style antiques accented by lovely fabrics—creating rooms that blend beautifully with the old-world ambiance of the villa. Although the surrounding area is not as pristinely rural as some parts of Tuscany, once you enter into the beautiful grounds (highlighted by cypress, pine, and olive trees) you enjoy a serene setting and accommodations with charm. *Directions:* From Florence go south on the A1. Take the Incisa exit. Turn right to Matassino. At the second roundabout turn left toward Vaggio. Pass Vaggio. Go toward San Giovenale. After crossing a bridge, the hotel is about 100 m on your right.

❋ ☕ ✗ ♨ 💳 ☎ 🐕 🏹 @ ⚱ P 🍴 🚫 ⚓ 🖼 👕 🚶 🚶 🐎 🍇

VILLA RIGACCI
Hosts: Kirsten & Federico Pierazzi
Loc. Vaggio, 75
Reggello–Vaggio, (FI) 50066, Italy
Tel: (055) 8656718, Fax: (055) 86 56 537
28 Rooms, Double: €95–€165
5 Suites: €145–€185
Open: all year, Credit cards: all major
HOTEL

Daniela and her architect husband, Piero, brought the family's ancient property back to life. Dating back to the 9th century the property contains a Romanesque church, now the site for concerts. The complex of stone houses is surrounded by vineyards, woods, olive groves (source of the family's prestigious olive oil), and a garden including a collection of English roses. Five suites and two apartments are attached to the main house. Each accommodate two to five persons. Simply furnished with the family's country antiques, wrought-iron beds, and original paintings by Daniela's father, a renowned fresco painter. They feature living rooms with fireplace and balconies with view to either the sweeping countryside, down to the sea, or out to the woods, All the units are rented on a self-catering basis but breakfast can be provided for a fee by request. Besides a pool with spectacular views and massage treatments, painting classes are organized in May and October. Along with Siena and Montalcino, there are plenty of off-the-beaten-track sights to see organized by son, Emiliano. Bikes can be rented. *Directions:* From Grosseto take Aurelia route 1 north and exit at Braccagni. Continue towards Montemassi and before town turn right for Caminino and Roccatederighi. After 1 km turn right at the gate for Caminino.

■ ✍ ☕ 💳@ W ￥ P 🚭 ≋ ⛷ ♨ ⚓ 🎣 🚶 🏇 ⛷ ⚘

PIEVE DI CAMININO
Hosts: Daniela Locatelli & Piero Marrucchi
Via Provinciale di Peruzzo
Roccatederighi, (GR) 58028, Italy
Tel: (0564) 569736, Fax: (0564) 568756
5 Suites: €130–€170
2 Apartments: €180–€230 daily
Minimum Stay Required: Suites: 2 nights, Apts: 7 nights
Open: all year, Credit cards: all major
History Traveller
B&B, SELF CATERING

The spectacular 2,500-acre hilltop farm property of Montestigliano is a rich combination of woods, cultivated fields, olive groves, and open meadows all surrounding the hamlet dating from 1730. British-born hostess Susan makes sure guests are comfortable in one of the ten independent apartments within the various houses scattered about the property. All retain their original Tuscan character in furnishings and have a combination of two or three bedrooms, kitchen, living room (some with fireplace), and essential modern amenities like washing machines and telephones. The granary has been restored and converted into a farm shop, recreation room, and dining room where meals are served upon request from Monday to Friday. Groups of up to 12 persons have the opportunity to reside in the main villa. Two swimming pools are at guests' disposal, plus many paths and trails. Montestigliano is a marvelous base for getting to know in depth a part of Tuscany whose traditions and lifestyles have remained intact, while still having Siena, San Gimignano, Pienza, Montalcino, and the Chianti area at one's fingertips. Plenty of places to dine are available in Rosia and Sovicille. Susan also arranges weddings. *Directions:* From Siena (12 km) take S.S.223 (towards Grosseto). After 12 km, just after a gas station, turn right and after 2 km turn left for Brenna, taking the unpaved road to the right up to the top of hill.

MONTESTIGLIANO
Host: Susan Pennington
Loc. Montestigliano
Rosia, (SI) 53010, Italy
Tel: (0577) 342189, Fax: (0577) 342100
10 Apartments: €545–€1780 weekly*
1 Villa: €1538–€3880 weekly*
*Breakfast not included
Minimum Stay Required: 5 to 7 nights depending on season
Open: all year, Credit cards: none
SELF CATERING

In the southeastern corner of Tuscany is a delightful, yet undiscovered pocket of absolutely stunning countryside. It was only natural that Andrea, with his expert culinary skills, and his lovely wife, Cristina, a born hostess, should open a bed and breakfast close to their vast 1,000-acre countryside property producing olive oil, wine, cereals and vegetables. La Crocetta sits at the crossroads leading up to the charming town of San Casciano, offering eight guestrooms. The small guestrooms with varying color schemes, each with a new bathroom, are pleasantly appointed with canopy beds and fresh country fabrics used for bedspreads and curtains. A pool has been added in the front garden. Inquire about the possibility of cooking and flower arranging courses. San Casciano dei Bagni is the home of several ancient thermal hot springs and is a real plus for those wanted to take a day off from touring to enjoy a swim in one of the thermal pools or take advantage of the many specialized treatments at the nearby luxury spa (Hotel Fonteverde mentioned in our hotel guide). Horseback riding or hiking through the Nature Park of Mount Rufeno are additional activities for lovers of the outdoors. Historic cities of Orvieto, Siena, and the hilltowns of Montepulciano, Pienza and Montalcino are all at easy touring distance. *Directions:* From the A1 autostrada, exit at Fabro from the south or Chiusi from the north, traveling towards Sarteano-Cetona, then San Casciano dei Bagni.

LA CROCETTA
Hosts: Cristina & Andrea Leotti
Localita: La Crocetta
San Casciano dei Bagni, (SI) 53040, Italy
Tel: (0578) 58360, Fax: (0578) 58353
8 Rooms, Double: €120–€140
Minimum Stay Required: 2 nights
Dinners: €28
Open: Mar 30 to Nov 12, Credit cards: MC, VS
B&B

Italy abounds in well-equipped spas concentrated around its many thermal water sources, yet the one at Fonteverde truly stands out among the rest. While most four and five star hotels now feature some kind of a wellness center, we added the Hotel Fonteverde for its combination of awesome setting, historic Medicean palazzo, and full-fledged Italian-style spa. The guestrooms, classically appointed and full of amenities, are spread about the original 17th-century home and an attached modern duplicate. A full buffet breakfast is served in the courtyard or indoors, while dinners are presented in an elegant restaurant highlighting fine local products: Porcini mushrooms, Pienza cheese, Brunello wine and Chianina meat. A spacious bar and lounges open out to a large terrace taking in a sweeping vista of the entire untouched valley with its occasional Tuscan farmhouse. This same view is savored from within one of the many thermal pools; one has its own circuit of hydro-jets created for specific body parts. This is a gorgeous lesser-known area of Tuscany called the Val d'Orcia with Mount Amiata looming on the horizon and many interesting medieval towns to explore. *Directions:* Exit Autostrada A1 from the north at Chiusi-Chianciano; then follow first signs for Sarteano, then San Casciano dei Bagni to the hotel.

HOTEL FONTEVERDE
Host: Antonio Politi
Località Terme 1
San Casciano dei Bagni, (SI) 53040, Italy
Tel: (0578) 57 241, Fax: (0578) 57 22 00
66 Rooms, Double: €330–€560
14 Suites: €690–€1340
Open: all year, Credit cards: all major
HOTEL

Perched atop a hill and enjoying a 360-degree view of perfectly unspoiled landscape, including a stunning medieval castle, sits the Le Radici farmhouse. Ex-urbanite Alfredo carefully chose this peaceful spot in order to offer accommodation to those who truly appreciate nature and the sense of well-being it inspires. The two farmhouses have been restored, maintaining most of the original rustic flavor, and divided into seven double rooms, three suites, and two apartments. The apartments include one or two bedrooms, living room with fireplace, kitchenette, and bathroom. The tastefully appointed rooms in muted colors are adorned by wrought-iron beds and antique furnishings, complemented by wood-beam and brick ceilings. Special attention has been given to landscaping around the immediate property, which includes vineyards and olive groves. The real treat is the absolutely gorgeous "borderless" swimming pool with cascading water, which fits harmoniously into its surroundings. A romantic candlelit dinner showing off Alfredo's passion for cooking is served in the dining room or out on the terrace, using fresh ingredients from the property. The hosts suggest many interesting itineraries in this area, which borders Umbria. One can relax in the thermal waters of San Casciano or venture out to the towns of Orvieto, Todi, or Pienza, among others. *Directions:* From San Casciano dei Bagni follow signs for Le Radici (4 km).

LE RADICI
Host: Alfredo Ferrari
San Casciano dei Bagni, (SI) 53040, Italy
Tel & Fax: (0578) 56038
7 Rooms, Double: €150–€250
3 Suites: €260–€300
2 Apartments: €1180–€1500 weekly
Minimum Stay Required: 2 nights
Dinners: €35–€55
Open: Apr to Nov, Credit cards: MC, VS
B&B, SELF CATERING

The Villa Il Poggiale is an intimate, elegant boutique hotel. This traditional Tuscan country villa dating to the Renaissance period has had such illustrious proprietors as noble families Corsini, Martini, and Ricasoli-Rucellai, and has been in the Vitta family for the past 50 years. Brothers Johanan and Nathanel have brought the family residence back to its former glory, transforming it from a private country home to an exclusive inn, with no expense spared on beauty, comfort and modern conveniences. On the ground floor you find the splendidly decorated grand main salon plus another smaller one off which three of the generous bedrooms and suites with antique furnishings and lovely new bathrooms are found. Soft-peach, olive-green, and pale-yellow color schemes are displayed in fine fabrics used for bedspreads, draperies, and upholstery. Other frescoed bedrooms upstairs are nicely spaced apart by three additional sitting rooms, the most desirable being those away from the main road. A full buffet breakfast featuring homemade cakes and local specialties is served in the garden terrace, which leads down to the swimming pool with its extraordinary views of the picture-perfect Tuscan landscape. This is a luxurious villa where you will feel like guest in a private home. May to October a traditional Tuscan buffet dinner is also offered. *Directions:* Drive through San Casciano following signs for Empoli. After 2 km, Villa Il Poggiale is on the left.

❄ ☕ ✄ ♨ 💳 ☎ 🛗 @ W Y P 🚭 ≈ 🖼 🐾 🏃 🚶 🐎 🍇

VILLA IL POGGIALE
Hosts: Johanan & Nathanel Vitta
Via Empolese, 69
Val di Pesa
San Casciano Val di Pesa, (FI) 50026, Italy
Tel: (055) 82 83 11, Fax: (055) 82 94 296
8 Rooms, Double: €130–€150
8 Suites: €195–€240
2 Apartments: €300–€1100 daily
Closed: Feb, Credit cards: all major
HOTEL

The luxurious Villa Mangiacane with its combination historic home, worldly décor, and high-tech amenities is, in a word, magnificent. Owner Glynn Cohen returned from years in South Africa and purchased the 15th century estate which encompasses 600 acres of surrounding land dedicated to the production of Chianti Classico wines and extra virgin olive oil. The stately villa once the residence of the Machiavelli family, is assumed to be the architectural work of Michelangelo. The eight sumptuous bedrooms and suites can be rented separately or as a full house rental and are exquisitely appointed with priceless antiques and artwork, finest fabrics and linens, and designer bathrooms. Besides grand but comfortable salons, dining room, library, wine cellars, terraces, swimming pool, and gym, spectacular Renaissance views are awarded at every window. In fact the home was designed on the same axis as the Duomo cathedral in Florence with the long driveway, villa entrance and exit to the back frescoed loggia, all perfectly aligned to frame the famous cupola through a pathway cut in the hilltop woods. Truly amazing. The additional 18 guestrooms and suites with private gardens are adjacent the Vineyard Villa. A very competent staff caters to your every whim. *Directions:* Exit A1 at Firenze Certosa, go straight towards Tavarnuzze. Pass Tavernuzze, drive over a the small bridge named "Scopet" on your right. At the first stop turn right and drive 50 m to the hotel.

VILLA MANGIACANE
Host: Paolo Barzagli
Via Faltignano 4
San Casciano Val di Pesa, (FI) 50026, Italy
Tel: (055) 82 90 123, Fax: (055) 82 90 358
26 Rooms, Double: €250–€460
Open: all year, Credit cards: all major
HOTEL

Without a doubt, San Gimignano is one of the most picturesque places in Tuscany: a postcard-perfect hilltop village punctuated by 14 tall towers. During the day, the town bustles with activity, but after the busloads of tourists depart, the romantic ambiance of yesteryear fills the cobbled streets. For the lucky few who spend the night, there is a jewel of small inn, the Hotel L'Antico Pozzo. What a pleasure to see a renovation with such excellent taste and meticulous attention to maintaining the authentic character of the original building. The name of the hotel derives from an antique stone well (pozzo), which is softly illuminated just off the lobby. The fact that only the most affluent families could afford the luxury of a private well indicates that this 15th-century townhouse was once a wealthy residence. A timeworn stone staircase leads up to the air conditioned bedrooms, tucked at various levels along a maze of hallways. Each one of the quietly elegant rooms has its own personality with thick stone walls, terracotta floors, and beautifully framed antique prints, plus satellite television. One of my favorites, number 20, has the palest of pastel-peach-colored walls, windows opening onto the terrace, and a fabulous domed ceiling painted with ancient Roman designs. Number 14 is also outstanding—a very large room with a canopy bed. Another advantage of L'Antico Pozzo is that this is a long time family-run hotel.

HOTEL L' ANTICO POZZO
Host: Emanuele Marro
Via San Matteo, 87
San Gimignano, (SI) 53037, Italy
Tel: (0577) 94 20 14, Fax: (0577) 94 21 17
18 Rooms, Double: €110–€180
Open: all year, Credit cards: all major
HOTEL

Il Casale is a highly efficient and very popular bed and breakfast, thanks to warm and dedicated host, Alessandro, who has combined his extensive hospitality experience with a desire to see his great-grandfather's lovely country property restored properly. Six double rooms and two small apartments including bedroom, kitchen/eating area, and bathroom are all housed within the extended stone farmhouse. Another section is reserved for Alessandro and the family who looks after the wine estate. Access to the guest entrance is through a well-kept garden around the back with a small chapel and lovely views over the soft hills. Main areas include a sitting room and beamed breakfast room with fireplace. The spotless home is appointed with scattered antiques and the very comfortable guestrooms, each with a different color scheme, have new bathrooms and either countryside views or garden or interior patio entrance. Infinite attention to details in both the aesthetics and service offered is given to guests. The entrepreneurial Alessandro has also restored the stone barn and cantina over in the olive grove, Rocca degli Olivi, creating an apartment, five lovely bedrooms with either mansard or vaulted ceilings and gorgeous views, and a breakfast room. An inviting swimming pool is hidden among the olive trees. Plenty of tourist information is on hand. *Directions:* From San Gimignano follow signs for Certaldo for 3 km. Il Casale is on the left and well marked.

❄ ☕ ✗ 💳 🔔 ☎ 🏠 @ W ⍣ P ⍢ 🚭 ≈ 🖼 🎿 🚶 🐎 🍇

IL CASALE DEL COTONE
Host: Alessandro Martelli
Localita: Cellole 59
San Gimignano, (SI) 53037, Italy
Tel & Fax: (0577) 943236
16 Rooms, Double: €100–€130
3 Suites: €120–€150
2 Apartments: €100–€150 daily
Minimum Stay Required: Apartments: 3 nights
Dinners: €35
Open: all year, Credit cards: all major
B&B

Due to the ever-increasing popularity of the stunning medieval village of San Gimignano, accommodations in the surrounding countryside have flourished. The Casanova is a typical square stone farmhouse with wood shutters and red-tile roof, which you'll grow accustomed to seeing throughout Tuscany. The bed and breakfast's exceptional feature is that it enjoys a privileged view of the towers of San Gimignano, an ancient town referred to as the "Manhattan" of the year 1000. The Fanciulini Family, who aim to offer quality accommodation at competitive rates, have the farmhouse, adding amenities in rooms such as air conditioning, satellite TV, and telephone, and have also installed a swimming pool with garden view. Breakfast and restaurant meals are served in the beautiful dining room or on the outside patio where guests can enjoy the breathtaking scenery. This is an authentic farm that produces a bounty of products: wine, olive oil, saffron-to name just a few! The property offers eight double rooms with private baths and one apartment for two persons. Country furniture characteristic of the region decorates the rooms, whose original architectural features have been preserved. *Directions:* From San Gimignano take the road toward Volterra. After 2 km, turn left at the sign for Casanova.

CASANOVA DI PESCILLE
Hosts: Monica & Roberto Fanciullini
Localita: Pescille
San Gimignano, (SI) 53037, Italy
Tel & Fax: (0577) 941902
8 Rooms, Double: €100–€105
1 Suite: €115–€125
Open: Mar to Dec, Credit cards: MC, VS
B&B, SELF CATERING

Accidentally coming upon the Casolare, tucked away in the unpopulated hills 8 kilometers past medieval San Gimignano, was a delightful surprise. Just before reaching the bed and breakfast, you'll see a half-abandoned stone convent dating back to 1100. The attractive renovated farmhouse, hosted by Andrea, a former art and antiques dealer, and his Spanish wife, Berta, retains all the features characteristic of the original structure. The five double rooms are extremely comfortable and tastefully appointed. Rooms are divided between the two floors of the house, with one being an independent structure poolside. The suites for two to four persons with terrace and living room have been decorated with refined antiques as well. Original watercolor paintings by a local artist adorn an entire wall in the inviting double living room. An extra bonus is the breathtaking swimming pool, with sweeping countryside panorama, surrounded by a manicured lawn, fruit trees, and terracotta pots overflowing with pink geraniums. It provides refreshment after a hot day of sightseeing, while you anticipate another appetizing candlelit meal at dusk under the pergola. Berta is an excellent cook and prepares very special Tuscan menus accompanied by an impressive wine list. This is a truly tranquil haven. *Directions:* From San Gimignano follow signs for Gambassi. Take road on left for Gambassi and Libbiano. After 3km turn left for Libbiano and the dirt road to the end.

CASOLARE DI LIBBIANO
Hosts: Berta & Andrea Bucciarelli
Localita: Libbiano 3
San Gimignano, (SI) 53037, Italy
Tel: (0577) 946002, Fax: (0577) 907122
4 Rooms, Double: €110–€130
4 Suites: €130–€170
1 Apartment: €140 daily, €980 weekly
Dinners: €24
Open: Apr 1 to Nov 2, Credit cards: MC, VS
B&B

San Gimignano is one of the most fascinating of the medieval Tuscany hilltowns. As you approach, this looks like a city of skyscrapers: come even closer and the skyscrapers emerge as 14 soaring towers—dramatic reminders of what San Gimignano must have looked like in all her glory when this wealthy town sported 72 giant towers. Most tourists come just for the day to visit this small town, but for those lucky enough to be able to spend the night, San Gimignano has a simple but very charming hotel, La Cisterna. The hotel is located on the town's main square and fits right into the ancient character of the surrounding buildings with its somber stone walls softened by ivy, arched shuttered doors, and red-tile roof. Inside La Cisterna, the medieval feeling continues with lots of stone, vaulted ceilings, leather chairs, and dark woods. The bedrooms are not fancy, but pleasant, and some have balconies with lovely views of the valley. Renovations added air conditioning and satellite TV (for European channels and CNN). La Cisterna is probably more famous as a restaurant than as a hotel and people come from far and wide because not only is the food delicious, but the dining rooms are delightful. Especially charming is the dining room with the brick wall, sloping ceiling supported by giant beams, and picture windows framing the gorgeous hills of Tuscany.

LA CISTERNA
Host: Salvestrini Family
Piazza della Cisterna, 24
San Gimignano, (SI) 53037, Italy
Tel: (0577) 94 03 28, Fax: (0577) 94 20 80
50 Rooms, Double: €80–€145
2 Suites: €115–€150
Restaurant closed Tue & Wed lunch
Open: Mar 14 to Jan 6, Credit cards: all major
HOTEL

Leaving San Gimignano on the road north towards Pancole-Certaldo, you come across La Fonte, the property of the Bergamasco family run by daughter Maria. This typical Tuscan farmhouse with cupola is surrounded by a nature reserve, vineyards, olive groves, and woods, yet is very close to many major sights and cities. Within the large main house are four fully-equipped apartments with coveted views for longer stays. Three have two bedrooms each with en suite bathrooms and one has one bedroom. Depending on guests' requests, Maria uses the seven bedrooms separately for bed-and-breakfast guests or as four apartments. Maria has enhanced the natural beauty of the home's original features —brick vaulted ceilings and floors—with appropriate country furnishings and smart, colorful fabrics. The cypress-backed swimming pool is nearby, and several patios within the English garden with its extensive lawns offer quiet places for relaxing after touring the many sights of the area. At your fingertips are Volterra, Lucca, the Chianti area, Siena, and many other Tuscan delights. Breakfast can be served outdoors or a pre-ordered tray is brought directly to rooms. *Directions:* 8 km from San Gimignano, 4 km from Certaldo. From Certaldo take the road to San Gimignano. Just as you leave town there is a gas station (ERG) and signs to Pancole and Il Monte. Take the road to Pancole and go for 2 km till you see the sign for La Fonte on the right.

LA FONTE
Host: Maria Bergamasco
Via Canonica 4
San Gimignano, (SI) 53037, Italy
Tel: (0577) 944845, Fax: (0577) 945044
7 Rooms, Double: €125*
4 Suites: €98–€190*
4 Apartments: €98 daily, €686 weekly*
*Breakfast not included
Minimum Stay Required: 3 nights
Open: Mar 1 to Oct 31, Credit cards: all major
B&B, SELF CATERING

The increasing popularity of this perfectly intact medieval town and the resulting availability of accommodations have made San Gimignano a hub from which tourists fan out to visit nearby, lesser-known treasures such as Volterra, Colle Val d'Elsa, and Monteriggioni. A pleasant, informal stay can be had at the Podere Villuzza, a reader favorite now owned by Salvatore Leanza, his sister Antonella and mother Pina, who recently purchased the 150-year-old stone farmhouse. Chairs are set up in front where visitors can enjoy the view of vineyard-covered hills leading up to the impressive multi-towered town. Common areas include the rustic living room with ceramic-tiled tables and fireplace where guests convene after a day of touring. While Pina prepares meals for guests upon requests, Salvatore produces top-quality wine and olive oil. Six double rooms, on ground and first floors accessed by several different entrances, are furnished in true country style with a mix of wrought-iron beds and antique armoires, complemented by mansard beamed ceilings and stone walls. Rooms have views out over the countryside and town or over hills. For weekly stays there are three small apartments within the house that include a living area and kitchen. A swimming pool is a great bonus for guests. *Directions:* Go through town and follow signs for Certaldo. After 2 km turn right and follow signs for Villuzza.

PODERE VILLUZZA
Host: Salvatore Leanza Family
Strada 25
San Gimignano, (SI) 53037, Italy
Tel & Fax: (0577) 940585
12 Rooms, Double: €98–€138
2 Apartments: €115 daily, €805 weekly
Dinners: €25
Closed: Jan 15 to Feb 15, Credit cards: MC, VS
B&B, SELF CATERING

The countryside around San Gimignano is becoming like the Alto Adige mountain area where practically every house offers some kind of accommodation, and the competition has created bed and breakfasts with high standards of quality and service. Among these, Il Rosolaccio (the local name for the poppies that cover the hill in springtime) is an 18th-century typical Tuscan farmhouse perched high above the road between Certaldo and San Gimignano. As expected, the view over the vineyards and hillsides is absolutely breathtaking. After a 30-year career running a hotel in Rome, Ingrid Music, with her son Steven, bought and very carefully restored the house which, by tradition, was added on to each time someone in the family got married. All the right ingredients are included for a perfectly delightful stay, with tastefully decorated bedrooms and apartments perfectly in tune with the simple beauty of the preserved farmhouse, warm and discreet hospitality, and marvelous views to be enjoyed either poolside or at sunset with a glass of wine. Common areas include the vaulted dining room and cozy upstairs living room with huge open fireplace and family antiques. *Directions:* From San Gimignano follow signs for Certaldo and after 7 km, turn right at the sign up to Il Rosolaccio. From Certaldo drive in the direction of San Gimignano for 5 km and turn left at Rosolaccio.

IL ROSOLACCIO
Hosts: Ingrid & Steven Music
Localita: Capezzano
San Gimignano, (SI) 53037, Italy
Tel: (0577) 944465, Fax: (0577) 944467
6 Rooms, Double: €97–€120
6 Apartments: €100–€130 daily, €650–€1200 weekly
Dinners: €28
Open: Mar to Oct, Credit cards: all major
B&B, SELF CATERING

La Locanda del Castello is a dreamy place to stay recently opened by Silvana Ravanelli, who took on the ambitious project of restoring part of the village's 13th-century castle (the municipal hall is housed in the other half) and transforming it into charming accommodations and a restaurant. The success she had with her previous, much smaller bed and breakfast in this guide created the desire to offer additional, more upscale rooms. She has a real talent for decorating and each individual room has been thoughtfully appointed with the family's antiques, gorgeous fabrics, and beautiful travertine bathrooms. Most have king-sized beds, double sinks, and generous showers. The golden hue chosen for the rooms' walls harmonize perfectly with the surrounding wheat-covered hillsides dotted with cypresses. The brick-vaulted restaurant, originally the olive press, is accessed through a delightful garden with dining tables right at the historic walls of the castle. The chef adds his own creativity to ancient Tuscan recipes using local percorino cheeses, white truffles, and other fresh local products. San Giovanni is right in the middle of some of Tuscany's most picture-perfect scenery. *Directions:* 35 km south of Siena, exit from autostrada A1 at Bettolle-Sinalunga and follow signs for San Giovanni d'Asso. Stairs from the town's main parking lot lead up to the inn.

❄ ☕ 🏌 CREDIT ☎ @ W Ⓨ P ¶ 🖼 ⚐ 🚶 🐎

LA LOCANDA DEL CASTELLO
Host: Silvana Ravanelli
Piazza Vittorio Emanuele II, 4
San Giovanni d'Asso, (SI) 53020, Italy
Tel: (0577) 802939, Fax: (0577) 802942
9 Rooms, Double: €120–€180
Half-board, per person: €160–€210
Open: all year, Credit cards: AX, MC, VS
B&B

For those seeking a self-catering base for exploring the hilltowns of Tuscany while sojourning in very characteristic accommodation with a rich historical past, the Lucignanello is a sublime choice. Imagine residing in one of the cluster of stone houses that make up the quaint village immersed in the type of picture-perfect, timeless Tuscan landscape seen in Renaissance paintings. The illustrious Piccolomini family still owns the 15th-century property where lovers of Italy can live out a dream. Five two-bedroom houses have been masterfully restored, preserving the original architectural features while ensuring modern facilities. The irregularly shaped interiors are filled with lovely antiques, beautiful tiled bathrooms, and kitchens with travertine counters, and all have large fireplaces. High above the village is a pool set among olive trees with inspiring views. Although breakfast ingredients are supplied, guests are self-sufficient (they find the hamlet's grocery shop and osteria most convenient) but a permanent staff is at their disposal for any suggestions or assistance. A separate five-bedroom farmhouse with private swimming pool is rented out by the week. Country charm exudes from every corner and the ambiance is so authentic you will feel almost Tuscan. *Directions:* From San Quirico go towards Siena, taking the first right to San Giovanni d'Asso. Two km before town, turn right for the 2-km drive to Lucignano d'Asso.

LUCIGNANELLO BANDINI
Host: Angelica Piccolomini Naldi Bandini
Lucignano d'Asso
San Giovanni d'Asso, (SI) 53020, Italy
Tel: (0577) 803068, Fax: (0577) 803082
5, 2-bed Houses: €290 daily, €1900 weekly*
1, 5-bed House: €700 daily, €4600 weekly*
*Breakfast not included
Minimum Stay Required: 2 to 7 nights depending on season
Open: all year, Credit cards: all major
Abitare La Storia
B&B, SELF CATERING

We instantly fell in love with Il Borro and decided that this gorgeous property would be perfect for those who want to nestle into Tuscany for a week or more in a "home away from home." Il Borro is owned by Ferruccio Ferragamo and managed by Leonardo Utari. This isn't your normal hotel at all—it is a huge estate with vineyards, walnut groves, olive trees, woodlands, and pastures. For such a vast property (1755 acres), it is amazing that there are only twenty-four suites, accommodating from two to six persons. Each has a bedroom (or bedrooms), kitchen, and living room. A wide variety of accommodations is offered: fourteen of the suites are in three houses nestled in the countryside, twelve are in individual cottages in the hamlet of Borro, and the last, a romantic, secluded little mill, stands by the river. My favorites are the twelve cottages in Borro, an adorable village with a cluster of enchanting stone buildings facing onto narrow, cobbled, pedestrian-only streets. This hamlet, reached by a beguiling stone bridge, is a real town with its own tiny plaza, artisan shops, boutiques, church, cobbler, goldsmith, restaurant, delicatessen and wine bar. Here, the twelve guest cottages are tucked among the villagers' homes. No matter where you stay, the decor and accommodations are outstanding, and in the off season prices drop dramatically. *Directions:* When you reach the town of San Giustino Valdarno, follow signs to Il Borro.

IL BORRO
Host: Leonardo Utari
San Giustino Valdarno, (AR) 52024, Italy
Tel: (055) 97 70 53, Fax: (055) 97 70 55
24 Rooms, Double: €200–€440
Open: all year, Credit cards: all major
HOTEL

In the countryside on the main road north of Arezzo (16 km) is the Villa Cassia di Baccano, a newly refurbished accommodation within a stately home and 16th century mill next door. The vaulted brick mill is where a buffet breakfast is served and where the reception area is located. Opposite the villa is a lovely borderless swimming pool overlooking a wide open countryside panorama, while the back opens up to face an umbrella pine tree garden. One and two-bedroom apartments within the main building are spread between two floors and are softly appointed with cool white and beige tones in a minimalist style. Wood floors and sleek travertine bathrooms harmonize well with the soothingly simple décor and canopy beds are made up with the finest linens available. All apartments have fully equipped kitchens and the ground floor accommodation includes a patio out in the garden. Rooms looking north have the same open view as that from the pool. Your hostess, Michela, is on hand to suggest itineraries in Arezzo, exploration of the immediate area or over to Chianti just across the tollway. *Directions:* From A1 autostrada, exit at Valdarno and follow for Terranuova and then S. Giustino Valdarno. The Villa Cassia is on this road just before town.

VILLA CASSIA DI BACCANO
Host: Sandro Bartolucci
Via Setteponti Levante, 132
San Giustino Valdarno, (AR) 52024, Italy
Tel: (055) 9772310, Fax: (055) 9772898
10 Apartments: €159–€229 daily, €1130-€1450 weekly*
*Breakfast not included
Open: all year, Credit cards: all major
SELF CATERING

This very special historic residence was once the summer villa of the Grand Duke of Tuscany, attracted to the bucolic countryside between Pisa and Lucca with its natural thermal waters. They are the same therapeutic waters enjoyed by Etruscans, Ancient Romans and nobility of Europe in later years up to today. Meticulous attention has been given to the restoration of this splendid palazzo, preserving high vaulted ceilings covered with frescoes, as presented in the main salon as well as in many of the sumptuous bedrooms and suites. Several rooms are bi-level with the loft bedroom elevated giving a closer look at the pastel-hued frescoes. Fine fabrics, linens, marble bathrooms and the latest amenities available are featured in all. Fine meals are served in the main dining room while aperitifs can be taken out on the terrace lined with potted lemon trees. A steep hillside backs the property with trails which take guests up to the terrace for views to the leaning tower. If this weren't already enough to satisfy the most demanding of guests, the hotel has its own adjoining full-fledged spa, a luxurious haven offering a long list of treatments ranging from traditional to oriental. Summer packages can include treatments and tickets to the Puccini Opera Festival. *Directions:* Exit at Lucca Est from the A11 autostrada then follow the signs for Terme di San Giuliano. After 10 km you enter the town of San Giuliano Terme, here follow the signs to "Terme".

❋ ▬ ⚞ ▦ ☎ 🐎 🛗 🍷 W Y P ⑪ 🚭 ☘ ≋ 🖼 ⚲ ♿ 🕺

BAGNI DI PISA NATURAL SPA RESORT
Host: Paolo Gutta
Largo Shelley, 18
San Guiliano Terme, (PI) , Italy
Tel: (050) 88 501, Fax: (050) 88 50 401
51 Rooms, Double: €310–€390*
8 Suites: €460–€600*
*Includes breakfast & dinner
Open: all year, Credit cards: all major
HOTEL

Staying at the Villa Arceno is truly like staying with friends in a sumptuous Italian villa. Although a luxurious property with stunning decor and impeccable service, the hotel exudes the warmth and charm of a small inn. The manager, Gualtiero Mancini, makes everyone feel at home. The mood of grandeur is set as you approach by a seemingly endless private road that winds through lovingly tended vineyards to a classic, three-story, ochre-colored villa. At one time the summer home of royalty, this 17th-century Palladian villa has been masterfully restored, both outside and within. The public rooms are more like lounges in a private home with a sophisticated, yet comfortable, elegance. The individually decorated guestrooms in the main villa are gorgeous—even the standard rooms are enormous and splendidly decorated. All the rooms are so outstanding it is difficult to choose, but I think my favorites are suites 104 and 204, both with sweeping vistas of vine-covered fields. Reveling in the utter peace and quiet, go sightseeing in nearby Siena, explore the wonders of Tuscany, or enjoy the hotel's bicycles, swimming pool, tennis court, and (best of all) the park. Here you can stroll for hours along romantic lanes shaded by rows of cypress trees or meander on paths through the forest, passing almost-hidden statues, to an idyllic, secluded lake. The hotel is being renovated and is set to open March 2009 with a lovely new spa. *Directions:* Ask hotel for directions.

RELAIS VILLA ARCENO
Host: Gualtiero Mancini
San Gusmè, (SI) 53010, Italy
Tel: (0577) 35 92 92, Fax: (0577) 35 92 76
16 Rooms, Double: €345–€525
Open: Apr to mid-Nov, Credit cards: all major
HOTEL

If you are looking for a place to stay in the heart of Tuscany that is moderately priced, yet does not sacrifice one ounce of charm or quality of accommodation, the family-run Hotel Belvedere di San Leonino is unsurpassable. Ceramic pots of geraniums, trellised grapevines, and climbing roses soften and add color to the weathered stone buildings, which were originally a cluster of 15th-century farmers' cottages. Off the central patio area you find a small reception area, a blandly decorated living room, and an attractive dining room with tiled floors, rustic beamed ceiling, and appropriately simple wooden tables and chairs. When the weather is warm, meals are served outside in the garden. Because the rooms are tucked into various parts of the old farmhouses, they vary in size and shape. They also differ in decor, but all have an antique ambiance with wrought-iron headboards, beautiful old armoires, and pretty, white curtains. What adds the icing to the cake is the setting of the Belvedere, nestled in the very heart of the Chianti wine region, surrounded by stunning scenery—in every direction you look there are idyllic, sweeping vistas of rolling hills dotted with vineyards, olive groves, and pine forests. Hotel Belvedere is conveniently located only a short drive from the freeway.

HOTEL BELVEDERE DI SAN LEONINO
Host: Signora C. Orlandi
San Leonino, (SI) 53011, Italy
Tel: (0577) 74 08 87, Fax: (0577) 74 09 24
29 Rooms, Double: €100–€156*
*Breakfast not included: €7
Open: mid-Mar to mid-Nov, Credit cards: all major
HOTEL

Easily accessed off one of the ancient roads leading from Rome to Florence (Via Cassia), Il Rigo farmhouse sits in its own 600-acre estate. It is ideally located as a base from which to explore the scenic landscapes south of Siena with their sparsely vegetated rolling hills. The large, rectangular stone and brick house dates back 500 years. Its inner courtyard sits on a hill overlooking fascinating vistas stretching to the distant horizons. Within are nine country-style bedrooms on both ground and upper floors, divided by several cozy sitting rooms. Country furnishings such as armoires and wrought-iron beds are very much in harmony with the simple, authentic farmhouse. Breakfast or a light lunch or dinner are served in a spacious dining room on the first floor. Ingredients from the farm include organic grains and beans and, of course, extra virgin olive oil and wine. Hostess Lorenza is an excellent cook and has conducted lessons both here and in the States. The Cipolla's live most of the year in the family palazzo (which has been owned by the family since 1684), Casa dell'Abate Naldi, in the charming village of San Quirico, where four lovely bedrooms with antiques are also available for guests. *Directions:* From San Quirico take the S.S. 2 south for 2 km and turn left at sign for Il Rigo. Continue on dirt road for 3 km up to cypress-lined driveway to the main house.

IL RIGO
Hosts: Vittorio & Lorenza Cipolla
Località: Casabianca
San Quirico d'Orcia, (SI) 53100, Italy
Tel: (0577) 897291, Fax: (0577) 898236
9 Rooms, Double: €105–€115
Open: all year, Credit cards: all major
B&B

The Residence San Sano is a very special small hotel in San Sano—a picturesque hamlet in the center of the Chianti wine-growing region. We were charmed by the hotel, which is incorporated into a cluster of 16th-century stone houses. A cozy dining room serves guests excellent meals featuring typically Tuscan-style cooking. Each of the bedrooms is delightfully furnished in antiques and each has a name incorporating some unique feature of the hotel, the name evolving from the time during reconstruction when each room was remembered by its special feature. One is called the Bird Room: here birds had claimed the room for many years and had nested in holes that went completely through the wall. With great imagination, the holes were left open to the outside, but on the inside were covered with glass. Another room is named for a beautiful, long-hidden Romanesque window that was discovered and incorporated into the decor and another for an antique urn uncovered during renovation. The hotel has upgraded the property with a beautiful swimming pool and several spacious new light and bright rooms with private terraces overlooking the garden and vineyards. This is a wonderful country house dipped in history.

HOTEL RESIDENCE SAN SANO
Host: Maurizio Amabili
San Sano, (SI) 53010, Italy
Tel: (0577) 74 61 30, Fax: (0577) 74 68 91
15 Rooms, Double: €130–€200
Meals for hotel guests only (not Sun)
Open: mid-Mar to Feb, Credit cards: AX, MC, VS
HOTEL

Poggio ai Santi has a magnificent view over a green valley down to the distant sea. Francesca has put her heart and soul into the place over the past 20 years with the emphasis being on the comfort and ease of her guests. In order to fulfill the needs of both families and couples she has divided the property into two separate accommodations, conveniently separated by a road. On the left is the Muccheria, two converted farms houses, bi-level family apartments with kitchen facilities, its own swimming pool and play area. On the right is the Poggio ai Santi with the family's stately main house, plus a one-story guest house with five junior-suite-sized rooms, all with independent entrances from the garden. A second guest house with additional suites is further down the hill. An immediate sense of calm and well-being is invoked by the views, the peaceful ambiance, the immaculate rooms appointed in soft earth tones with their spacious bathrooms with natural stone tiles and rain showers. The pool area is landscaped primarily with aromatic herbs and lavender. Breakfast is served out on the veranda; lunch and dinner can be enjoyed in the wonderful Il Sale restaurant. *Directions:* Exit from the Aurelia freeway S.S.1 at San Vicenzo Sud and drive north to San Vicenzo on the S.S.1 Aurelia for 1 km. Take a right turn for San Carlo and continue for 3 km. Poggio ai Santi is just before San Carlo.

POGGIO AI SANTI
Host: Francesca Vierucci
Via San Bartolo, 100
San Vincenzo, (LI) 57027, Italy
Tel: (0565) 798032, Fax: (0565) 798090
11 Suites: €140–€430
11 Apartments: €400–€1540 weekly
Minimum Stay Required: 3 nights high season, 7 in Apts
Open: all year, Credit cards: MC, VS
B&B, SELF CATERING

As more travelers realize how close together destinations of interest throughout Italy are, weekly house rentals to use as a home base for excursions have become more popular. One such ideal base is La Sovana, bordering Tuscany and Umbria and equidistant to Siena, Perugia, Assisi, Arezzo, and many other smaller hilltowns such as Montepulciano, Pienza, and Montalcino—the area where Italy's finest wines are produced. Two stone farmhouses were carefully restored to provide comfortable suites for two to six people. Tastefully decorated with local antique beds and armoires, matching floral bedspreads and curtains, each has a fully equipped kitchenette and eating and living area. Guests can dine by candlelight in the dining room in the main house, whose enormous arched window takes in the expansive view of vineyards, wheat fields, and impeccable landscaping. Giovannella and Giuseppe Olivi, dedicated and amiable hosts, and their two grown children, Riccardo and Francesca, dine with their guests each evening. Potted flowers abound around the pool and Jacuzzi where on Saturday nights a sumptuous barbecue is organized to enable guests to meet one another. Two tennis courts, a small fishing lake, and bikes are available. There are more bi-level suites in a large converted barn in the woods a short walk away from the main farmhouse. *Directions:* Just 2 km from the Chiusi exit of the A1 autostrada. La Sovana is just before Sarteano on the right.

LA SOVANA
Host: Giuseppe Olivi Family
Localita: Sovana
Sarteano, (SI) 53047, Italy
Tel: (0578) 274086, Fax: (0578) 275005
9 Rooms, Double: €116–€208
5 Suites: €174–€297
Minimum Stay Required: 3 nights, 7 nights Jul & Aug
Dinners: €39
Open: Mar 13 to Nov 2, Credit cards: all major
B&B

Tenuta La Bandita is set amid 150 acres of woods, olive groves, orchards and meadows within a beautifully undisturbed area south of Livorno near the sea and just a few kilometers from the historic and picturesque villages of Castagneto Carducci and Bolgheri. Dino and Daniela, with their former business and hotel experience, have brought the estate back to its original splendor. The 18th-century main villa is where most of the guest bedrooms are situated. Their idea was to transform the villa into a bed and breakfast while leaving as much as possible of the original structure and atmosphere of the private residence intact. Ten furnished bedrooms with bathrooms, situated down one long corridor upstairs, are appointed with original period furniture, chandeliers, and matching golden brocade drapes and bedspreads. Guests can lounge on the front terrace with wide countryside views or in the gracious arched living and dining room downstairs with gray-stone fireplace and framed portraits. Fifteen additional rooms are divided within two adjacent houses, Gli Uliui and La Foresteria, between the villa and swimming pool. *Directions:* Exit from S.S.1 at Donoratico and head for Sassetta/Castagneto for 11 km on a winding mountain road. Take the turnoff left for Larderello/Monteverdi (not Sassetta) for 1 km to the La Bandita property. Pass through the gate and go past the first group of private homes to the villa at the end of the road.

☕ 🍴 ☕ 💳 ☎ 🐕 @ W Ⓨ P ‖ ≈ 🏃 🖼 🐾 ⚓ 🎿 🐴 ⛴ 🍷

TENUTA LA BANDITA
Hosts: Daniela & Dino Filippi
Via Campagna Nord 30
Sassetta, (LI) 57020, Italy
Tel: (0565) 794224, Fax: (0565) 794350
22 Rooms, Double: €100–€170
3 Suites: €170–€220
Open: Apr 4 to Nov 2, Credit cards: all major
B&B

Saturnia's thermal waters have been gushing from an underground volcano for over 2,000 years, yet only recently have it and the enchanting surrounding Maremma area become internationally famous, leading to new accommodations springing up. One such is the charming Villa Clodia, once home to nobility, now run by former restaurateur Giancarlo Ghezzi. The villa is a curiosity, seemingly built out of the limestone rock, one side overlooking the street and the other an expansive valley of grapevines and olive trees. Because of its unusual proportions, each room is unique in size and decor. A small winding stairway takes guests up or down to rooms, some of which have been literally carved out of the rock. All bedrooms feature scattered antiques, new bathrooms, and valley views, and a fortunate few boast a terrace. Amenities include air conditioning, TVs, and mini-bars. Breakfast is offered in a sweet, luminous room next to the sitting room. A lush rose garden and fruit orchard surround the inviting star-shaped pool. Advance reservations are a must and weekly stays preferred. *Directions:* From Rome take the Aurelia highway north, turning off to the right at Vulci following signs for Manciano, Montemerano, and Saturnia. Villa Clodia is in the middle of town.

VILLA CLODIA
Host: Giancarlo Ghezzi
Via Italia 43
Saturnia, (GR) 58050, Italy
Tel: (0564) 601212, Fax: (0564) 601305
12 Rooms, Double: €100–€110
1 Suite: €130
Minimum Stay Required: 4 nights
Closed: Jan 9 to Feb 1, Credit cards: VS
B&B

The Maremma, an intensely scenic area in the coastal foothills of southern Tuscany, offers a wealth of sightseeing possibilities: walled villages, Etruscan ruins, archaeological sites, and marvelously unspoiled landscapes. The congenial Pellegrini family converted a 200-year-old stone farmhouse into a hotel and over the years, into a veritable country resort. The "Castagneta" restaurant is the heart of the inn and has tables set in a beamed-ceilinged room filled with sunlight from large French doors opening onto a panoramic terrace where meals are served on warm days. A real bonus are the delectable typically local meals coupled with fine regional wines. Learn the kitchen's secrets firsthand by participating in the cooking classes. The singles and some double bedrooms are found in the main house in addition to the spacious guestrooms in two nearby annexes, comfortably appointed with wrought iron beds, artisan-made furnishings and many amenities. Self-catering villas are also available for rent on the property. There is also a full spa offering a variety of oriental philosophy based treatments, indoor heated salt-water pool, sauna, and outdoor pool. Down the hill from the hotel you find the equestrian center where horses are groomed each day for guests, ready for countryside excursions. Plenty to keep one happy here. *Directions:* From Scansano, take S.S. 322 towards Manciano. The hotel is on the right after 3 km.

❋ ☕ ⚒ ♨ 💳 ☎ 🐕 @ W Ⓨ P 🍴 ✿ ≋ 🖼 ⛷ ♿ ⚓ 🧍 🚶 🏇 🏌

ANTICO CASALE DI SCANSANO
Hosts: Massimo Pellegrini & Family
Loc. Castagneta
Scansano, (GR) 58054, Italy
Tel: (0564) 50 72 19, Fax: (0564) 50 78 05
28 Rooms, Double: €130–€190
4 Suites: €195–€260
14 Apartments: €550–€1250
Minimum Stay Required: 7 nights in Aug
Open: all year, Credit cards: all major
HOTEL

The Grand Hotel Continental Siena, an elegant small hotel that opened in early 2002, is one of the most exciting properties to come on the scene in Siena in many years. Although there are lovely places to stay on the periphery, there has never been an outstanding hotel in the heart of Siena, within steps of all of its fabulous sights. To say that this need for an exceptional property has now been fulfilled is an understatement: the Grand Hotel Continental Siena is an absolute dream and would be a sensation anywhere in the world. Located just off the Piazza del Campo, the building dates back to 1600 when it was designed as a magnificent palace for the noble Chigi family. After years of labor by countless artisans, the palace has been returned to its original splendor. The grandeur and opulence of the rooms are breathtaking. Fine fabrics, exquisite furnishings, and priceless antiques create a setting of unsurpassed grandeur. At the heart of the palace a central courtyard, protected by a glass roof, allows the sunlight to fill the hotel with sunshine. Off the courtyard the various parlors and ballrooms are gorgeous. A sweeping, wide staircase leads upstairs to the sumptuous bedrooms and suites, some of which feature magnificent, museum-quality, frescoed ceilings.

GRAND HOTEL CONTINENTAL SIENA
Host: Giuseppe Artolli
Banchi di Sopra, 85
Siena, (SI) 53100, Italy
Tel: (0577) 56 011, Fax: (0577) 56 01 555
51 Rooms, Double: €440–€590*
5 Suites: €900–€1600*
*Breakfast not included: €28
*Tax: 10%
Open: all year, Credit cards: all major
HOTEL

Siena is a fascinating walled, hilltop city filled with a wealth of fabulous museums, intriguing squares, and breathtaking churches. If you want to stay within walking distance of the all the major sights and your budget precludes a splurge at the deluxe Grand Hotel Continental, the Palazzo Ravizza pensione makes an excellent choice. The brick exterior of the hotel looks quite plain but inside, the beauty of this once-grand 17th-century palace is immediately revealed. Belonging to the same family for 200 years, the mansion exudes the warmth of a home, with an intimate parlor, card room, music lounge, cozy bar, handsome ceiling frescos, old family portraits, and fresh flowers on polished antique tables. The Palazzo Ravizza is a simple hotel and some of the fabrics show a well-worn look, but overall it is well kept and appealing and for the price, it is an excellent choice. The individually decorated bedrooms vary in size, but all are furnished with antiques, down comforters, and have flat screen TVs. The choice rooms are those that overlook the back garden—I especially liked rooms 14 and 11. The most outstanding feature of the Ravizza is its splendid large garden. This is the heart of the hotel where guests can enjoy a cold drink at one of the tables on the terrace or relax on one of the benches strategically placed for capturing a sweeping view of the Tuscany hillside. *Directions:* Near the Porta San Marco gate. Ask hotel for exact directions.

❄ 🍵 🚴 💳 ☎ @ W ⅄ P 🍴 🖼 🔔 👫 🏇 🍇

PALAZZO RAVIZZA
Host: Francesco Grottanelli
Pian dei Mantellini, 34
Siena, (SI) 53100, Italy
Tel: (0577) 28 04 62, Fax: (0577) 22 15 97
30 Rooms, Double: €150–€270
Open: all year, Credit cards: all major
HOTEL

The Locanda dell'Amorosa, a charming small hotel with great warmth and excellent management, makes a super base for exploring Tuscany and Umbria. From the Locanda dell'Amorosa it is an easy drive to such sightseeing delights as Siena, Pienza, Orvieto, Todi, and Assisi. The Locanda dell'Amorosa is actually a tiny town located a few kilometers south of Sinalunga. You approach along a cypress-lined road that cuts through fields of grapes. Park your car and enter through the gates into the walled 14th-century medieval village where you are greeted by an enormous courtyard with its own little church—exquisite inside with its soft pastels and its lovely fresco of the Madonna. A rustic wine bar next to the church features a selection of the estate's wines and can provide guests a light meal when the restaurant is closed. On the right side of the courtyard are the stables, which have been converted to a stunning restaurant whose massive beams and natural stone-and-brick walls are tastefully enhanced by arched windows, thick wrought-iron fixtures, and wooden tables. The guestrooms, located in a separate building, are tastefully appointed with a few antiques and matching bedspreads and draperies. The rest of this tiny village spreads out behind the main square and the buildings are used for the production of wine. *Directions:* Exit the A1 at Sinalunga. Just before town turn left toward Torrita. After 2 km, the hotel is on your right.

❄ 🍺 ✗ ♨ 💳 ☎ @ W ⧖ P ⫼ ≈ 🖼 ⟳ 🐴 🍇

LOCANDA DELL'AMOROSA
Host: Carlo Citterio
Sinalunga, (SI) 53048, Italy
Tel: (0577) 67 72 11, Fax: (0577) 63 20 01
19 Rooms, Double: €255–€375
8 Suites: €412–€660
Restaurant closed Mon, Tue lunch
Closed: Jan 10 to Mar 11, Credit cards: all major
History Traveller
HOTEL

In yet another lesser-known pocket of Tuscany halfway between Siena and the sea is the absolutely stunning 1,000-acre property of the Visconti family. Dating back to the 1400s, in its heyday it was a village in itself, complete with the noble family's main villa, farmers' houses, church, nuns' quarters, oil press, and blacksmith and carpenter's shops. These stone buildings are all attached to the villa in a U-shape formation with a beautiful formal garden within. Terracotta pots with lemon trees and red geraniums give spots of color among the greenery. Vitaliano and Vittoria, whose home has been in the same family since its origins, welcome guests in the restored part of the villa where eight bedrooms with private bathrooms have been created including three large triples. All with beamed ceilings and brick floors, they are simply appointed with beds and armoires, looking out either to the garden or woods at the back. Common areas are the living room with enormous fireplace, the dining room where delectable Tuscan country meals are served (€20), and an upstairs loggia with a panoramic view over the countryside, which seems to take in all of Tuscany. Apartments are available for weekly stays. For those who enjoy spectacular scenery in a very special, historical setting, this is the place. *Directions:* From the Florence-Siena highway exit at Colle Val d'Elsa Sud. Follow signs for Grosseto-Radicondoli-Castelnuova Val di Cecina, then Fattoria Solaio.

FATTORIA SOLAIO
Hosts: Vittoria & Vitaliano Visconti
Solaio–Radicondoli, (SI) 53030, Italy
Tel: (0577) 791029, Fax: (0577) 791015
2 Rooms, Double: €80–€90
3 Suites: €105–€115
4 Apartments: €680–€800 weekly
Minimum Stay Required: 3 nights
Open: Mar to Nov, Credit cards: all major
B&B, SELF CATERING

If the idea of staying in an extraordinary medieval fortress that crowns a spectacular hilltown far off the beaten path appeals, you will fall in love with the Hotel della Fortezza—it is an absolute jewel. This tiny hotel is in a splendid part of Tuscany called Maremma, little known to the casual tourist, but well worth exploration. There are many walled villages in the hills that lie between Orvieto and the coast, all beckoning you to drive within their walls, but one of the most beautiful of all is Sorano. The town is nestled into a pocket of the hill, a jumble of ancient stone and stucco buildings that form a striking architectural design, and crowning the top of the town is the imposing Orsini Fortress. You enter through an impressive gate, cross a stone bridge over what was once a moat, then pass through a tower gate and into the fortress where you find the hotel. This is not a deluxe hotel nor does it pretend to be, but the interior is extremely appealing, with the guestrooms decorated with great taste, appropriate to the charm of the building. Almost all of the bedrooms have a breathtaking view of the town and beyond to the densely wooded hills. Number 16 is an especially attractive corner room, larger than most, with handsome antique headboards and windows on two sides. However, even the smaller rooms have sensational views. This area is well known for its many walking trails. *Directions:* In Sorano, look for signs to the Fortezza Orsini.

HOTEL DELLA FORTEZZA
Host: Luciano Caruso
Piazza Cairoli, 5
Sorano, (GR) 58010, Italy
Tel: (0564) 63 20 10, Fax: (0564) 63 32 09
15 Rooms, Double: €120–€200
Closed: Jan & Feb, Credit cards: all major
HOTEL

La Taverna Etrusca is in an intriguing, picturesque, little-known part of Tuscany called Maremma, where you find ancient towns with very old stone houses, wrapped by dense green woodlands, tucked into the landscape. Throughout this region, hiking, biking, and horseback riding are popular ways to discover the countryside. Etruscan ruins are found everywhere, making this an especially interesting area to explore. This property's emphasis is not as a hotel, but rather as a restaurant. It's housed in a rustic stone building situated in the center of a tiny village that seems to be suspended in time. The restaurant, which specializes in traditional Tuscan and Maremman dishes, faces onto a tiny piazza where a stone church, topped by a whimsical bell tower, sits at one end. Within, the restaurant abounds with medieval allure. High ceilings are enhanced by wood beams and huge stone archways divide the room into romantic dining areas. When the weather is mild, meals are also served outside on the terrace. Many dining guests never realize that there are also a few hotel rooms upstairs. These are small and simply decorated, but are very nice for the price. *Directions:* Located in the center of the village, facing the piazza.

LA TAVERNA ETRUSCA
Host: Luciano Caruso
Piazza del Pretorio 16
Sovana, (GR) 58010, Italy
Tel: (0564) 61 61 83, Fax: (0564) 61 41 93
7 Rooms, Double: €90–€130
Restaurant closed Wed
Closed: Jan & Feb, Credit cards: all major
HOTEL

It was love at first sight as I drove up the long graveled road through forest and vineyard and suddenly caught my first glimpse of the Borgo Pretale, a tiny cluster of weathered stone buildings nestled next to their medieval watchtower. My first impression was more than justified—this small inn is truly paradise. There are absolute serenity and beauty here with nothing to mar the perfection. Civilization seems far away as the eye stretches over a glorious vista of rolling hills forested with oaks, juniper, and laurel, interspersed with square patches of vineyards. But although this small village is seemingly remote, it is only a short drive south of Siena, thus a perfect hideaway from which to enjoy the magic of Tuscany. The rooms in the tower are showplaces of fine country antiques and splendid designer fabrics, blended together with the artful eye of a skilled decorator. Every piece is selected to create a sophisticated yet rustic elegance. The rooms in the surrounding cottages are furnished in a more "country" style, though maintaining standards of elegance and comfort. The lounge beckons guests to linger after dinner by the roaring fire. A path leads to a groomed tennis court and farther on to a swimming pool on a hillside terrace. NOTE: The closest town on most maps is Rosia, which is about 8 kilometers southeast of Borgo Pretale. To reach the hotel, go through Rosia and follow signs to Borgo Pretale.

BORGO PRETALE
Host: Daniele Rizzardini
Localita: Pretale - Tonni
Sovicille, (SI) 53018, Italy
Tel: (0577) 34 54 01, Fax: (0577) 34 56 25
27 Rooms, Double: €120–€170
7 Suites: €150–€210
Open: Apr to Oct, Credit cards: all major
HOTEL

Halfway between Florence and Siena in the heart of the Chianti region is the Sovigliano farm, restored by a gracious couple from Verona, Claudio Bicego and his wife, Patrizia, and daughter, Claudia. Guests have an independent entrance to the four bedrooms with kitchenette, each very much in keeping with the pure simplicity of this typical farmhouse. Exposed-beam ceilings and worn terracotta floors, antique beds and armoires, and bucolic views make time stand still here. Besides three apartments (two with air conditioning) in a separate farmhouse, there is also a spacious two-bedroom apartment within the house with kitchen and dining area and fireplace. At guests' disposal are a living room, kitchen with country fireplace, TV, large surrounding garden with swimming pool and hydro-jet, exercise trail, and outdoor eating area overlooking the characteristic hills of Chianti. Signor Bicego is actively involved in the production of top Tuscan wines in conjunction with several other wine estates, and also coordinates with other area residents to organize lessons in language, history, and culinary arts with local professors. *Directions:* From Siena, exit the superstrada at San Donato in Poggio; from Florence at Tavarnelle Val di Pesa. Drive through the village of Tavarnelle following the directions to Certaldo-Marcialla. At the end of Tavarnelle, at the fourth traffic circle, veer to the left (blue sign says Magliano), following signs for Sovigliano.

❄ 🚲 ☕ CREDIT @ 🍸 P 🍴 🚭 🏊 🖼 🏃 🏇 🎿 🍷

SOVIGLIANO
Hosts: Patrizia & Claudio Bicego
Via Magliano 9
Tavarnelle Val di Pesa, (FI) 50028, Italy
Tel & Fax: (055) 8076217
4 Rooms, Double: €130–€190
4 Apartments: €870–€1520 weekly
Minimum Stay Required: 3 nights
Dinners: €35
Closed: Jan 15 to 31, Credit cards: MC, VS
B&B, SELF CATERING

Country tourism has flourished in the last decade, especially in the highly popular region of Tuscany. However, most travelers still flock to the Chianti area, leaving many other parts of Tuscany wide open to discovery. Such is the gorgeous virgin territory of the Valdera Valley between stunning Volterra with its Etruscan origins and Pisa where everything has remained remarkably unspoiled. Affable host Sandro and his family bought a 100-acre farm property here and are restoring the ancient farmhouses piece by piece with guests' comfort foremost in mind. So far, eight neat apartments with one or two bedrooms and five guest bedrooms have been completed within three adjacent stone houses and are tastefully appointed with local antiques. Within one of the houses is the pleasant dining room with large arched windows where breakfast and dinners upon request are served, all prepared by Sandro's mother, who also conducts cooking lessons. Olive oil, wine, fruits, and vegetables all come directly from the farm. There is a beautiful borderless swimming pool and Sandro supplies guests with mountain bikes and a long list of interesting local itineraries. Easy day trips include Florence, Siena, San Gimignano, Lucca, Pisa and Volterra, famous for its alabaster artisans. *Directions:* Il Selvino is located off the main road 439 from Volterra (20 km) between Terricciola and La Sterza at Pieve a Pitti (marked on most maps).

IL SELVINO
Host: Alessandro Sgherri Family
Localita: La Sterza, Via Pieve a Pitti 1
Terricciola, (PI) 56030, Italy
Tel: (0587) 670132, Fax: (0587) 670817
7 Rooms, Double: €100–€115
8 Apartments: €150–€200 daily
Open: all year, Credit cards: MC, VS
B&B, SELF CATERING

Returning to his native Italy after running a resort in Mexico, Matteo continues using his expertise in anticipating guest's needs in this latest endeavor at the Lupaia. Finishing touches have been made after a thorough restoration project of the family's vast Tuscan property overlooking the ancient hilltown of Montepulciano. With two stone farmhouses with beamed ceilings and brick floors as a base, and Matteo's mother's flair for details in decorating, each guest room has been given its own distinct character. Bold colors range from celestial blues, chartreuse greens, solar yellows and rusty reds mixed with hot oranges and are found in every single object or piece of furniture cleverly restored by hand. All seven rooms, most with fireplaces, are accessed independently from the outside, each with a terrace or garden. Features such as extra space, extraordinary views, loft beds, kitchen corners and spacious showers are divided among the rooms. Breakfast is served in the garden or in the large dining room with a fireplace. A lovely bi-level pool for simply lounging and taking in the breathtaking scenery has been specially designed to hug the hillside. Cooking classes and wine and cheese tastings are arranged, as well as sumptuous Tuscan fare. With all these marvelous ingredients, you simply cannot go wrong. *Directions:* Exit A1 autostrada at Val di Chiana; pass Torrita; pass the turn for Montefollonico. After 2 km turn left; travel 3.5 km to the house.

HOTELITO LUPAIA
Host: Matteo Murzilli
Località: Lupaia 74
Torrita di Siena, (SI) 53049, Italy
Tel: (0577) 668028, Fax: (0577) 668900
5 Rooms, Double: €240–€290
2 Suites: €360–€390
Open: all year, Credit cards: AX, MC, VS
B&B

The Aiola opened its doors to guests several years ago when the Campellis restored the farmers' houses on the wine estate's vast property in Chianti. The family's villa with its ancient origins sits across the street from the guest quarters, almost completely hidden by enormous oak and cypress trees, where the bedrooms, one of which sleeps four persons, all have separate outside entrances. Original architectural features have been preserved and rooms are decorated with wrought-iron beds and antique or reproduction armoires. The vineyards come right up to the house and a wide, open view of the hills is offered to the other side. The barn next door includes common areas such as the breakfast room, where Federica's fresh-baked coffee cakes are served, and a living room. Part of the founding members of the Wine Tourism Association, visits to the cellar and the villa, and wine tasting begin right here at the Aiola. Federica and Enrico aim to make each guest feel special, dedicating much time to suggesting itineraries with maps and making reservations at restaurants, museums, and local concerts. At 12 kilometers from Siena and an easy distance from the highlights of the region, the Aiola serves as an excellent touring base. Total silence reigns here, with only the buzz of cicadas breaking it. *Directions:* From Siena follow route 222, then 102 just past Vagliagli—the Aiola property (well marked) is on this same road.

CASALI DELLA AIOLA
Hosts: Federica & Enrico Campelli
Vagliagli, (SI) 53019, Italy
Tel: (0577) 322797, Fax: (0577) 322509
7 Rooms, Double: €95
1 Suite: €120–€140
Open: Mar to Nov, Credit cards: AX, MC, VS
B&B

With great finesse and determination, Lucia and Paolo, an editor and art collector, managed to purchase Villa Campestri, a magnificent Renaissance villa—no easy feat, considering the 400-acre property had been in one family for 700 years. The cream-colored villa with handsome lawns and surrounding cypress woods commands a spectacular view over the immense valley and Mugello mountain range in an area north of Florence known for its concentration of Medici villas. The guestrooms in the villa have been restored to their original splendor, with high Florentine woodworked ceilings, carefully selected antiques, and delightful blue-and-white-tiled bathrooms. The honeymoon suite features a grand, gold-crowned, red canopy bed. Equally characteristic rooms are located in the side wing and small independent house. A sitting room adorned with rich paintings leads to the elegant, stencil-painted dining rooms where original combinations of fresh local produce are served with great attention to detail, accompanied by an excellent selection of wines. They have created Italy's first "Oleoteca" devoted to the culture of olive oil, offering courses in its history, science, and cuisine. Villa Campestri offers refined, romantic accommodations with professionalism and hospitality given by daughter, Viola. *Directions:* Exit A1 at Barberino di Mugello and follow signs for Borgo San Lorenzo, then to Vicchio, then Campestri.

VILLA CAMPESTRI
Hosts: Lucia & Paolo Pasquali
Manager: Gabriele Vaccaro
Localita: Campestri 19/22
Vicchio di Mugello, (FI) 50039, Italy
Tel: (055) 84 90 107, Fax: (055) 84 90 108
21 Rooms, Double: €150–€270
2 Suites: €280–€400
Open: Mar to Nov, Credit cards: all major
Abitare La Storia
HOTEL

For years Andrea and Silvia have literally opened their entire home to guests, welcoming and re-welcoming guests to their bed and breakfast. International guests gather together in the evenings out on the patio or in the converted barn for one of Silvia's delightful meals based on fresh vegetables and meats enhanced with their own extra-virgin olive oil. Conversation is never lacking with meals accompanied by La Volpaia's own Chianti (all beverages are included in the half-board rate). Andrea, a native Roman architect and sculptor, bought the wine estate with its 16th-century farmhouse 19 years ago and his pieces in olive wood are displayed in and about the property. The five cozy bedrooms are appointed with antiques, as is the large living room with fireplace. Beyond the patio where meals are served is the spectacular swimming pool with its heavenly views of what can only be described as a truly classic Tuscan landscape. Guests are made to feel immediately right at home in this informal setting and so it is no wonder that many become "regulars" to this idyllic spot so close to the highlights of Tuscany. *Directions:* From the town of Vico d'Elsa follow Via della Villa (on the right) for 2 km, turning left at the wooden signpost for La Volpaia.

LA VOLPAIA
Hosts: Silvia & Andrea Taliaco
Strada di Vico 5-9
Vico d'Elsa, (FI) 50050, Italy
Tel: (055) 8073063
5 Rooms, Double: €150–€190*
Minimum Stay Required: 2 nights
*Includes breakfast, dinner & drinks
Open: all year, Credit cards: none
B&B

Volterra, a walled medieval hilltown, is not as well known as its ever-popular neighbor, San Gimignano, but it too exudes great authentic medieval character. Although not quite as colorful, it benefits from fewer tourists and offers a wealth of museums and many boutiques selling items made of alabaster, for which the town is renowned. Conveniently located within the walled city, very near the gate called Porta Florentina, the Hotel La Locanda is intimate and very attractive. The exterior is a pretty pinkish-beige color with arched doorway, flower boxes at the windows, green shutters, and a wrought-iron light sconce. You enter into a small foyer with gorgeous parquet floors and fresh flowers accenting the antique reception desk. Just beyond are a small lounge and then the cheerful room for breakfast, the only meal served (the restaurant for the hotel, under the same ownership, is the Etruria, just a short walk up the street). Throughout the hotel you find original art, with the work of local artists on display in all of the rooms. An elevator leads up to three floors of guestrooms, all as fresh and pretty as can be. Each level has its own color scheme—green, red, or blue—established by the carpeting and the richly hued, handsome coordinating fabrics used for draperies and bedspreads. The marble bathrooms are excellent and the suites even have Jacuzzi tubs. *Directions:* Inside the city walls, on the street leading to, and close to, Porta Florentina.

HOTEL LA LOCANDA
Host: Assenza Andrea
Via Guarnacci, 24
Volterra, (PI) 56048, Italy
Tel: (0588) 81 547, Fax: (0588) 81 541
19 Rooms, Double: €93–€250
Open: all year, Credit cards: all major
HOTEL

Places to Stay in Umbria

Having made the decision to return to her native Italy after years in Venezuela, Liria elected to do it in style. She bought a 200-acre estate in the virgin hills north of Orvieto and set about restoring the four abandoned stone houses which once made up a farmer's village. Her natural flare for integrating soft muted color tones, gorgeous French fabrics and selected antiques has resulted in a refined and romantic country ambiance throughout. The five spacious bedrooms with canopy beds in the main house are tastefully appointed and harmonize well with handmade terracotta brick floors and original stone walls so typical of an Umbrian home. Two 2-bedroom apartments are found in an adjacent house complete with kitchenette and living room for longer stays. Alternatively you could rent an entire two-story house with three bedrooms. Sweeping valley views over soft green hills are enjoyed from any position whether it be out in the lavender garden surrounding the curved swimming pool or on the main terrace where most meals are served. The farm produces organic olive oil, wine, grain, honey and fruits. *Directions:* From the A1 autostrada exit at Fabro and turn right for Allerona. Pass through the town center of Fabro and continue for 5 km and fork left for Allerona Scalo. After 3.2 km turn right and stay to the right for the next two forks until you come to Monticchio.

I CASALI DI MONTICCHIO
Host: Liria Costantino Family
Vocabolo Monticchio 34
Allerona, (TR) 05011, Italy
Tel & Fax: (0763) 628365
11 Rooms, Double: €300–€380
3 Suites: €380–€520
2 Apartments: €500–€1000 daily
Open: all year, Credit cards: AX, MC, VS
B&B, SELF CATERING

The beautifully renovated Relais Tenuta del Gallo (which opened its doors to guests in 2008) has an excellent location: convenient to the romantic hill towns of Umbria and Tuscany, and also nearby the Sabine Hills which lie just to the south. This 17th-century country farmhouse sits on a gentle rise of a hill surrounded by a magnificent 20-hectare private estate. The setting is supreme with absolutely nothing to mar the natural beauty of the landscape. In every direction all you see are vast olive groves, fruit orchards, fields of wheat, gently rolling hills, and distant wooded mountains. The handsome, creamy-beige stone exterior of this farmhouse gives little hint of the luxurious elegance you will find within including 15th-century furniture, sumptuous fabrics, fine paintings, soft lighting, oriental carpets, and hand-painted ceilings. Much of the food served in the attractive restaurant is freshly prepared from produce grown on the property. To accompany your meal, you have the choice an extensive selection of fine wines (ask to see the incredible wine cellar). The guestrooms are all tastefully decorated and offer views of the countryside. The hotel opens to a garden that is highlighted by a pretty swimming pool with sweeping valley vistas. *Directions:* Exit the A1 at Orte. Take the E45 toward Terni. Exit at Amelia. Go past Amelia in the direction of Orvieto for about 2 km and turn right at the Roman Bridge toward Macchie. Go straight about 6 km and turn right.

※ ♨ ✍ ☕ 💳 ☎ 🐕 @ W Ⴤ P ⊺ 🚭 ≈ 🖼 👫 🏇 🍇 ⚘

RELAIS LA TENUTA DEL GALLO   New
Host: Francesco Catalano Family
Strada Ortacci # 34
Macchie fraz. di Amelia
Amelia–Macchie, (TR) 05022, Italy
Tel: (0744) 98 71 11, Fax: (0744) 98 79 28
7 Rooms, Double: €145–€195
2 Suites: €215–€305
Open: all year, Credit cards: MC, VS
HOTEL

A reader highly recommended La Fortezza, saying that it was a wonderful bargain and that he enjoyed the best meal of his entire trip there. We too were immediately captivated by this simple, charming place to stay in the center of Assisi. The restaurant seems to be the star attraction, with Guglielmo Chiocchetti in the kitchen cooking while his wife, Tina, takes care of the many dinner guests. Their two wonderful sons, Luca and Lorenzo, are also totally involved in this family operation, helping out wherever needed, assisted by Luca's pretty wife who was serving the day we stopped by. Without a doubt, it is the gentle, caring Chiocchetti family with their exceptional warmth that makes La Fortezza so special. Their restaurant's superior food features many Umbrian dishes, served in a cozy dining room with vaulted stone ceiling and wooden chairs painted a cheerful red. The guestrooms, which are an outstanding value, are located on two floors above the restaurant. Although not large, each is spotlessly clean and very tastefully decorated in a simple, country style. The choice bedroom even has its own little terrace. The hotel is hidden up a lane of stone steps at the northeast corner of the Piazza del Comune. There are lots of steps getting to the hotel, but then this is true throughout Assisi, which seems pasted to the side of the hillside. Just remember, bring a small suitcase. Closest parking: Piazza Matteotti.

LA FORTEZZA
Host: Chiocchetti Family
Above NE corner of Piazza del Comune
Assisi, (PG) 06081, Italy
Tel: (075) 81 24 18, Fax: (075) 81 98 035
7 Rooms, Double: €65
Restaurant closed Thu
Closed: Feb, Credit cards: all major
HOTEL

The delightful Malvarina farm with its charming, country-style accommodations, excellent local cuisine, warm and congenial host family, and ideal location has been a long-time favorite of our readers. Just outside town, yet immersed in lush green vegetation at the foot of the Subasio Mountains, the property is comprised of the 15th-century stone farmhouse where the family lives and four independent cottages (converted barn and stalls) divided into bedrooms and suites with en suite bathrooms, plus three apartments with kitchenettes for two to four persons. Casa Angelo has several bedrooms plus a sweet breakfast room with a corner fireplace and cupboards filled with colorful Deruta ceramics. Great care has obviously been taken in the decor of rooms, using Mamma's family heirloom furniture. The old wine cellar has been cleverly converted into a cool and spacious taverna dining room with long wooden tables for dining "en famille" if not out on the veranda terrace. Cooking classes are very popular here. A collection of antique farm tools and brass pots cover walls near the enormous fireplace. Horses are available for three- to seven-day trekking trips into the scenic national park just beyond the house, led by gregarious hosts, Claudio and Filippe. A welcome feature is a swimming pool. *Directions:* Exit at Rivotorto from the Perugia-Spello route 75. Turn right then left on Via Massera (Radio Subasio sign) and follow the road up to Malvarina.

MALVARINA
Host: Claudio Fabrizi Family
Localita: Malvarina 32
Assisi, (PG) 06080, Italy
Tel & Fax: (075) 8064280
9 Rooms, Double: €95
3 Suites: €120–€160
3 Apartments: €98 daily; €670 weekly
Minimum Stay Required: 3 nights
Open: all year, Credit cards: MC, VS
B&B, SELF CATERING

Il Palazzo, a three-star hotel in the heart of Assisi, offers surprisingly attractive accommodations for a modest price. Built in the 1500s as a palace for the prosperous Bindangoli-Bartocci family, its foundations date back even further. Amazingly, the hotel is still owned by Bartocci descendants. Indications of the palace's rich heritage can still be seen in the many important oil paintings and 18th-century tempera mythical scenes. As you enter off the street there is a simple reception area. Beyond is a large, beamed-ceilinged living room with comfortable sitting areas. The right wing of the palace has been turned into a restaurant serving local dishes. A buffet breakfast is served on the main level. To reach the bedrooms, you walk out into a central courtyard and then up an exterior steel staircase. I assure you the climb is worthwhile because once you throw open the shutters of your bedroom, you are treated to a stunning panorama of the Umbrian countryside. Definitely splurge—request one of the superior bedrooms, all very spacious and attractively furnished with appealing antiques. One of my favorites, 204, has twin beds with pretty, painted iron headboards. Room 203, a corner room, is also a real winner with a canopy bed—it would be my first choice except that the bathroom is not very large. As with all the hotels in Assisi, take just a small overnight suitcase. Closest parking: Piazza San Francesco.

IL PALAZZO
Host: Arianna Bartocci Fontana
Via San Francesco, 8
Assisi, (PG) 06081, Italy
Tel: (075) 81 68 41, Fax: (075) 81 23 70
11 Rooms, Double: €100–€140
1 Suite: €130–€160
Dinner by prior request
Closed: mid-Nov to mid-Mar
Credit cards: AX, MC, VS
HOTEL

Fabrizio and Bianca, the Milanese hosts originally from this part of Umbria, restored their farmhouse, situated in the very desirable location just 2 km from Assisi, with their guests' comfort foremost in mind. With careful attention to detail, six comfortable apartments and two guestrooms were fashioned within the three stone houses. Each apartment has one or two bedrooms, bathroom, fully equipped kitchenette, and eating area. Interesting decorating touches such as parts of antique iron gates hung over beds, terracotta and white ceramic tiles in the immaculate bathrooms, and antique armoires give the accommodations a polished country flavor. Le Pannocchie includes a corner fireplace, while Papaveri looks out over the flat cornfields up to magnificent Assisi and the Subasio Mountains beyond. Ambra looks after guests when the owners are away. A small dining room has been created on the ground floor, next to the 18th-century wood oven, for morning breakfast. At guests' request cooking classes and guided tours are arranged to Umbria's top sights. A lovely swimming pool, barbecue area, small gym, bikes, ping pong, and games for children are available for guests. *Directions:* From Perugia-Spoleto highway 75, exit at Ospedalicchio on route 147, turn left for Tordibetto after the bridge, then right for Assisi and follow signs for La Fornace.

PODERE LA FORNACE
Hosts: Bianca & Fabrizio Feliciani
Via Ombrosa 3
Tordibetto
Assisi, (PG) 06081, Italy
Tel: (075) 8019537, Fax: (075) 8019630
2 Rooms, Double: €65–€95*
6 Apartments: €70–€195 daily, €430–€1200 weekly*
*Breakfast not included: €6
Minimum Stay Required
Closed: Jan & Feb, Credit cards: all major
B&B, SELF CATERING

Assisi is one of our favorite places to stay and our guide can never recommend enough hotels here, so we were delighted to find the Residenza d'Epoca San Crispino, a fabulous, enchanting new hotel. Dating back to the 14th century when it was a religious site for the order of San Crispino, the hotel has been tenderly restored to maintain its rich heritage while adding every comfort for the 21st century. Almost all of the furnishings are beautiful antiques previously used in a nunnery. Throughout this tiny inn you find uncluttered, tasteful decor with white walls, stone floors, bouquets of fresh flowers, and handsome antiques. The mood is set as you enter through very old double doors into a courtyard, bound on one side by the small, 5th-century church of San Biagio. From the courtyard, steps lead up to the foyer where the reception desk is an antique confessional. Accommodations are all suites, varying in size from a studio to a two-bedroom, two-bath apartment. Every room has an armoire, which conceals a small refrigerator, minibar, espresso machine, hot plate, dishes, and utensils for preparing light snacks. Breakfast is servied in the cozy "Domus" restaurant where guests can relax throughout the day. Laundry service is available upon request. Each room is a dream, but my very favorite is The Moon and The Stars, which not only has a lovely view, but also its own huge private garden. This small hotel is really special and a marvelous value.

RESIDENZA D'EPOCA SAN CRISPINO
Host: Anna Maria Baldoni
Via San Agnese, 11
Assisi, (PG) 06081, Italy
Tel & Fax: (075) 81 55 124
7 Rooms, Double: €160–€340
Open: all year, Credit cards: all major
HOTEL

For a moderately priced place to stay in the heart of Assisi, the Hotel Umbra is an unbeatable choice. The hotel is located just a few steps down a narrow little alley that leads off the Piazza del Comune, one of the central plazas in town. The entrance is through wrought-iron gates that open to a tiny patio where you are treated to an idyllic oasis with tables set under a trellis covered by vines creating a lacy pattern of shadows. There is a lovely view from this intimate terrace. After passing through the patio, you enter into a lounge/reception area with doors opening into the dining room where very good meals are served. The public rooms have accents of antiques, but have a homey rather than grand ambiance. Steps lead to the simple bedrooms, which are individually decorated and very pleasant. Splurge and ask for a room (such as 34) with a panoramic vista of the Umbrian valley. However, do not be disappointed if one is not available—the rooms (such as 35) overlooking the jumble of tiled roofs are also very nice. If you like small, family-run hotels that are not decorator-perfect in every detail, but offer great heart and hospitality, the Hotel Umbra is an excellent choice. The delightful Alberto Laudenzi family oversees every detail of this small inn and makes guests feel at home. The staff too is extremely gracious and accommodating. The location is absolutely perfect.

❄ ☕ ✦ ♨ CREDIT ☎ @ W Y ∥ ⫟ ⍤ 🍇

HOTEL UMBRA
Host: Alberto Laudenzi Family
Via Degli Archi, 6-Piazza del Comune
Assisi, (PG) 06081, Italy
Tel: (075) 81 22 40, Fax: (075) 81 36 53
24 Rooms, Double: €100–€125
Restaurant closed Sun
Closed: mid-Jan to mid-Mar, Credit cards: all major
HOTEL

As the road twists and turns ever further into the wooded hills above Assisi, one can't help wondering what treasure awaits at the trail's end, or if anyone could possibly have found this romantic hideaway before you. What a surprise then to finally turn off the graveled road and discover the parking lot filled with luxury cars. In this glorious hillside setting with its sweeping panorama of wooded hills, worldly cares quickly melt away. Although the hotel is built into a cluster of 10th-century stone houses, all the modern-day luxuries are present including a beautiful swimming pool on the right as you enter and, on a lower terrace, tennis courts. Behind the main building is a separate stone house where you find a most appealing lounge with deep-green sofas and chairs grouped around a giant fireplace. Doors from the lounge lead into an intimate little bar and beyond to a dining room with honey-colored stone walls, beamed ceiling, and terracotta floors with tables dressed in the finest of linens. Marvelous meals are served, prepared almost totally from ingredients from the hotel's own farm, which is part of the property. The individually decorated bedrooms sport a rustic, yet elegant, ambiance. The hotel is located 10 km outside of Assisi in the charming village of Armenzano. *Directions:* From Assisi follow signs toward Gualdo-Tadino and as you leave the town walls of Assisi take the road to the right signposted Armenzano. From Armenzano, the hotel is well marked.

ROMANTIK HOTEL LE SILVE DI ARMENZANO
Host: Marco Sirignani Family
Assisi–Armenzano, (PG) 06081, Italy
Tel: (075) 80 19 000, Fax: (075) 80 19 005
21 Rooms, Double: €160–€220
13 Apartments: €600 weekly
Open: Mar to mid-Nov, Credit cards: all major
Romantik Hotels
HOTEL

The expansive Pomurlo farm covers 370 acres of hills, woods, and open fields and is an excellent base for touring Umbria. A winding dirt road leads to the typical stone house, which contains a restaurant featuring organically grown, farm-fresh specialties. An antique cupboard and old farm implements on the walls enhance the rustic setting. A nearby converted stall houses two adorable independent rooms looking out over the lake. Other guestrooms and apartments with kitchens are found in two large hilltop homes commanding a breathtaking view of the entire valley with its grazing herds of longhorn cattle. The main house, a 12th-century tower fortress where the inn's personable hostess Daniela resides, accommodates guests in three additional suites of rooms. Breakfast fixings are provided in apartments. The acquisition of the neighboring property has resulted in a center (Le Casette) offering more service—two stone farmhouses containing 16 additional rooms and a restaurant around a large swimming pool (there's a second pool at Pulicchio). Comfortable and cheerful, all rooms are decorated with wrought-iron beds, colorful bedspreads, and typical regional country antiques. Enjoy the pool and activities such as tennis, soccer, and mountain biking. Very affordable. *Directions:* The farm is located near the Rome-Florence autostrada. Take the Orvieto exit from the A1 and follow signs for Todi, not for Baschi. On route S.S.448 turn right at the sign for Pomurlo.

POMURLO VECCHIO
Hosts: Lazzaro Minghelli & Family
Localita: Lago di Corbara
Baschi, (TR) 05023, Italy
Tel: (0744) 950190, Fax: (0744) 950500
18 Rooms, Double: €65–€85
13 Apartments: €65–€85 daily
Open: all year, Credit cards: MC, VS
B&B, SELF CATERING

The vast Torre Burchio property is immersed in 1,500 acres of wooded wildlife preserve where wild boar, deer, hare, and pheasant abound. Seemingly far away from civilization, this Italian version of a ranch offers a relaxing holiday in close touch with nature, while still being in reach of Umbria's top sights. The reception, restaurant, and six guest bedrooms are within the main 18th-century farmhouse, which maintains the ambiance of the original hunting lodge with hunting trophies on the walls, large open fireplace, cozy living room, and library. The upstairs breakfast room, from which the bedrooms lead, is lined with colorful Deruta ceramics. An additional ten bedrooms are found in a single-story house just across from the lodge, while the very comfortable apartments with kitchenettes are in a beautifully restored 230-year-old stone house with inner courtyard 4 kilometers down the road. The rooms and apartments are very nicely appointed with antiques, pretty fabrics, paintings, and large bathrooms, and have telephones and televisions. Guests gather in the busy restaurant in the evening for a hearty meal based on organic products from the farm. Many activities such as cooking classes, horseback-riding weeks, and sports are available. *Directions:* 20 km from either Perugia or Assisi. From the center of Bettona, follow signs for 5 Cerri-Torre Burchio and follow the dirt road through the woods for 5 km to the main house/reception.

TORRE BURCHIO
Host: Alvaro Sfascia
Bettona, (PG) 06084, Italy
Tel: (075) 9885017, Fax: (075) 987150
16 Rooms, Double: €77–€104
13 Apartments: €672–€878 weekly*
*Apartment rental, breakfast not included
Closed: Jan & Feb, Credit cards: all major
B&B, SELF CATERING

L'Orto degli Angeli is a rare jewel. Located in the historic center of Bevagna (a small, picture-perfect walled village of Roman origin), this intimate inn exudes the genuine warmth of a private home, yet offers the comfort and sophistication of a fine hotel. The handsome stone house has been in the family of your gracious host, Francesco Antonini, since 1788. He and his sweet wife, Tiziana, welcome guests with such a gentle kindness that you will be immediately captivated by their charm. An impressive staircase leads up to the guest lounge, which has a stunning frescoed ceiling and comfortable sofa and chairs grouped around an immense stone fireplace. Main meals are served in the Redibis restaurant set in a well-preserved part of the ambulatory of the ancient Roman theater built in the 1st century A.D. All of the individually decorated guestrooms have pretty, tiled bathrooms, some antique furnishings, fireplaces, and color-coordinating fabrics on the bedspreads and curtains. Many of the rooms overlook a central garden, built upon the old Roman theatre. Bevagna is rich in historical importance—don't miss the stunning little 19th-century opera house, the well-preserved mosaics in the Roman baths, and the picturesque churches. *Directions:* From Perugia take 75 to Assisi-Foligno. Exit to the 316 to Bevagna and look for L'Orto degli Angeli signs.

❄ 🍺 ✂ ☕ CREDIT ☎ 🐕 @ 🍷 🍴 🎋 🚶 🐎 🍇

L' ORTO DEGLI ANGELI
Hosts: Tiziana & Francesco Antonini
Via Dante Alighieri, 1
Bevagna, (PG) 06031, Italy
Tel: (0742) 36 01 30, Fax: (0742) 36 17 56
5 Rooms, Double: €200–€220
9 Suites: €280–€350
Restaurant closed Tue
Open: all year, Credit cards: all major
History Traveller
HOTEL

Relais Il Canalicchio is snuggled within a medieval village on a hilltop overlooking a breathtaking vista of vineyards, olive groves, tiny villages, and forested hills that melt into the horizon. Because the hotel occupies almost the entire romantic village, it has secret little terraces and enchanting nooks to explore. The castle dates back to the 13th century and in its excellent restoration great care was taken to preserve its original architectural features such as terracotta floor tiles, beamed ceilings, thick stone walls, massive fireplaces, and arched brick doorways. The ancient Roman fortified walls of the village are incorporated into one side of the hotel and allow for a romantic lush garden that stretches to the edge of the wall and, on a lower terrace, a splendid swimming pool and a panoramic restaurant. Giant terracotta pots filled with brilliant red geraniums add color to the immaculately tended grounds. Inside, everything is decorator-perfect with a homelike, comfortable ambiance created by the use of fine antiques and lovely fabrics. The spacious bedrooms have the feel of an English country manor, with pretty floral fabrics, coordinating wallpapers, and accents of antiques. A footbridge takes you to an adjacent building with 16 new country suites, all with private entrances. *Directions:* From Perugia go south on E45 in the direction of Roma/Terni, exit at Ripabianca-Foligno, and follow signs to the hotel.

RELAIS IL CANALICCHIO
Host: Orfeo Vassallo
Via della Piazza, 4
Canalicchio di Collazzone, (PG) 06050, Italy
Tel: (075) 87 07 325, Fax: (075) 87 07 296
47 Rooms, Double: €170–€240
3 Suites: €230–€350
Open: all year, Credit cards: all major
HOTEL

A stay at the Villa Aureli with Count di Serego Alighieri (descendant of Dante) can only be memorable. With its back to the town and looking out over the Italian Renaissance garden and surrounding countryside, the imposing brick villa has been standing for the past 300 years. When it was bought by the di Serego family in the 18th century, it was meticulously restored and embellished with plasterwork, decorative painted ceilings, richly painted fabrics on walls, ornately framed paintings and prints, colorful tiles from Naples, and Umbrian antiques. Left intentionally intact by the Count, who disdains overly restored historical homes, the elegant apartments for guests maintain their original ambiance. They can accommodate from four to eight persons and are spacious, having numerous sitting rooms with fireplaces; although don't expect updated bathrooms or kitchens. A small swimming pool set against the villa's stone walls is a refreshing spot for dreaming. The villa serves as an ideal base from which to explore Umbria and parts of Tuscany, as well as special local itineraries prepared for guests by the Count. *Directions:* Exit from the Perugia highway at Madonna Alta and follow route 220 for Citta della Pieve. After 6 km, turn left for Castel del Piano Umbro.

VILLA AURELI
Host: Sperello di Serego Alighieri Family
Via Cirenei 70
Castel del Piano, (PG) 06132, Italy
Tel: (340) 6459061, Fax: (075) 5149408
4 Apartments: €700–€1500 weekly*
*Breakfast not included
Open: all year, Credit cards: MC, VS
SELF CATERING

In the hills between Tuscany and Umbria, overlooking the Tiber and Chiana valleys, you find the Nannotti family's typical farm property. Renato and Maria Teresa used to run a restaurant nearby before deciding to open a bed and breakfast and serve delicious Tuscan-Umbrian recipes at home. The three adjacent red-stone houses include six guestrooms, two apartments, and the family's private quarters. Rooms, many with terrace or garden space, are all decorated in a simple, pleasant country style with a mix of reproduction armoires, wrought-iron beds, and some modern pieces. Ernesto and Renato specialize in organic produce and make their own honey, jams, grappa, D.O.C. red wine (Colli del Trasimeno), and extra-virgin olive oil, which are brought directly to their restaurant next door with large panoramic terrace, Le Due Valli, for Maria Teresa to use in her authentic homemade cooking. She creates an easy, informal ambiance and young daughter Aureliana helps out. Being close to the charming, historical village and having easy access to the autostrada make this a super touring location. There are also bikes, a swimming pool, hiking trails, a special spa package at nearby thermal waters, a park for children, many farm animals, a fitness track, and horses to ride. *Directions:* Exit at Chiusi from the north or Fabro from the south and follow signs for Citta della Pieve. In town follow signs for San Casciano Dei B., the B&B is signposted.

MADONNA DELLE GRAZIE
Host: Renato Nannotti Family
Via Madonna delle Grazie 6
Citta della Pieve, (PG) 06062, Italy
Tel: (0578) 299822, Fax: (0578) 297749
6 Rooms, Double: €100–€140
2 Apartments: €600–€1100 weekly
Open: all year, Credit cards: MC, VS
B&B, SELF CATERING

Just on the border between Umbria and Tuscany and conveniently close to the walled town of Citta della Pieve, the Relais dei Magi is an excellent choice for accommodations in this enchanting part of Italy. A quiet, tree-lined lane leads up to the handsome 18th-century yellow villa with symmetrical windows accented by green shutters and roof adorned by rustic tile. The setting is utterly tranquil, with idyllic views in every direction—over 160 acres of woodlands, olive groves, and meadows stretch out as far as the eye can see. To the right of the villa, perfectly positioned to capture the view, is a stunning swimming pool romantically nestled on a grassy terrace amongst beds of flowers and towering cypresses. In the villa there are five deluxe suites, two with stunning view terraces and all with fireplaces and Jacuzzi tubs. Also in the villa are comfortable lounges and a beautiful dining room where a set-menu dinner is offered. A homelike ambiance prevails, with comfortable yet decorator-perfect furnishings throughout. Additional suites are found in a wing of rooms near the pool, while for longer stays or for families/friends there are apartments for two to six persons with kitchens complete with dishwashers and every modern amenity. Spa facilities include a fitness center, sauna, Turkish bath, and small heated pool. *Directions:* From Citta della Pieve take N220 toward Perugia. The hotel is on the left side of the road.

RELAIS DEI MAGI
Host: Paolo De Marchis
Localita Le Selve Nuove, 45
Citta della Pieve, (PG) 06062, Italy
Tel: (0578) 29 81 33, Fax: (0578) 29 88 58
8 Rooms, Double: €170–€195
5 Suites: €300–€350
Closed: Jan & Feb, Credit cards: all major
HOTEL

Leaving behind the road from Perugia with its developing industries, a country gravel road takes you up to the splendid 17th-century Villa di Montesolare overlooking in all directions its hilly estate of olive groves and vineyards. A wide, gray-stone staircase leads up to an elegant salon with marble fireplace and crystal chandelier off which are eight lovely guestrooms and two suites on two floors. They are individually appointed with authentic period antiques, which harmonize perfectly with the original features of the villa left intact. Seven newer suites and nine bedrooms are located within two 350-year-old farmhouses just down the road, offering magnificent views and utter tranquility. A separate breakfast room is inside one of these two houses. Back at the main house, guests enjoy a drink at the bar before dinner served in one of the two intimate, frescoed dining rooms where varied Umbrian cuisine is presented along with a selection of 400 Umbrian wines. Summer concerts are held in a chapel in the formal Italian garden. Enjoy activities such as swimming in one of two hillside pools, tennis, theme menus, and the on site spa and beauty farm. Gracious and warm hosts Filippo and Rosemarie do an absolutely superb job of making guests feel totally pampered at their romantic retreat. *Directions:* From Perugia take S.S. 220 toward Citta di Pieve. After Fontignano (3 km), turn right at Colle Sao Paolo to the villa (4 km).

❄ ☕ ✄ ♨ 💳 ☎ 🐕 @ W ⌾ P ⦙⦙ ⚘ ≈ 🚶 🖼 🧍 👥 🐴 💐

HOTEL VILLA DI MONTE SOLARE
Hosts: Rosemarie & Filippo Iannarone
Via Montali 7
Panicale
Colle San Paolo, (PG) 06068, Italy
Tel: (075) 83 23 76, Fax: (075) 83 55 462
25 Rooms, Double: €200–€280
9 Suites: €300–€450
Open: all year, Credit cards: AX, MC, VS
HOTEL

The Antica Fattoria came highly recommended by several readers who stayed there in the first year it opened. It is indeed a delightful combination of pretty countryside, strategic touring position, comfortable rooms, excellent meals, and warm hospitality. Following the increasingly popular lifestyle trend of abandoning the city for a rural pace, Roman couple Alessandro and Anna left their offices to become, essentially, farmers. They bought and restored two connected stone farmhouses and incorporated a combination of five rooms and two apartments, decorated pleasantly with a characteristic country flavor, for guests. While Alessandro tends to the crops and farm animals, Anna lives out her passion for cooking, much to guests' delight. Meals are served either outside at one long table or in the transformed cow stalls below with cozy sitting area and fireplace. At times the allegria and good food keep guests at the table until the wee hours. A lovely swimming pool looks over the wooded hills to the valley. The busy hosts take time to assist guests with the many local itineraries and organize a wide variety of games. Perfect for families and a great base for exploring Umbria. The town of Deruta is world famous for its painted ceramic pottery and filled with workshops and stores. *Directions:* From Perugia (18 km), exit from E45 at Casalina. Take the first right and follow signs to the Santuario Madonna dei Bagni and then to the Fattoria.

ANTICA FATTORIA DEL COLLE
Hosts: Anna & Alessandro Coluccelli
Strada Colle delle Forche 6
Deruta, (PG) 06053, Italy
Tel & Fax: (075) 972201
5 Rooms, Double: €90–€110
2 Apartments: €850–€1100 weekly
Minimum Stay Required: 2 nights, 7 nights Aug
Half-board, per person: €75–€85
Dinners: €30
Open: Easter to Jan 10, Credit cards: none
B&B, SELF CATERING

L'Antico Forziere in the capable hands of Daniela and her industrious family, formerly the manager of another hotel in the guide, is a pleasant and strategic place from which to tour the highlights of Umbria. The ancient stone fortress building on the Tiber river, is located just off the main road which leads to Deruta, one of Italy's most famous ceramic centers. The views from the house and swimming pool over the valley are quite lovely. Attention has been given to the preservation of the centuries-old building, with exposed stone walls, handmade brickwork, wood beamed ceilings. Accommodation within 3 suites with independent garden entrance or 6 double rooms are appointed in typical Umbrian style with iron wrought beds, hand-woven local fabrics and simple country furniture and many amenities including wireless internet access. High emphasis has been given to the restaurant where sons, Stefano and Andrea continue to work wonders, serving excellent local fare including fish and meat specialties within the vaulted brick and stone dining room where many come for a specially-prepared regional meal. Daniela's husband and third son, Samuele, take care of the general property and serve in the restaurant. Perugia, Assisi, Todi, Orvieto and Spoleto are all within 30 minutes of this base. Excellent value and hospitality. *Directions:* From Perugia, exit at Casalina just after Deruta and follow signs to the hotel for 1 km.

L' ANTICO FORZIERE
Hosts: Daniela Taddia & Alessandro Rodella Family
Via Rocca, 2 – Località Casalina
Deruta, (PG) 06051, Italy
Tel: (075) 97 24 314, Fax: (075) 97 29 392
6 Rooms, Double: €90–€100
3 Suites: €125–€150
Restaurant closed Mon
Open: all year, Credit cards: all major
HOTEL

Best friends Luciano and Tommaso, refugees from city life, have transformed the 1,000-acre property, La Casella, made up of woods, rivers, and valleys, into a veritable countryside haven for vacationers. Foremost attention has been given to the 32 rooms, which are divided between four separate stone houses. The Noci house contains seven doubles upstairs appointed with country antiques, and a large vaulted room downstairs used for small meetings or dining. La Terrazza, originally a hunting lodge, has nine rooms, one with namesake terrace looking over the oak woods. On the highest point sits San Gregorio, with a small pool, where guests revel in the utter silence and a spectacular 360-degree view over the entire property. The lively dining room offers delectable cuisine, with ingredients direct from the farm. The many sports facilities include a beautiful big swimming pool, tennis, and an equestrian center where numerous special outings and events are organized. There is also a spa program with natural treatments. Well-marked trails lead the rider, biker, or hiker to such marvels as Todi, Orvieto, or even Perugia. *Directions:* Exit at Fabro from the Rome-Florence A1 autostrada. Follow signs for Parrano (7 km), turning right at the Casella sign, and continue for another 7 km on a rough gravel road.

LA CASELLA
Hosts: Luciano Nenna & Tommaso Campolmi
Localita: La Casella
Ficulle, (TR) 05016, Italy
Tel & Fax: (0763) 86588
32 Rooms: €70–€90, price per person
Minimum Stay Required: 7 nights Aug
Open: all year, Credit cards: all major
B&B, SELF CATERING

After many years working as managers of multinational corporations in separate cities, gracious hosts Stefano and Paola Zocchi changed lifestyles and location. They decided on Umbria—midway between Milan and Rome—and bought the Palazzetta property sitting on a hill near Todi. Complete with 360-degree countryside views, their beautifully restored 17th-century stone home is a gem where guests enjoy spacious bedrooms with all the amenities. While enhancing the original features, and capitalizing on the views, each romantic room has been styled with a muted color scheme enhanced by delightful hand-loomed local fabrics for curtains and bedspreads. The bathrooms are accented with lovely mosaic tiles. Guests enjoy breakfast in the lovely dining room or out on the terrace facing an infinity pool that seems to look out on all of Umbria. The sitting rooms on each floor, with similar inviting country chic décor, offer relaxing spots for reading or chatting. Besides sightseeing in the area, arrangements can be made for massages, personal trainers, helicopter transfers from the airport, vineyard visits and cooking lessons with Paola. *Directions:* Exit the E45 (Todi-Perugia) at Fratta Todina/Montecastello di Vibio for the 7 km drive to Fratta Todina. Pass the walls of the town and turn left to Spineta. Go through Spineta past the convent and after the vineyard turn right at the gate.

LA PALAZZETTA DEL VESCOVO
Hosts: Stefano & Paola Zocchi
Via Clausura, 17
Fratta Todina, (PG) 06054, Italy
Tel: (075) 8745183, Fax: (075) 8745042
7 Rooms, Double: €170–€230
2 Suites: €210–€260
Rent the entire Villa: from €8500 weekly
Minimum Stay Required: 2 nights
Dinners: €38
Open: Feb to Jan 6, Credit cards: all major
B&B

La Ghirlanda is an enchanting country home, glowing with warmth and color, charm and romance. The sprawling country estate home of Riccardo and Amalija who encourage you to make their house your home. From the hill top position, the rust-red stately home, originally the family hunting lodge, takes in sweeping views of the alternating wooded and cultivated landscapes, thankfully all theirs and therefore left unspoiled. The secluded pool area is an agreeable spot from which to literally breath in this inspiring scene. Each individually decorated bedroom has been thoughtfully appointed with antique pieces, fine linens and color coordinated fabrics. A cozy wine bar, dining room, library and sitting room with fireplaces are all open to guests and meals are enjoyed either within the golden hued dining room or out in the garden under the stars. Guests are offered freshly made totally Umbrian recipes accompanied by their own top-rated Sagrantino di Montefalco wine. Most ingredients come right from the farm, including meats, vegetables, fruits and of course, the extra virgin olive oil. *Directions:* From the S.S.3 Todi-Perugia, exit at the second Todi exit from the south, or Ripabianca from the north and follow signs for San Terenziano, then Saragano.

LA GHIRLANDA
Hosts: Riccardo Pongelli & Amalija Tomassini Barbarossa
Localita: Saragano
Gualdo Cattaneo, (PG) 06035, Italy
Tel: (0742) 98731, Fax: (06) 233231544
8 Rooms, Double: €108–€128
4 Suites: €124–€210
Open: all year, Credit cards: all major
B&B

If you are searching for a property that is one hundred percent Umbria, you have come to the right place. Le Terre del Verde incorporates the best of what this marvelous region offers: genuinely warm hospitality, characteristic accommodation within historic dwellings, a noteworthy restaurant featuring its own organic products. All these elements, including full spa facilities, is found literally immersed in 1500 acres of pure green landscapes. The Carnevali family and partners understandably enamored with the natural beauty of the surroundings switched gears in mid-career to devote their time to the restoration of the ancient abbey, mill and outlying buildings. The 50 guestrooms and suites are divided among the stone houses maintaining their original Umbrian features. Daughter Federica is at the helm and manages the estate with finesse. Roads within the vast property lead to wooded hills, walking and biking trails, past grazing sheep, cattle, and the small factories where the farm's foods are processed. Gubbio, Perugia and smaller villages are withing a half hour's drive. *Directions:* From Perugia (40 km) follow signs for Valfabbrica and Gualdo Tadino. After Cerasa take a right turn at the sign for hotel, 7 km before actually reaching Gualdo.

❄ ☕ 🍽 💳 📷 🏠 ♿ @ 🍸 P 🍴 🚭 🌸 🏊 🎿 🖼 🐕 ♿ 🚶 🏇 🎯

LE TERRE DEL VERDE   New
Host: Federica Carnevali
Loc. Badia Val di Rasina
Gualdo Tadino, (PG) 06023 , Italy
Tel: (075) 91 07 01, Fax: (075) 91 07 05 17
50 Rooms, Double: €108–€212
6 Suites: €182–€400
Open: all year, Credit cards: all major
HOTEL, SELF CATERING

Emanuela and Paolo left behind advertising careers and a period of time living in Mexico and returned to their native Italy with the idea of changing lifestyles and opening a B&B. They purchased and carefully restored Casa Branca, a hilltop stone house surrounded by woods and a soothing babbling brook. Just above the house is a peaceful spot poolside which enjoys spectacular countryside views. The main house is divided between the couple's own residence and the guest quarters which are made up of six double rooms with nice new bathrooms. Down on the main floor is a large stone-walled room with tables to one side and a sitting area to the other. A separate cottage in back has two bedrooms with adjoining bathroom. Their Latin American stay has had a definite influence on décor decisions with yellow, orange, and red prominent in sofas and wall colors, an effective contrast to traditional brick, stone and wood materials. It is well worth staying for dinner as Emanuela is an exceptional cook, preparing a four-course meal with ingredients from the vegetable garden at an impeccable table either out on the terrace or in the dining room. Besides Gubbio there is lots to explore in this area bordering the Marches. *Directions:* From Spoleto follow signs for Foligno, then Nocera Umbra, then Branca. From Branca, turn right at the sign for Casa Branca up past new houses to the top. Gubbio is 12 km away.

CASA BRANCA
Hosts: Emanuela Notari & Paolo Coppola
Voc. San Simeone, 8|A
Gubbio, (PG) 06020, Italy
Tel: (075) 9270016, Fax: (075) 9270037
5 Rooms, Double: €90
2 Suites: €100–€120
Dinners: €25
Open: all year, Credit cards: all major
B&B

The address says Gubbio but actually the Locanda, of ancient origins, is immersed in the wooded hills halfway between Gubbio and Perugia (each 20km away) where it once played a strategic role protecting the territory. Take the scenic road up to the group of stone houses (once an entire village with chapel) overlooking this peaceful landscape, a haven for those wanting to just take it easy. You can dine on healthy organic foods and recharge your batteries, literally immersed in noiseless nature. Furnished comfortably in Asian style, pleasantly blending in with the original stone, brick and wood architecture, gracious hosts Paola and Eric have faithfully and lovingly restored the residence, creating ten double pastel-colored bedrooms. Meals are served in the dining room or on the terrace at tables set with crisp yellow linen cloths and picture-perfect foods prepared by amiable Chef Jimmy. If guests are not out viewing the highlights of Umbria, they have given in and chosen just to relax; walking in the surroundings or lounging poolside, taking in the magical, undisturbed scenery and waiting for another spectacular sunset. Everyone seems content at this very special place and it is the owners and the setting that make it that way. *Directions:* From Perugia, follow for Cesena and after 15 km exit at Ponte Pattoli and follow for "Casa del Diavolo", then Santa Cristina. Continue for another 7 km and turn left into the Locanda after the restaurant, "La Dolce Vita".

LOCANDA DEL GALLO
Hosts: Paola & Erich Breuer
Loc. S. Cristina
Gubbio, (PG) 06020, Italy
Tel & Fax: (075) 9229912
10 Rooms, Double: €130–€140
Open: all year, Credit cards: MC, VS
B&B

Gubbio is one of Umbria's many jewels: a small, wonderfully intact medieval town that presses against the wooded hillside. A not-to-be-missed sight in Gubbio is the Piazza Grande, considered to be one of the boldest examples of medieval town planning, and facing onto this awesome masterpiece is the Relais Ducale. Gazing from the square, you would hardly know that a hotel is secreted within the building, but you will notice a large, open, stone passageway. Enter here and climb up the stairs through a tunnel-like corridor where you will emerge into a little lane. Continue on until you come to a hotel sign by the gate on a stone wall. Ring the bell for entrance and suddenly the hotel reveals itself with a charming inner garden courtyard off which you find the discreet reception office. The hotel, once the guest quarters for the Ducale Palace, has been sleekly renovated, but impressive features of its past are seen throughout with massive thick walls, high vaulted ceilings, and stone archways. On the fourth level of the hotel there is a romantic garden with one side enclosed by a carved stone balustrade, where you can gaze out to a beautiful panoramic view. Fine antique furniture is used for accent, handsome oil paints adorn the walls, and Oriental carpets brighten the floors. The pretty guestrooms have a sedate, refined decor, showing an effort to preserve the aristocratic aura of the hotel's heritage. All guestrooms have LCD TVs and Internet access.

❄ ▣ 🍵 ♨ CREDIT ☎ 🐕 🏨 @ ☏ 🍴 🖼 ⬮ ⛷ ♿ 🧍 👥 🐎 🍇

RELAIS DUCALE
Host: Rodolfo Mencarelli
Via Ducale, 2
Gubbio, (PG) 06024, Italy
Tel: (075) 92 20 157, Fax: (075) 92 20 159
32 Rooms, Double: €155–€275
Open: all year, Credit cards: all major
HOTEL

When Lois Martin, a retired teacher, spotted the lovely restored farmhouse at San Martino, she knew it literally had her name on it and purchased it immediately. The house is completely open to guests, from the upstairs cozy living room with large stone fireplace to the downstairs country kitchen and large family room. Ingredients for a full country breakfast await you in the kitchen with its impressive display of Deruta ceramics. One bedroom with king bed is joined by a bathroom to a small room with twin beds, ideal for a family. Each of the other two doubles has a bathroom, with one being en suite. Besides a swimming pool overlooking the wooded hills and valley, other extras are satellite TV, a travel library, American washer and dryer, bikes, guest bathrobes, and dinner upon request. Casa San Martino also offers onsite cooking and painting with a visiting professional teacher in off-season. Being right on the border of Umbria and Tuscany, Lake Trasimeno and towns such as Gubbio, Perugia, Cortona, Assisi, and Deruta are all easily accessible. The entire house can also be rented weekly for a group of up to eight persons. *Directions:* From Lisciano square, pass the bar and turn left for San Martino. Continue for 2 km and take a right up the hill at the sign for San Martino for just over 1.5 km to the house.

CASA SAN MARTINO
Host: Lois Martin
Localita: San Martino 19
Lisciano Niccone, (PG) 06060, Italy
Tel: (075) 844288, Fax: (075) 844422
4 Rooms, Double: €140–€150
1 House: €2000–€3000 weekly
Minimum Stay Required: 3 nights
Open: all year, Credit cards: none
B&B, SELF CATERING

Still another undiscovered area is the peaceful countryside northeast of Todi, where you find the Castello di Loreto. After having meticulously restored part of this medieval fortress castle as a country home, Nino Segurini now coordinates restoration work on ancient buildings, besides continuing his own business as a consultant to antiques dealers. Nino is very knowledgeable on many subjects, and delights in introducing guests to the undiscovered treasures he has found in the immediate area. Nino and Francesca's home is a veritable museum, with collections of ancient artifacts naturally inhabiting the historical building. Within the base of the thick-walled fortress you find the main living room, two small bedrooms (one twin, one double) connected by a sitting area, and three bathrooms. The kitchen leads outside to the spacious patio with grape pergola overlooking the landscaped garden and swimming pool. The preferred and largest bedroom, arranged as a suite with its own sitting room, is reached by two flights of stairs past another living room with fireplace, appointed with antique armor and weaponry and an enclosed loggia. A fourth guestroom features a 16th-century carved, gilded bed of a noble Venetian family who once had Napoleon as a house guest. *Directions:* Leave highway E45 at Todi/Orvieto, heading for Pian di Porto, then San Terenziano. After 2 km, fork right towards Loreto for another 4 km. The entrance gate is opposite the church.

CASTELLO DI LORETO
Hosts: Nino & Francesca Segurini
Loreto—Todi, (PG) 06059, Italy
Tel & Fax: (075) 8852501
4 Rooms, Double: €110–€130
Minimum Stay Required: 2 nights
Open: all year, Credit cards: none
B&B

The scenic approach to the Fattoria di Vibio passes through lush green hills, by picturesque farms, and is highlighted by a romantic view of the quaint town of Todi, 20 kilometers away. The houses sit side by side and share between them 14 double rooms with private baths. Common areas for guests include a cozy, country-style living room with fireplace, games room, and country kitchen. The accommodations are enhanced by preserved architectural features such as terracotta floors and exposed-beam ceilings, and typical Umbrian handicrafts such as wrought-iron beds, renovated antiques, and Deruta ceramics. On the assumption that guests may find it difficult to leave this haven, the hosts offer half board plus lunch and snacks, along with SPA facilities (massages and Turkish bath) indoor and outdoor heated swimming pools, tennis, hiking, horseback riding, fishing, and biking. Signora Gabriella, with a passion for cooking, gets all the richly deserved credit for the marvelous meals served either poolside or on the panoramic terrace. Four houses are also available for rent. *Directions:* From either Todi or Orvieto follow route S448 until the turnoff for Vibio at the sign for Prodo-Quadro and follow the well-marked dirt road for 10 km up to the farmhouse.

FATTORIA DI VIBIO
Host: Giuseppe Saladini
Localita: Buchella-Doglio
Montecastello di Vibio, (PG) 06057, Italy
Tel: (075) 8749607, Fax: (075) 8780014
14 Rooms, Double: €140–€160
3 Suites: €180–€200
4 Villas: €980–€2100 weekly
Open: Mar to Jan 8, Credit cards: all major
B&B, SELF CATERING

The Villa Zuccari, the childhood home of owner Paolo Zuccari, opened its doors in 2005 to guests. With the admirable success of their other nearby hotel, San Luca in Spoleto, it was natural that he and his gracious wife, Daniela, decided to transform the spacious pink villa into a small hotel. The back side of the villa is attached to the small town, while the front looks out over the garden, swimming pool and outlying fields. The main hall leads past the reception area, two cozy vaulted living rooms to the main dining room with its original terracotta tiled ceiling and sun-colored walls. Genuine local recipes are savored here with special attention given to the use of locally grown products. Individually styled bedrooms are found on the ground and first floors. While one daughter oversees the hotel in Spoleto, the other daughter, an architect, supervised the renovation project. Comfortable rooms are purposely on the large size, have antique furnishings and feature terraces or garden patios. Each bathroom has been created with a different combination of marble patterns, many with both bathtub and separate shower. A separate house in the garden can be rented for 8-10 guests. Before a full day of touring Umbria from this centrally located spot, a full breakfast awaits guests in the trellis-painted bar and breakfast room. *Directions:* From the Spoleto-Perugia highway S.S. 3 exit at Trevi/Montefalco and follow signs to Madonna della Stella/Montefalco for 4 Km.

VILLA ZUCCARI
Hosts: Daniela & Paolo Zuccari
Località San Luca
Montefalco, (PG) 06036, Italy
Tel: (0742) 39 94 02, Fax: (0742) 39 91 94
31 Rooms, Double: €110–€240
3 Suites: €210–€350
Open: all year, Credit cards: all major
HOTEL

La Locanda del Capitano is a tiny inn romantically tucked in the historic center of a medieval, picture-perfect walled village perched on a hilltop overlooking a serene, gentle, Umbrian landscape. The hotel is at heart a restaurant, which has quickly gained well-deserved publicity for the outstanding quality of the kitchen but, luckily for guests, there are also a few bedrooms. The guestrooms are small, but sweetly decorated in an appropriately simple, country style. All have pretty wrought-iron headboards with floral paintings hand-done by a local woman. The choice guestrooms are the two with a small terrace tucked up amongst the ancient tiled rooftops. La Locanda is the creation of your charming hosts, Carmen and Giancarlo Polito, who decided at the tender ages of 26 and 27 to begin their life together in the countryside and discovered in a newspaper ad the perfect site for their inn, a centuries-old stone house in the idyllic town of Montone. As soon as they saw the house, their hearts were won. Carmen and Giancarlo are wonderful with their guests, and even organize tours for a minimum of seven people into the countryside for truffle hunting during the season. *Directions:* Heading north from Perugia on the E45, take the Montone exit. The hotel is just a block from the town square.

LA LOCANDA DEL CAPITANO
Hosts: Carmen & Giancarlo Polito
Via Roma, 7
Montone, (PG) 06014, Italy
Tel: (075) 93 06 521, Fax: (075) 93 06 455
10 Rooms, Double: €120–€140
Closed: Jan 10 to Feb 10, Credit cards: all major
HOTEL

In a small pocket of land in the southernmost point of Umbria is the Podere Costa Romana property, immersed in the green hillsides south of ancient Narni. Dynamic hostess Anna Maria left her native Naples for the peace and quiet of the Umbrian hills and meticulously restored the stone 18th-century farmhouse where she now hosts guests within six well-appointed apartments. Rooms have been thoughtfully decorated with antique country furnishings, which harmonize perfectly with the rustic quality of the original farmhouse. Each individual apartment (named for women) can accommodate from two (Giovanna is an adorable love nest) to five guests (Paola has two bedrooms) and is equipped with a kitchenette. Soft-peach and pale-yellow walls highlight exposed stones, beamed ceilings, and brick floors. The large main living room with fireplace and double arches opens out to the surrounding garden and swimming pool overlooking the hills. Travelers can easily reach many lesser-known Umbrian villages as well as the cities and from Orte frequent trains depart for either Rome or Florence. *Directions:* Exit the A1 autostrada at Magliano Sabina and turn right for Otricoli. 8 km after Otricoli turn right at the Narni-Testaccio-Itieli sign and then right again for the Podere Costa Romana.

PODERE COSTA ROMANA
Host: Anna Maria Giordano
S.S. Flaminia, Strada per Itieli
Narni, (TR) 05035, Italy
Tel: (0744) 722495, Fax: (0823) 797118
6 Apartments: €110 daily, €400–€600 weekly
Minimum Stay Required: 2 nights
Open: all year, Credit cards: none
SELF CATERING

The town of Orvieto, just off the main expressway between Rome and Florence, is one of the most picturesque of all the Umbrian hilltowns. This small city is perched on the top of a hill—an intriguing sight that can be viewed from many kilometers away. Less than a ten-minute drive south of Orvieto is a 12th-century Gothic abbey that has been converted into a hotel where you can stay surrounded by the romantic ruins of yesteryear. Although there is a commercial air to La Badia, the reception is caring and friendly. The manager, Ettore Pelletti, has been with the hotel for over 20 years, as has the chef, so, as you can see, there is a real continuity of management. Although this is not a cozy, small hotel, you are bound to enjoy the setting, the pool, the old-world ambiance, and the food. The dining room is one of the most attractive rooms in the hotel. It has an enormous, high-vaulted stone ceiling, wrought-iron fixtures, heavy wooden beams, eye-catching copper accents, and, at one end, a cavernous fireplace complete with a roasting spit. The standard bedrooms, although not large or with inspired decor, are comfortable and many have a stunning view up to the town of Orvieto. If you want to splurge, ask for one of the romantic suites, which have much prettier furnishings. In the meadows behind the monastery there is a lovely pool. *Directions:* From Orvieto, follow signs for Viterbo. The hotel is 4 km south of Orvieto.

❄ ☕ ✄ 💳 ☎ @ 🍸 P 🍴 🚫 ≈ 🏃 🖼 👟 ♿ 🚶 🐴 ⛷ 💃

LA BADIA
Host: Contessa Luisa Fiumi
Localita: La Badia, 8
Orvieto, (TR) 05019, Italy
Tel: (0763) 30 19 59, Fax: (0763) 30 53 96
18 Rooms, Double: €180–€280
9 Suites: €280–€400
Restaurant closed Wed
Closed: Jan & Feb, Credit cards: AX, MC, VS
Abitare La Storia
HOTEL

The Locanda Palazzone distinguishes itself from the more standard agriturismo or bed and breakfast choices by its contemporary interiors wrapped up in a 14th-century building. Once a cardinal's home and a stopover on a pilgrimage to Rome, the hillside residence takes in wide open views over the valley. The Dubini family, originally from Milan, returned from abroad and settled in on their grandfather's property, surrounded by the vineyards which produce a pleasant Orvieto Superiore wine. The unusual limestone brick structure resembling a church was completely restored to its original dimensions by having a part of the roof raised. Interiors were carefully studied by a group of architects and were given a clean minimalist décor. Guests walk into an enormous open space, cross-sectioned by large arches with a central staircase and glass elevator. Spacious rooms and suites upstairs have designer bathrooms, hardwood floors and some have loft space for beds. The enoteca below is where breakfast is served or wine-tastings are arranged. Hosts Lodovico and Patrizia reside in the adjacent house and are on hand to assist guests. While dining by candlelight on the front terrace, guests delight at the magical view of illuminated Orvieto and its dominating Cathedral. *Directions:* From the A1 Autostrada, exit at Orvieto and follow for Orvieto then Allerona and just after stay left at the gas station. Continue for 2.5 km turning left at the Locanda sign.

LOCANDA PALAZZONE
Hosts: Lodovico & Patrizia Dubini
Rocca Ripesena 67
Orvieto, (TR) 05019, Italy
Tel: (0763) 393614, Fax: (0763) 394833
7 Suites: €165–€290
Minimum Stay Required: 2 nights Jun, Jul & Aug
Dinners: €38
Open: Mar to Jan, Credit cards: AX, VS
B&B

A very high rating goes to the Locanda Rosati on the border of Umbria and Lazio, and just steps away from Tuscany. Giampiero and sister, Alba, with their respective spouses, Luisa and Paolo, sold their cheese production business in Lucca and returned to Orvieto to transform the family farmhouse into a deluxe bed and breakfast. The results are splendid and guests, taking priority over the agricultural activity in this instance, are treated with extra-special care. The downstairs common areas include two cozy living rooms with fireplace and a large stone-walled dining room divided by a brick archway leading down to the "tufo" stone cellar. Seven bedrooms upstairs (one with access and bathroom for the handicapped) have been decorated with an animal theme evident in the carvings on bed boards and lamps. Three more bedrooms were added for guests on the top floor with mansard ceilings, leaving the entire home to the bed and breakfast business. Most rooms face the lush gardens to the back where a large open lawn space leads to the inviting swimming pool. Paolo produces appetizing pastas, soups, and other specialties all written up in a recipe book for guests who can also sign up for impromtu cooking lessons. *Directions:* Exit from the A1 autostrada at Orvieto and follow signs for Viterbo-Bolsena. Skirt town and continue towards Bolsena for about 8 km on route 71. After a series of sharp curves, the locanda comes up on the right.

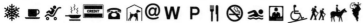

LOCANDA ROSATI
Host: Rosati Family
Localita: Buonviaggio 22
Orvieto, (TR) 05018, Italy
Tel: (0763) 217314, Fax: (0763) 217783
10 Rooms, Double: €100–€140
Open: all year, Credit cards: MC, VS
B&B

With a rich history dating back to the 16th century, the Hotel Palazzo Piccolomini in the historic center of Orvieto, an incredible, walled city perched atop a high hill, was once home to the wealthy Piccolomini family. At the end of the 1980s the palace was rescued from neglect and after many years of restoration, opened in 1999 as a hotel. In the entrance some of the original architectural features remain, accented by a few pieces of antique furniture, but overall the mood is contemporary. From the reception hall, a flight of steps leads up to a large lounge where the frescoed ceiling again attests to the hotel's glamorous past. However, the room that most portrays the age of the building is the breakfast room in the cellar. It has a giant stone pillar supporting a coved ceiling, an ancient well tucked in a corner, and a carefully preserved medieval stone staircase leading to secret places far below. The standard bedrooms are moderate in size and well equipped in the style of a modern hotel with good lighting, writing desks, satellite TVs, mini-bars, air conditioning, and hairdryers. The hotel sits on a corner facing the small Piazza Ranieri and from here it is a delightful stroll through picturesque little squares to Orvieto's crown jewel, the stunning, not-to-be-missed cathedral. *Directions:* From the A1, exit at Orvieto and follow signs to the center. When the road splits, take the road to the right. Follow signs to the hotel.

HOTEL PALAZZO PICCOLOMINI
Host: Roberto Mazzolai
Piazza Ranieri, 36
Orvieto, (TR) 05018, Italy
Tel: (0763) 34 17 43, Fax: (0763) 39 10 46
29 Rooms, Double: €154–€280
Open: all year, Credit cards: all major
HOTEL

A convenient stopover while heading either north or south along the main artery—the A1 autostrada—is the Villa Ciconia inn. Located below the historical center of Orvieto, in the newer commercial outskirts, the property maintains its tranquil setting thanks to the fortress of trees protecting the 16th-century stone villa. The first floor includes reception area, breakfast room, and two large high-ceilinged dining rooms. These latter, with their somber gray-stone fireplaces, tapestries, heavy dark-wood beams, and subdued-color frescoes depicting allegorical motifs and landscapes, give the place a medieval castle's air. The 12 air conditioned bedrooms on the second floor are appointed either in appropriate style, with antique chests and wrought-iron beds, or with more contemporary furnishings (lower rates) and all the amenities of the four-star hotel that this is. Most rooms are quiet and look out onto the 8 acres of woods behind the villa. There are also two enormous beamed sitting rooms on this floor for guests and a beautiful new swimming pool. The restaurant has a solid reputation for creating excellent Umbrian specialties. Manager Anna Elena Petrangeli is always on hand to assist guests. *Directions:* Exiting from the autostrada, turn right towards Orvieto and right again where marked Arezzo, Perugia, passing under the tollway. The Ciconia is just after the river on the left-hand side of the road.

VILLA CICONIA
Host: Petrangeli Family
Via dei Tigli 69
Orvieto, (TR) 05019, Italy
Tel: (0763) 30 55 82, Fax: (0763) 30 20 77
12 Rooms, Double: €100–€150
Restaurant closed Mon
Closed: Jan 7 to Feb 28, Credit cards: all major
HOTEL

Owner Claudia Spatola does an admirable job of single-handedly running a bed and breakfast in the complex of stone houses known as Borgo Spante, which dates back to the 15th century and has been in her family since 1752. Consisting of a main villa, connecting farmers' houses, chapel, barns, swimming pool, and garden, it is isolated in 500 acres of woods and hills, the true heart of Umbria, yet is located only 16 kilometers from Orvieto and not far from Assisi, Todi, and Perugia. Guests stay in a combination of rooms or apartments in the former farmers' quarters with their irregular-sized rooms, sloping worn-brick floors, and rustic country furnishings—very charming in its way. Authentic Umbrian meals (half-board required), prepared by local women, are served in the dining room with long wooden tables and fireplace. A larger dining area has been added in the former barn, along with four additional mini-apartments, simply and characteristically decorated. Memorable evenings are spent in the garden or poolside conversing with other guests or listening to an impromptu concert or lecture. *Directions:* From the A1 autostrada exit at Orvieto and follow signs for Arezzo on route 71. After 4 km, turn right at Morrano, Route 101, and proceed for 12 km to the sign for Spante. Turn left and continue for 2 km.

BORGO SPANTE
Host: Claudia Spatola
Loc. Spante
Ospedaletto, (TR) 05010, Italy
Tel: (075) 8709134, Fax: (075) 8709201
4 Rooms, Double: €120*
5 Apartments: €60 per person daily*
Minimum Stay Required: 3 nights
*Includes breakfast & dinner
Open: all year, Credit cards: none
B&B, SELF CATERING

A truly classic hotel with old-world charm, the 120-year-old Brufani Palace was once two hotels sitting back to back in the main piazza of Perugia's historic center. Joined together like Siamese twins, the hotel has been recently restored to its original splendor with, of course, double of everything, including many spacious sitting rooms, two bars, a restaurant, and enormous formal breakfast room. Unlike many newly restored accommodation, obvious effort has been made to retain its old-fashioned flavor while updating amenities and maintaining a five-star level. Carpeted bedrooms are spacious and elegantly appointed with antiques, gilded mirrors, and marble bathrooms, most with lovely views over historic Perugia or the Umbrian countryside. Guests can choose from standard doubles, suites and junior suites with high ceilings, or cozy beamed mansard rooms. All guests can enjoy the full 360-degree views from the highest point in the city, the Brufani's rooftop terrace. Another unique feature of this hotel is the swimming pool down in the original cantinas with brick vaulted ceilings. Etruscan relics were found while digging and now the glass-bottom pool proudly displays this discovery! The hotel also has a gym and sauna. Step out of the hotel and you are right on the main street of charming Perugia. *Directions:* Follow hotel signs up to the historic center to the Piazza Italia. Hotel staff will take care of parking.

❄ 🚲 📇 ☎ 🛎 🍽 @ ☉ P 🍴 🏊 🖼 🐾 ♿

HOTEL BRUFANI PALACE
Piazza Italia, 12
Perugia, (PG) 06100, Italy
Tel: (075) 57 32 541, Fax: (075) 57 20 210
59 Rooms, Double: €325–€385*
20 Suites: €460–€980*
*Breakfast not included: €33
*Tax: 10%
Open: all year, Credit cards: all major
History Traveller
HOTEL

The sleepy village of Solomeo, located between Perugia and Lake Trasimeno, had been almost completely abandoned until a well-known cashmere company bought and restored most of the town to its original charm, using the individual houses and apartments for offices and workshops. Pier Luigi Cavicchi, an import/export consultant, and his friendly wife Donatella (who runs the family's farm) inherited a turn-of-the-last-century villa, located right in the heart of town. Pier Luigi (who had spent many happy summers at the villa) and his wife thoroughly renovated the property and opened it as an inn. Their wish was to maintain the original character of the beloved residence while adding all possible amenities (including air conditioning). The result is a compact and quaint hotel that has it all. The 12 English-style country bedrooms are named after flowers and this theme is followed through in stenciled borders, bedspread fabrics, and bathrooms. Preserved stencil work on walls and ceilings in the entrance, tea room, and upstairs sitting room were done by the same artist who decorated the town's church across the street. The bright breakfast room downstairs has stone walls and beams and leads to terraces overlooking the countryside where a garden, swimming pool, exercise room, meeting room, and four garden bedrooms are situated. In the immediate area are a golf club and horseback-riding facilities. The hotel is 10 km outside of Perugia in Solmeo.

❄ ☕ ⚒ ♨ 💳 ☎ ❦ @ ♈ P ⅋ 🚭 ≈ 🖼 🐾 🚶 🐎 🍇

LOCANDA SOLOMEO
Hosts: Pier Luigi & Donatella Cavicchi
Piazza Carlo Alberto dalla Chiesa
1 Loc. Solomeo
Perugia, (PG) 06070, Italy
Tel: (075) 52 93 119, Fax: (075) 52 94 090
12 Rooms, Double: €110–€140
Restaurant by prior reservation
Closed: Christmas & Jan 6 to 31
Credit cards: all major
HOTEL

Accessed by a steep, winding road, the 18th-century rectangular Palazzo Terranova, which dominates the northern Tiber valley and seemingly all of Umbria, is softened by surrounding terraced gardens filled with roses, lavender, cascading geraniums, and magnolia trees. This stylish country house was lovingly restored back to life by an English family some years ago and is filled with precious antiques and paintings from England and Italy. The current owners continue this passion for beauty and art in this tranquil, Italian countryside setting. Each masterpiece of a bedroom, with its stenciled and painted designs, holds some enchanting feature and, just as in the creation of a painting, utmost attention has been given to color scheme, composition, and lighting. Most of the rooms have king-sized wrought-iron beds, soft linens and stunning views. The restaurant is open to guests for lunch and dinner with meals being prepared using fresh, seasonal ingredients, highlighting the special dishes of the area. There is a scenic pool taking advantage of views and spa treatments available. Delightful staff is on hand to satisfy any whim. *Directions:* Ask the hotel to send you detailed driving instructions.

PALAZZO TERRANOVA
Host: Valentina Morriconi
Localita: Ronti near Morra
Città di Castello
Ronti, (PG) 06010, Italy
Tel: (075) 8570083, Fax: (075) 8570014
6 Rooms, Double: €220–€590
4 Suites: €390–€730
Open: Mar 1 to Nov 15, Credit cards: AX, MC, VS
HOTEL

As you twist up the steep, narrow road from Spoleto toward Monteluco, you will see on your left an appealing, ochre-colored villa. The setting looks so fabulous that you will hope this is your hotel. It is, and you won't be disappointed. The Eremo delle Grazie is an astounding property—truly a living museum, with history simply oozing from every nook and cranny. The property has been the home of the Lalli family for many years, but its roots hark back to the 5th century when a small grotto where religious hermits came to live occupied the site. The grotto still exists, but now serves as a wine cellar behind the bar. From its humble beginnings the importance of this grotto grew, becoming so well known that one of Italy's important cardinals, Camillo Cybo, lived here (his bedroom is now one of the guestrooms). The cardinal enjoyed his comfort so instead of residing in the small damp grotto, he slept in a lovely bedroom, which he had painted to look like a cave. One of my favorite places in Eremo delle Grazie is the tiny, incredibly beautiful, vaulted chapel with beautifully preserved 15th-century paintings of the life of Mary. Another favorite is the splendid terrace with a sweeping view of the glorious Umbrian landscape. According to Signor Lalli, Michelangelo was once a guest here. In his letter to Vasari, Michelangelo wrote that he left part of his heart at Eremo delle Grazie—as you will, too.

⬛🏌📇☎🐴@W P 🍴🏊🚶🐴🍇

EREMO DELLE GRAZIE
Host: Professor Pio Lalli
Spoleto, Monteluco, (PG) 06049, Italy
Tel: (0743) 49 624, Fax: (0743) 49 650
6 Rooms, Double: €190–€210
4 Suites: €230–€320
Open: all year, Credit cards: all major
Abitare La Storia
HOTEL

The walled hill town of Spoleto is a must on any trip to Umbria. What Spoleto has that is so outstanding is its Bridge of Towers (Ponte delle Torri), an absolutely awesome feat of engineering. Built in the 13th century on the foundations of an old Roman aqueduct, this bridge, spanning a vast crevasse, is supported by ten Gothic arches that soar into the sky. The Hotel Gattapone (a mustard-yellow building with dark-green shutters) is built into the hillside and provides a box-seat location to admire this architectural masterpiece. As you enter, there is a cozy reception area. To the left is a bright, sunny lounge with modern black-leather sofas, a long black-leather bar, very pretty deep-blue walls, large pots of green plants, an antique grandfather clock, and, best of all, an entire wall of glass which provides a bird's-eye view of the bridge. To the right of the reception area, steps sweep down to another bar and lounge where breakfast is served. This room is even more starkly modern, with deep-red wall coverings. The newer wing of the hotel houses the superior-category bedrooms, each with a sitting area and large view windows. In the original section of the hotel the bedrooms are smaller, but also very attractive and every one has a view. Although most of the hotels in this guide have more of an antique ambiance, the Gattapone is highly recommended—a special hotel offering great warmth of welcome and superb vistas.

HOTEL GATTAPONE
Host: Dr. Pier Hanke Giulio
Via del Ponte, 6
Spoleto, (PG) 06049, Italy
Tel: (0743) 22 34 47, Fax: (0743) 22 34 48
15 Rooms, Double: €120–€230
Open: all year, Credit cards: all major
HOTEL

Le Logge di Silvignano, a stunning castle of creamy-beige stone, embraces one side of a tiny 12th-century village with a population of about 85 people tucked high in the hills north of Spoleto. It is not surprising to learn the building was originally a strategic lookout to guard against enemy attack since the setting is breathtaking, with a sweeping view of the narrow valley far below. Although termed a "castle" the structure is not in the least foreboding, but rather a splendid edifice with a handsome, open, arched gallery supported by ornately carved, octagonal pillars stretching across the front. There are six beautiful, individually decorated suites, all extremely attractive with medieval stone floors accenting handsome furniture which is either antique or handcrafted locally of wood or wrought iron. The fine bed linens and fabrics are woven locally from the Montefalco looms. A huge terrace, magically transformed into a romantic, manicured garden enhanced by fragrant, colorful roses, spreads in front of the castle to the edge of the bluff. Although Le Logge would be a winner by any standards, it is the genuine warmth and charm of your lovely hosts that make a stay here so outstanding. For dinner, guests can prepare a light meal in their own kitchenette or dine in a local restaurant. The hotel has a beautiful pool with views of the valley and a club house where guests can relax or dine upon reservation. *Directions:* Ask for detailed driving instructions.

LE LOGGE DI SILVIGNANO
Hosts: Diana & Alberto Araimo
Frazione Silvignano, 14
Spoleto, (PG) 06049, Italy
Tel & Fax: (0743) 27 40 98
1 Room, Double: €140
6 Suites: €200–€280
4 Apartments: €750–€1600 weekly
Minimum Stay Required: 2 nights
Closed: Nov to Mar, Credit cards: all major
HOTEL

The town of Spoleto has gained international fame thanks to the July Due Mondi festival, a month-long series of cultural events including ballet, theater, opera, and concerts with renowned artists, which attracts a worldwide audience. Accommodations are reserved from one year to the next. For the rest of the year, however, Spoleto holds its own along with nearby Assisi, Spello, Todi, and Perugia as an enchanting medieval stone town, rich in its historical past. The 14th-century Palazzo Dragoni, situated on a quiet little street in the heart of the town near the famous cathedral, was completely renovated by the Diotallevi family and offers charming accommodation within 15 bedrooms. Son Roberto manages the property while his parents reside in a section of the palazzo. The spacious bedrooms (larger ones are considered suites) are spread out among the three floors, reached by elevator, and have new bathrooms and many modern amenities including air conditioning. Everything possible has been done to maintain the original architecture and ambiance of a private home, with vaulted and frescoed high ceilings, antique furnishings, Oriental carpets, and Murano chandeliers. The real treat is breakfast served in the glassed-in loggia, taking in splendid views of the tiled rooftops and bell tower of the Duomo. *Directions:* Follow signs for the center of Spoleto, by way of Via P. Bunilli, passing the football field (campo sportivo). Follow white signs for the hotel.

PALAZZO DRAGONI
Host: Roberto Diotallevi Family
Via del Duomo 13
Spoleto, (PG) 06049, Italy
Tel: (0743) 222220, Fax: (0743) 222225
15 Rooms, Double: €125–€150
Open: all year, Credit cards: MC, VS
B&B

Spoleto is always a favorite with tourists, not only during the music festival (end of June until mid-July), but throughout the year. Due to its popularity, there used to be a shortage of charming places to stay within the walled city but happily that problem was solved with the opening of the Hotel San Luca in 1995. The family-owned San Luca is a splendid small hotel—very polished, very sophisticated, yet exuding great personal warmth and friendliness. Built within a 19th-century tannery, the hotel (which is painted yellow and has a traditional red-tiled roof) only hints at its past. The renovation has been so extensive that much of what you see today is of new construction, but the ambiance is old world. From the moment you enter, there is a fresh, luminous atmosphere with pastel walls reflecting light streaming in through large arched windows opening onto a central courtyard. The reception lounge is especially appealing, with comfortable chairs upholstered in cheerful peach fabric grouped around a large fireplace and a few choice antiques adding greatly to the homelike feeling. A pair of canaries in an antique birdcage repeats the color scheme. The spacious, pastel-colored, completely soundproofed guestrooms are all equally attractive and well equipped with lots of closets, excellent lighting, and large, exceptionally modern bathrooms. And the surprise is that the price for such high quality is amazingly low.

HOTEL SAN LUCA
Host: Daniela Zuccari
Via Interna delle Mura, 21
Spoleto, (PG) 06049, Italy
Tel: (0743) 22 33 99, Fax: (0743) 22 38 00
33 Rooms, Double: €110–€240
2 Suites: €210–€300
Open: all year, Credit cards: all major
HOTEL

Italy abounds with romantic places to stay, but none can surpass the outstanding beauty of the Villa Milani. This stunning property, on a hill overlooking Spoleto, just about has it all: enchanting architecture, breathtaking 360-degree view, splendid decor, gorgeous antiques, and owners who shower their guests with kindness. The villa was built in 1880 by one of Rome's most famous architects, Giovanni Battista Milani, the grandfather of your hostess Giovanna Milani Capobianchi. Milani obviously poured both his talent and heart into his countryside retreat, embellishing his home with splendid ceilings, fireplaces, columns, marble statues, romantic gardens, and ancient Roman artifacts. The result is splendid. The current owners lived for many years in Rome then changed their lifestyle completely and moved to Spoleto, where they tenderly restored the home to its original splendor, adding beautiful bathrooms to each bedroom and a fantastic pool, perched on a terrace looking out to the soft wooded hills of Umbria. Giovanna must have inherited some of her grandfather's talent, for she has decorated each room to perfection. The smallest room is also the most romantic, located in the tower with windows on four sides. *Directions:* On S.S.3, coming from the north turn right at the second exit; while coming from the south, turn left at the first exit (opposite the Monteluco road). At the first intersection turn left and go uphill following signs to the villa.

VILLA MILANI
Hosts: Giovanna & Luigi Capobianchi
Localita Colle Attivoli, 4
Spoleto, (PG) 06049, Italy
Tel: (0743) 22 50 56, Fax: (0743) 49 824
11 Rooms, Double: €190–€570
Meals for hotel guests only
Open: Apr-Oct, Credit cards: all major
HOTEL

In order to stand out among the crowd of recently opened bed and breakfasts in Italy, many hosts have begun to specialize according to their own personal interests. This is true for enthusiastic and friendly hosts, Alberto and his Brazilian wife Luzia, who opened a gourmet vegetarian bed and breakfast on their isolated 27-acre farm up on a mountain ridge between Perugia and Lake Trasimeno, the first of its kind in Umbria. A 4-kilometer gravel road ends at the panoramic property with its main house, two stone guesthouses, and cultural center where courses on yoga and meditation and ethnic music concerts are held. An informal ambiance prevails and the total respect for nature and tranquility is evident among guests who take hikes in the surrounding woods or read poolside, enjoying both sunrise and sunset over the opposite valleys. The ten neat rooms with independent outside entrances are comfortably decorated with teakwood beds and armoires and the paintings of a reputed artist. The sun-filled dining room is where guests convene for Luzia's and Alberto's famed fare based on strictly organic produce from the farm. So unique is this bed and breakfast that the BBC did a documentary on it, and it has been acclaimed one of the ten best vegetarian destinations in a US magazine. *Directions:* From Perugia follow route 220 for approximately 22 km and turn right before Tavernelle at Colle San Paolo.

COUNTRY HOUSE MONTALI
Hosts: Luzia & Alberto Musacchio
Via Montali 23
Tavernelle di Panicale, (PG) 06068, Italy
Tel: (075) 8350680, Fax: (075) 8350144
10 Rooms, Double: €180–€220*
Minimum Stay Required: 3 nights
*Includes breakfast & dinner
Open: Mar to Oct, Credit cards: MC, VS
B&B

Crowning the top of a small hill near the enchanting walled village of Todi (which you can see in the distance), the Relais Todini has a breathtaking, 360-degree view of wooded hills, soft valleys, manicured fields, vineyards, and tiny villages. You will be captivated at first sight of this charming, 14th-century stone hotel with architectural roots going back to the Etruscan-Roman period. Although built of rustic, tan-colored stone, there is nothing rustic about this hotel. From the moment you walk through the manicured gardens and into the beautiful frescoed lobby, you are surrounded by elegance and luxury. You register at an intimate table rather than a hotel-like counter before being shown to your room. All the guestrooms are beautifully decorated and the suites are especially opulent, with fine antique furniture and lush fabrics. The public rooms are also handsomely furnished, particularly the dining room with its tall-back chairs upholstered in tapestry and charming chandeliers embellished with clusters of grapes. One wall has windows of glass that open out to a terrace and beyond to a large swimming pool. On the estate tennis, biking, walking, swimming and a gorgeous health and body center with Turkish baths are just a few of the options available to guests. *Directions:* From Rome, take the A1 north, exit at Orte. Follow E45 toward Perugia. Exit at Casigliano-Collevalenza and follow signs toward Todi. Turn left Rosceto Scalo to the hotel.

❄ ☕ 🎿 💳 ☎ 🍴 @ 🍷 P ⁇ 🚭 🌿 🏊 🚶 🖼 💰 🐎 🍇

ROMANTIK HOTEL RELAIS TODINI
Host: Clementi Paolo
Collevalenza
Todi, (PG) 06050, Italy
Tel: (075) 88 75 21, Fax: (075) 88 71 82
12 Rooms, Double: €180–€360
Restaurant open Thu to Sun
Open: all year, Credit cards: all major
Romantik Hotels
HOTEL

Fortunate guests at the fascinating Tenuta di Canonica are assured of an unforgettable stay. Maria and Daniele, with son Michelangelo, have transformed a massive stone tower with foundation dating to the ancient Roman period and adjoining century-old house into a bed and breakfast of dreams. The spacious living room with stone fireplace and vaulted ceiling is reached down a few stairs from the entryway and looks out over the stunning valley down to Lake Corbara. Outstanding medieval architectural features such as stone walls, brick floors, and high, beamed ceilings have been enhanced by Provence-inspired colors. Stairs lead up to the library and bedrooms are divided between the three-story tower and house, respecting the epoch of each: bathrooms in the medieval quarters have gray stone tiles and travertine, while the others have white tile alternating with terracotta pieces. Each tastefully decorated, antique-filled room has some attractive feature, whether it be the more suite-like arrangements with sitting area or the smaller corner rooms with head-spinning views over hills and up to Todi. Common areas include a dining room and large swimming pool with 360-degree views. Cooking classes can also arranged.

Directions: From Todi take the road for Orvieto, turning right at the sign for Prado/Titignano. After 2 km turn left for Cordigliano and follow the signpost for Tenuta di Canonica to the end of the road (1 km).

TENUTA DI CANONICA
Hosts: Maria & Daniele Fano
Localita: Canonica
Todi, (PG) 06059, Italy
Tel: (075) 8947545, Fax: (075) 8947581
8 Rooms, Double: €160–€195
3 Suites: €200–€250
2 Apartments: €950 weekly
Dinners: €40
Closed: Dec 1 to Mar 1, Credit cards: MC, VS
B&B, SELF CATERING

Umbria's most international acclaimed wines are without doubt those of Lungarotti, whose 600 acres of vineyards produce a long list of both reds and whites, grappa, and olive oil. Besides a 5 star hotel, the Tre Vaselle, and a wine museum, the family has now branched out to offer accommodation on the farm in the center of their vineyards. At a short distance from Torgiano, the Lungarotti center, the typical elongated stone farmhouse dating to the 1700's has been converted into ten refined country apartments with swimming pool. A separate house at the entrance contains a reception area and breakfast room. Breakfast is served on the terrace overlooking the vines in warmer weather. Your friendly and accommodating hostess (very little English spoken), Gabriella, lives on the property and assists guests. The apartments can sleep from two to six and have living rooms with kitchenette corners, basic white tiled bathrooms and outdoor garden space. A clean country look is achieved with striped cushions on wicker or wrought iron furniture, an occasional antique, painted accents on white walls and Deruta hand-painted hanging plates. For larger groups or families consider renting I Pometo a rustic farmhouse with four bedrooms and a pool. *Directions:* Exit the S.S.3 highway Perugia-Todi at Torgiano. Go past town towards Brufa. After 1.5 km turn left onto the estate.

POGGIO ALLE VIGNE
Host: Chara Lungarotti
Via del Colle, 46
Localita: Montespinello
Torgiano, (PG) 06089, Italy
Tel: (075) 982994, Fax: (075) 9887014
10 Apartments: €470–€840 weekly
Country House: €850–€1600 weekly
Minimum Stay Required: 7 nights Jul & Aug
Open: all year, Credit cards: all major
B&B, SELF CATERING

The elegant Le Tre Vaselle is located in Torgiano, a small wine village not far from Assisi. The interior reflects the ambiance of a graceful country manor with sophisticated furnishings and exquisite taste displayed in every detail. The hotel belongs to the Lungarotti family who are famous for their production of superb wines and who own all of the vineyards surrounding Torgiano for as far as the eye can see. Excellent meals, accompanied by fine Lungarotti wines, are served in the beautiful dining room. The guestrooms are attractively decorated and offer every amenity of a deluxe hotel, including wireless Internet. Le Tre Vaselle also has outstanding conference rooms furnished in antiques with adjacent dining rooms. The Lungarotti family has thought of everything—to keep the wives happy while their husbands are in meetings, with a new spa and cooking classes are sometimes offered. Other diversions include an outdoor swimming pool, an indoor pool with whirlpool, a sauna, a gym, and even a small outdoor amphitheater. The Lungarottis also have a private wine museum that would be a masterpiece anywhere in the world. Not only do they have an incredible and comprehensive collection of anything pertaining to wine throughout the ages, but the display is a work of art. If you are interested in the production of wine, the museum alone would be worth a detour to Le Tre Vaselle. *Directions:* The hotel is well marked in the center of town.

❊ ☕ ✗ ♨ 💳 ☎ 🏨 🏋 @ W ♉ P ‖ ✿ ≈ ⚓ 🏃 🐎 🦌

LE TRE VASELLE
Host: Lungarotti Family
Via Garibaldi, 48
Torgiano, (PG) 06089, Italy
Tel: (075) 98 80 447, Fax: (075) 98 80 214
60 Rooms, Double: €215–€245
13 Suites: €285
Open: Mar 1 to Dec 31, Credit cards: all major
HOTEL

Just off the busy road that connects the major towns of Umbria—Perugia, Assisi, Spoleto, and Todi—is the elegant country house Giulia, which has been in the Petrucci family since its 14th-century origins. Later additions were built on to the main stone villa, one of which Signora Caterina has opened up to guests. Time seems to have stood still in the six bedrooms, all but one with en suite bathroom, and filled with lovely antique wrought-iron beds, armoires, and period paintings. They are divided among two floors, accessed by a steep stone staircase, the largest having a ceiling fresco depicting the local landscape. Another room with handicapped facilities has been added on the ground floor. Breakfast is served either in the chandeliered dining room upstairs, with Oriental carpets, lace curtains, and a large fireplace, or under the oak trees in the front garden during the warmer months. Part of the barn has been converted into two independent units for up to four persons, including a fully equipped kitchenette. Although the large swimming pool overlooks a rather barren field and the distant main road, it is a welcome respite after a full day of touring, which guests do a lot of from this strategically convenient location. *Directions:* Just off the Perugia-Spoleto route 75 between Trevi and Campello.

CASA GIULIA
Host: Caterina Alessandrini Petrucci
Loc. Corciano, 1
Trevi, (PG) 06039, Italy
Tel: (0742) 78257, Fax: (0742) 381632
6 Rooms, Double: €88–€108
1 Suite: €95–€125
3 Apartments: €155 daily, €900 weekly
Open: all year, Credit cards: AX, MC, VS
B&B, SELF CATERING

When the Marti family from Rome came across the abandoned castle of Montegualandro 20 years ago, it was love at first sight—only pure passion could have driven them to tackle such an overwhelming project as the entire restoration of the property following original plans. A winding dirt road (1.5 kilometers) leads up to the gates of the walled 9th-century castle. As you enter into the courtyard, the main building and family residence lies to the left and immediately to the right is a cluster of stone dwellings, originally farmers' quarters, with small tower, stable, pottery kiln, dove house, and private chapel. There are four rustic guest apartments, cleverly incorporating all original architectural features. All different, each has a living area with fireplace, very basic kitchen facilities, and bathroom, and is furnished with country-style antiques. A walk up in the turreted walls gives a glimpse of the spectacular view out over olive groves to the lake. An internet point has been set up in the newly restored library. The Martis take special interest in guests' needs, providing a breakfast basket upon arrival, and can also suggest easy day trips. Cortona is just 10 kilometers away. *Directions:* Montegualandro is marked on most maps. Leave the A1-Perugia highway at Tuoro. Take the road 75 bis towards Cortona and Arezzo. After 3 km, at km sign 44,700, follow the signs up to the castle or call from town.

CASTELLO DI MONTEGUALANDRO
Hosts: Franca & Claudio Marti
Loc. Montegualandro 1
Tuoro Sul Trasimeno, (PG) 06069, Italy
Tel & Fax: (075) 8230267
4 Apartments: €700–€800
Minimum Stay Required: 3 nights
Open: all year, Credit cards: none
SELF CATERING

Index

A

Abbazia di Monte Oliveto Maggiore, 38
Abbey Sant'Antimo, 37
Accommodation
  B&B, 17
  Hotels, 19
  Self Catering, 20
Affiliations, 5
Agnolo, L', Montepulciano, 138
Airfare, 5
Albergo Pietrasanta, Pietrasanta, 154
Albergo Villa Marta, Lucca, 121
Albergotto, Hotel, Florence, 86
Alla Corte degli Angeli, Lucca, 122
Allerona
  I Casali di Monticchio, 214
Amelia-Macchie
  Relais La Tenuta del Gallo, 215
Antella-Florence
  Villa Il Colle, 54
Antica Casa dei Rassicurati, Montecarlo, 131
Antica Dimora Firenze, Florence, 87
Antica Dimora Johlea, Florence, 88
Antica Fattoria del Colle, Deruta, 231
Antica Torre Di Via Tornabuoni, Florence, 89
Antico Borgo Poggiarello, Monteriggioni, 142
Antico Casale di Scansano, Scansano, 197
Antico Forziere, L', Deruta, 232
Antico Pozzo, Hotel L', San Gimignano, 176
Arezzo, 43
Assisi, 46
  Fortezza, La, 216
  Malvarina, 217
  Palazzo, Il, 218
  Podere La Fornace, 219
  Residenza d'Epoca San Crispino, 220
  Rocca Medioevale, 47
  Santa Chiara, 47
  St. Francis's Basilica, 46
  Umbra, Hotel, 221
Assisi-Armenzano
  Romantik Hotel Le Silve di Armenzano, 222

B

Badia a Passignano Abbey, 26
Badia, La, Orvieto, 246
Bagni Di Pisa Natural Resort, San Guiliano Terme, 188
Bagno a Ripoli
  Villa Olmi Resort, 55
Bagno Vignoni, 37
  Locanda del Loggiato, La, 56
Bagnone
  Villa Mimosa, 57
Bagnorégio, 51
Banks, 6
Barberino Val d'Elsa, 31
  Fattoria Casa Sola, 58
  Paretaio, Il, 59
Baschi
  Pomurlo Vecchio, 223
Belvedere di San Leonino, Hotel, San Leonino, 190
Benozzo Gozzoli, 48
Bettolle
  Locanda La Bandita, 60
Bettona
  Torre Burchio, 224
Bevagna, 47
  Orto degli Angeli, L', 225
Bibbona
  Podere Le Mezzelune, 61
Borghetto Country Inn, Il, Montefiridolfi, 132
Borgo Argenina, Gaiole in Chianti, 114
Borgo Elena, Cortona, 79
Borgo Iesolana, Bucine, 63
Borgo Il Melone, Cortona, 80
Borgo Pretale, Sovicille, 204

Borgo San Lorenzo
  Monsignor della Casa, 62
Borgo Spante, Ospedaletto, 251
Borro, Il, San Giustino Valdarno, 186
Boscarecce, Le, Castelfiorentino, 69
Botticelli, Hotel, Florence, 90
Brufani Palace, Hotel, Perugia, 252
Brunello, 23, 34
Brunello di Montalcino, 38
Bucine
  Borgo Iesolana, 63
Buonconvento
  Ripolina, La, 64

C

Caldana
  Montebelli, 65
Campagnatico
  Villa Bellaria, 66
Canalicchio di Collazzone
  Relais Il Canalicchio, 226
Canonica a Cerreto
  Canonica a Cerreto, 67
Capalbio
  Ghiaccio Bosco, 68
Car Rental, 6
Casa Bolsinina, Monteroni d'Arbia, 144
Casa Branca, Gubbio, 237
Casa del Garbo, La, Florence, 91
Casa Giulia, Trevi, 266
Casa Mezzuola, Greve in Chianti, 120
Casa Palmira, Feriolo, 85
Casa San Martino, Lisciano Niccone, 240
Casale del Cotone, Il, San Gimignano, 177
Casale Il Caggio, Civitella in Val di Chiana, 78
Casali della Aiola, Vagliagli, 208
Casalone, Il, Orbetello Scalo, 146
Casanova di Pescille, San Gimignano, 178
Casella, La, Ficulle, 233
Casolare di Libbiano, San Gimignano, 179

Castel del Piano
  Villa Aureli, 227
Castelfiorentino
  Boscarecce, Le, 69
Castelletto di Montebenichi, Montebenichi, 130
Castellina in Chianti, 31
  Fattoria Tregole, 70
  Locanda Le Piazze, 71
  Tenuta di Ricavo, 72
Castello d'Albola, 33
Castello di Brolio, 31
Castello di Loreto, Loreto—Todi, 241
Castello di Meleto, Gaiole in Chianti, 34, 115
Castello di Montegualandro, Tuoro Sul Trasimeno, 267
Castello di Ripa d'Orcia, Castiglione d'Orcia, 76
Castello di Spaltenna, Gaiole in Chianti, 116
Castello di Tornano, Gaiole in Chianti, 117
Castello di Vicarello, Poggi del Sasso, 157
Castello di Volpaia, 32
Castelnuovo Berardenga, 31
  Fontanelle, Hotel le, 73
  Relais Borgo San Felice, Hotel, 74
Castelnuovo dell'Abate, 37
Castiglion Fiorentino
  Relais San Pietro, 75
Castiglione d'Orcia
  Castello di Ripa d'Orcia, 76
Cetona
  Frateria di Padre Eligio, La, 77
Chianti Classico, 27, 31, 34
Chianti Wine, 31
Chiusa, La, Montefollonico, 39, 135
Cisterna, La, San Gimignano, 180
Citta della Pieve
  Madonna delle Grazie, 228
  Relais dei Magi, 229
Civita di Bagnorégio, 51
Civitella in Val di Chiana
  Casale Il Caggio, 78
Colle San Paolo
  Villa di Monte Solare, Hotel, 230
Collepino, 47

Cortona, 44
    Borgo Elena, 79
    Borgo Il Melone, 80
    Falconiere Relais e Ristorante, Il, 81
    Piazza della Repubblica, 44
    Villa di Piazzano, 82
    Villa Marsili, 83
Cortona-Petrignano del Lago
    Relais alla Corte del Sole, 84
Country House Montali, Tavernelle di Panicale, 261
Credit Cards, 7
Crocetta, La, San Casciano dei Bagni, 171
Currency, 6

D

Della Fortezza, Hotel, Sorano, 202
Deruta
    Antica Fattoria del Colle, 231
    Antico Forziere, L', 232
Dionora, La, Montepulciano, 139
Doccia, La, Pelago, 150
Domenico di Bartolo, 29
Driving, 7
    Road Signs, 14
    Tolls, 14

E

Eastern Umbria, 43
ENIT, 11
Eremo delle Grazie, Spoleto, 255
Euro, 6

F

Fagiolari, Panzano in Chianti, 148
Falconiere Relais e Ristorante, Il, Cortona, 81
Fattoressa, La, Galluzzo, 119
Fattoria Casa Sola, Barberino Val d'Elsa, 58
Fattoria dei Barbi, 37
Fattoria di Petrognano, Pomino, 158
Fattoria di Vibio, Montecastello di Vibio, 242
Fattoria La Loggia, Montefiridolfi, 133
Fattoria La Palazzina, Radicofani, 167

Fattoria Solaio, Solaio-Radicondoli, 201
Fattoria Tregole, Castellina in Chianti, 70
Feriolo
    Casa Palmira, 85
Ficulle
    Casella, La, 233
Finding Your Accommodation, 8
Finding Your Bed and Breakfast
    Directions, 8
Florence, 23, 31
    Places to Stay:
        Albergotto, Hotel, 86
        Antica Dimora Firenze, 87
        Antica Dimora Johlea, 88
        Antica Torre Di Via Tornabuoni, 89
        Botticelli, Hotel, 90
        Casa del Garbo, La, 91
        Helvetia and Bristol, Hotel, 92
        Hermitage, Hotel, 93
        In Piazza della Signoria, 94
        Lungarno, Hotel, 95
        Marignolle Relais & Charme, 96
        Niccolini al Duomo, 97
        Orto de'Medici, Hotel, 98
        Palazzo dal Borgo—Hotel Aprile, 99
        Palazzo Galletti, 100
        Palazzo Magnani Feroni, 101
        Regency, Hotel, 102
        Relais Uffizi, 103
        Silla, Hotel, 104
        Torre di Bellosguardo, 105
        Torricella, La, 106
        Villa La Massa, Hotel, 107
        Villa La Vedetta, 108
    Sightseeing
        Baptistry, 24
        Duomo, 24
        Galleria dell'Accademia, 23
        Michelangelo's David, 23
        Palazzo Vecchio, 23
        Piazza della Signoria, 23
        Pitti Palace, 25

Index

Florence, 23, 31 (continued)
   Sightseeing:
      Ponte Vecchio, 23
      Uffizi Museum, 24
Florence-Fiesole
   Pensione Bencista, 109
   Villa Fiesole, Hotel, 110
   Villa San Michele, 111
Fontanelle, Hotel le, Castelnuovo Berardenga, 73
Fontanelle, Le, Montemerano, 136
Fonte, La, San Gimignano, 181
Fonteverde, Hotel, San Casciano dei Bagni, 172
Forcoli
   Villa Il Torrino, 112
Forte dei Marmi
   Hotel Byron, 113
Fortezza, La, Assisi, 216
Franchini, Nicole, 13
Frateria di Padre Eligio, La, Cetona, 77
Fratta Todina
   Palazzetta del Vescovo, La, 234

G

Gaiole in Chianti, 31, 32, 34
   Borgo Argenina, 114
   Castello di Meleto, 115
   Castello di Spaltenna, 116
   Castello di Tornano, 117
   Ultimo Mulino, L', 118
Galluzzo
   Fattoressa, La, 119
Gasoline Prices, 9
Gattapone, Hotel, Spoleto, 256
Ghiaccio Bosco, Capalbio, 68
Ghirlanda, La, Gualdo Cattaneo, 235
Grand Hotel Continental Siena, Siena, 198
Greve in Chianti, 31
   Casa Mezzuola, 120
Grotta Giusti Natural Resort, Monsummano Terme, 129
Gualdo Cattaneo
   Ghirlanda, La, 235

Gualdo Tadino
   Le Terre del Verde, 236
Gubbio, 45
   Casa Branca, 237
   Locanda Del Gallo, 238
   Relais Ducale, 239
Guido Monaco, 43

H

Haunting Beauty of Umbria, The, Itinerary, 41
Helvetia and Bristol, Hotel, Florence, 92
Hermitage, Hotel, Florence, 93
Hidden Treasures of Italy, 13
Holidays, 9
Hotel Byron, Forte dei Marmi, 113
Hotelito Lupaia, Torrita di Siena, 207

I

I Casali di Monticchio, Allerona, 214
In Piazza della Signoria, Florence, 94
Information on Italy, 11
Italian Government Travel Offices, 11
Itineraries, 4
   Haunting Beauty of Umbria, The, 41
   Romantic Tuscany, 21

L

Lake Trasimeno, 44
   Castiglione del Lago, 44
Languages Spoken, 7
Lisciano Niccone
   Casa San Martino, 240
Locanda del Capitano, La, Montone, 244
Locanda del Castello, La, San Giovanni d'Asso, 184
Locanda del Gallo, Gubbio, 238
Locanda del Loggiato, La, Bagno Vignoni, 56
Locanda dell'Amorosa, Sinalunga, 200
Locanda La Bandita, Bettolle, 60
Locanda Le Piazze, Castellina in Chianti, 71
Locanda L'Elisa, Lucca, 123
Locanda Palazzone, Orvieto, 247
Locanda Rosati, Orvieto, 248

Locanda Solomeo, Perugia, 253
Locanda, Hotel La, Volterra, 211
Locanda, La, Radda in Chianti, 162
Logge di Silvignano, Le, Spoleto, 257
Loreto—Todi
    Castello di Loreto, 241
Lucca
    Albergo Villa Marta, 121
    Alla Corte degli Angeli, 122
    Locanda L'Elisa, 123
    Palazzo Alexander, 124
    Romea, La, 125
Lucignanello Bandini, San Giovanni d'Asso, 185
Lungarno, Hotel, Florence, 95

M

Madonna delle Grazie, Citta della Pieve, 228
Malvarina, Assisi, 217
Maps, 12
    Itineraries
        Haunting Beauty of Umbria, The, 41
        Romantic Tuscany, 21
    Michelin Maps, 12
Marignolle Relais & Charme, Florence, 96
Massa Marittima
    Tenuta Il Cicalino, 126
    Villa Il Tesoro, 127
Mercatale Val di Pesa
    Salvadonica, 128
Michelin Maps, 12
Monsignor della Casa, Borgo San Lorenzo, 62
Monsummano Terme
    Grotta Giusti Natural Spa Resort, 129
Montalcino, 38
Montebelli, Caldana, 65
Montebenichi
    Castelletto di Montebenichi, 130
Montecarlo
    Antica Casa dei Rassicurati, 131
Montecastello di Vibio
    Fattoria di Vibio, 242

Montefalco, 47
    Villa Zuccari, 243
Montefiridolfi
    Borghetto Country Inn, Il, 132
    Fattoria La Loggia, 133
    Villa Sant'Andrea, 134
Montefollonico, 39
    Chiusa, La, 39, 135
Montemerano
    Fontanelle, Le, 136
    Villa Acquaviva, 137
Montepulciano, 23, 34, 35
    Agnolo, L', 138
    Dionora, La, 139
    Montorio, 140
    Palazzo Comunale, 35
    Palazzo Contucci, 35
    Piazza Grande, 35
    Temple of San Biagio, 35
    Villa Poggiano, 141
    Wineries, 35
Monteriggioni, 26
    Antico Borgo Poggiarello, 142
    Romantik Hotel Monteriggioni, 143
Monteroni d'Arbia
    Casa Bolsinina, 144
Montestigliano, Rosia, 170
Monticchiello, 36
Montone
    Locanda del Capitano, La, 244
Montorio, Montepulciano, 140

N

Narni
    Podere Costa Romana, 245
Niccolini al Duomo, Florence, 97

O

Olmo, L', Pienza, 151
Orbetello
    San Biagio Relais, 145

Orbetello Scalo
  Casalone, Il, 146
Orto degli Angeli, L', Bevagna, 225
Orto de'Medici, Hotel, Florence, 98
Orvieto, 49, 51
  Places to Stay:
    Badia, La, 246
    Locanda Palazzone, 247
    Locanda Rosati, 248
    Palazzo Piccolomini, Hotel, 249
    Villa Ciconia, 250
  Sightseeing
    Chapel of San Brizio, 51
    Duomo, 51
    St. Patrick's Well, 51
Ospedaletto
  Borgo Spante, 251
Ottone (Portoferraio)
  Villa Ottone, Hotel, 147

P

Palazzetta del Vescovo, La, Fratta Todina, 234
Palazzo Alexander, Lucca, 124
Palazzo dal Borgo—Hotel Aprile, Florence, 99
Palazzo Dragoni, Spoleto, 258
Palazzo Galletti, Florence, 100
Palazzo Magnani Feroni, Florence, 101
Palazzo Piccolomini, Hotel, Orvieto, 249
Palazzo Ravizza, Siena, 199
Palazzo Terranova, Ronti, 254
Palazzo, Il, Assisi, 218
Panzano in Chianti
  Fagiolari, 148
  Villa Le Barone, 149
Paretaio, Il, Barberino Val d'Elsa, 59
Passignano in Chianti, 26
Pelago
  Doccia, La, 150
Pellicano, Il, Porto Ercole, 159
Pensione Bencista, Florence-Fiesole, 109

Perugia, 45
  Brufani Palace, Hotel, 252
  Fontana Maggiore, 45
  Locanda Solomeo, 253
  Piazza IV Novembre, 45
Pienza, 36
  Olmo, L', 151
  Relais Il Chiostro di Pienza, Hotel, 152
  Traverse, Le, 153
Pietrasanta
  Albergo Pietrasanta, 154
Pieve di Caminino, Roccatederighi, 169
Pisa
  Relais dei Fiori, 155
  Relais dell'Orologio, Hotel, 156
Places to Stay, Classifications, 12
Podere Costa Romana, Narni, 245
Podere La Fornace, Assisi, 219
Podere Le Mezzelune, Bibbona, 61
Podere Terreno, Radda in Chianti, 163
Podere Val delle Corti, Radda in Chianti, 164
Podere Villuzza, San Gimignano, 182
Poggi del Sasso
  Castello di Vicarello, 157
Poggibonsi, 31
Poggio ai Santi, San Vincenzo, 193
Poggio alle Vigne, Torgiano, 264
Poggio Antico, 38
Pomino
  Fattoria di Petrognano, 158
Pomurlo Vecchio, Baschi, 223
Pope Clement VII, 51
Pope Pius II, 36
Pornanino, Radda in Chianti, 165
Porto Ercole
  Pellicano, Il, 159
Porto Santo Stefano
  Torre di Cala Piccola, Hotel, 160
Prato
  Villa Rucellai di Canneto, 161

R

Radda in Chianti, 27, 31, 32, 33
   Locanda, La, 162
   Podere Terreno, 163
   Podere Val delle Corti, 164
   Pornanino, 165
   Relais Vignale, 166
Radici, Le, San Casciano dei Bagni, 173
Radicofani
   Fattoria La Palazzina, 167
Regency, Hotel, Florence, 102
Reggello-Vaggio
   Villa Rigacci, 168
Regions of Italy
   Tuscany, 2
Relais alla Corte del Sole, Cortona-Petrignano del Lago, 84
Relais Borgo San Felice, Htl, Castelnuovo Berardenga, 74
Relais dei Fiori, Pisa, 155
Relais dei Magi, Citta della Pieve, 229
Relais dell'Orologio, Hotel, Pisa, 156
Relais Ducale, Gubbio, 239
Relais Il Canalicchio, Canalicchio di Collazzone, 226
Relais Il Chiostro di Pienza, Hotel, Pienza, 152
Relais La Tenuta del Gallo, Amelia-Macchie, 215
Relais San Pietro, Castiglion Fiorentino, 75
Relais Uffizi, Florence, 103
Relais Vignale, Radda in Chianti, 166
Relais Villa Arceno, San Gusmè, 189
Reservations, 12
   Email, 13
   Fax, 13
   Hidden Treasures of Italy, 13
   Telephone, 13
Residence San Sano, Hotel, San Sano, 192
Residenza d'Epoca San Crispino, Assisi, 220
Rigo, Il, San Quirico d'Orcia, 191
Ripolina, La, Buonconvento, 64
Roads
   Autostrada, 14
   Raccordo, 14
   Strada Statale, 14
   Superstrada, 14

Roccatederighi
   Pieve di Caminino, 169
Romantic Tuscany, Itinerary, 21
Romantik Hotel Le Silve di Armenzano, Assisi-Armenzano, 222
Romantik Hotel Monteriggioni, Monteriggioni, 143
Romantik Hotel Relais Todini, Todi, 262
Romea, La, Lucca, 125
Ronti
   Palazzo Terranova, 254
Rosia
   Montestigliano, 170
Rosolaccio, Il, San Gimignano, 183

S

Safety, 15
Salvadonica, Mercatale Val di Pesa, 128
San Biagio Relais, Orbetello, 145
San Casciano dei Bagni, 31
   Crocetta, La, 171
   Fonteverde, Hotel, 172
   Radici, Le, 173
San Casciano Val di Pesa
   Villa Il Poggiale, 174
   Villa Mangiacane, 175
San Gimignano, 28
   Antico Pozzo, Hotel L', 176
   Casale del Cotone, Il, 177
   Casanova di Pescille, 178
   Casolare di Libbiano, 179
   Cisterna, La, 180
   Fonte, La, 181
   Podere Villuzza, 182
   Ristorante Dorando, 28
   Ristorante Il Pino, 28
   Rosolaccio, Il, 183
San Giovanni d'Asso
   Locanda del Castello, La, 184
   Lucignanello Bandini, 185
San Giustino Valdarno
   Borro, Il, 186
   Villa Cassia di Baccano, 187

Index

San Guiliano Terme
    Bagni Di Pisa Natural Spa Resort, 188
San Gusmè
    Relais Villa Arceno, 189
San Leonino
    Belvedere di San Leonino, Hotel, 190
San Luca, Hotel, Spoleto, 259
San Quirico d'Orcia, 37
    Horti Leonini, 37
San Quirico d'Orcia
    Rigo, Il, 191
San Sano
    Residence San Sano, Hotel, 192
San Vincenzo
    Poggio ai Santi, 193
Sarteano
    Sovana, La, 194
Sassetta
    Tenuta La Bandita, 195
Saturnia
    Villa Clodia, 196
Scansano
    Antico Casale di Scansano, 197
Selvino, Il, Terricciola, 206
Siena, 28, 31, 34
    Places to Stay:
        Grand Hotel Continental Siena, 198
        Palazzo Ravizza, 199
    Sightseeing
        Baptistry, 30
        Duomo, 29
        Museo Civico, 30
        Museo dell'Opera Metropolitana, 30
        Ospedale di Santa Maria della Scala, 29
        Palazzo Pubblico, 29
        Palio delle Contrade, 28
        Piazza del Campo, 28
        Piccolomini Library, 29
Silla, Hotel, Florence, 104
Sinalunga
    Locanda dell'Amorosa, 200

Solaio-Radicondoli
    Fattoria Solaio, 201
Sorano
    della Fortezza, Hotel, 202
Southern Tuscany, 34
Sovana
    Taverna Etrusca, La, 203
Sovana, La, Sarteano, 194
Sovicille
    Borgo Pretale, 204
Sovigliano, Tavarnelle Val di Pesa, 205
Spoleto, 48
    Cathedral, 48
    Eremo delle Grazie, 255
    Gattapone, Hotel, 256
    Logge di Silvignano, Le, 257
    Palazzo Dragoni, 258
    Ponte delle Torri, 48
    San Luca, Hotel, 259
    Villa Milani, 260
St. Francis, 46

T

Tangenziale, 14
Tavarnelle Val di Pesa, 31
    Sovigliano, 205
Taverna Etrusca, La, Sovana, 203
Tavernelle di Panicale
    Country House Montali, 261
Telephones, 15
Tenuta di Canonica, Todi, 263
Tenuta di Ricavo, Castellina in Chianti, 72
Tenuta Il Cicalino, Massa Marittima, 126
Tenuta La Bandita, Sassetta, 195
Terre del Verde, Gualdo Tadino, Le, 236
Terricciola
    Selvino, Il, 206
Tipping, 16
Todi, 49
    Cathedral, 50
    Roman/Etruscan Museum, 50
    Romantik Hotel Relais Todini, 262

Todi, 49 (continued)
   San Ilario Church, 50
   Tenuta di Canonica, 263
Torgiano, 48
   Poggio alle Vigne, 264
   Tre Vaselle, Le, 48, 265
Torre Burchio, Bettona, 224
Torre di Bellosguardo, Florence, 105
Torre di Cala Piccola, Hotel, Porto Santo Stefano, 160
Torricella, La, Florence, 106
Torrita di Siena
   Hotelito Lupaia, 207
Travel Insurance, 13
Traverse, Le, Pienza, 153
Tre Vaselle, Le, Torgiano, 48, 265
Trevi
   Casa Giulia, 266
Tuoro Sul Trasimeno
   Castello di Montegualandro, 267
Tuscany, 2

U

Ultimo Mulino, L', Gaiole in Chianti, 118
Umbertide, 44
Umbra, Hotel, Assisi, 221
Umbria, 3

V

Vagliagli
   Casali della Aiola, 208
Vicchio di Mugello
   Villa Campestri, 209
Vico d'Elsa
   Volpaia, La, 210
Villa Acquaviva, Montemerano, 137
Villa Aureli, Castel del Piano, 227
Villa Bellaria, Campagnatico, 66
Villa Campestri, Vicchio di Mugello, 209
Villa Cassia di Baccano, San Giustino Valdarno, 187
Villa Ciconia, Orvieto, 250
Villa Clodia, Saturnia, 196
Villa di Monte Solare, Hotel, Colle San Paolo, 230

Villa di Piazzano, Cortona, 82
Villa Fiesole, Hotel, Florence-Fiesole, 110
Villa Il Colle, Antella-Florence, 54
Villa Il Poggiale, San Casciano Val di Pesa, 174
Villa Il Tesoro, Massa Marittima, 127
Villa Il Torrino, Forcoli, 112
Villa La Massa, Hotel, Florence, 107
Villa La Vedetta, Florence, 108
Villa Le Barone, Panzano in Chianti, 149
Villa Mangiacane, San Casciano Val di Pesa, 175
Villa Marsili, Cortona, 83
Villa Milani, Spoleto, 260
Villa Mimosa, Bagnone, 57
Villa Olmi Resort, Bagno a Ripoli, 55
Villa Ottone, Hotel, Ottone (Portoferraio), 147
Villa Poggiano, Montepulciano, 141
Villa Rigacci, Reggello-Vaggio, 168
Villa Rucellai di Canneto, Prato, 161
Villa San Michele, Florence-Fiesole, 111
Villa Sant'Andrea, Montefiridolfi, 134
Villa Zuccari, Montefalco, 243
Vino Nobile, 23, 34
Volpaia, La, Vico d'Elsa, 210
Volterra, 30
   Locanda, Hotel La, 211
   Sightseeing
      Museo Etrusco Guaracci, 30
      Piazza dei Priori, 30
      Porta all'Arco, 30

W

Western Umbria, 49
When to Visit, 16
Wineries, 31
   Cantina del Redi, 35
   Castello d'Albola, 33
   Castello di Brolio, 31
   Castello di Meleto, 34
   Castello di Volpaia, 32
   Dei, 36
   Fattoria dei Barbi, 37
   Poggio Antico, 38

KAREN BROWN wrote her first travel guide in 1976. Her personalized travel series has grown to 17 titles, which Karen and her small staff work diligently to keep updated. Karen, her husband, Rick, parents to Alexandra and Richard, live in a small town on the coast south of San Francisco.

CLARE BROWN was a travel consultant for many years, specializing in planning itineraries using charming small hotels in the countryside. Her expertise is now available to a larger audience—the readers of her daughter Karen's travel guides. When not traveling, Clare and her husband, Bill, divide their time between northern California, Colorado, and Mexico.

JUNE EVELEIGH BROWN hails from Sheffield, England and lived in Zambia and Canada before moving to northern California where she lives in San Mateo with her husband, Tony, their German Shepherd.

NICOLE FRANCHINI was born in Chicago and raised in a bilingual family (her father being Italian), but she has been residing in Italy for many years. Currently living in the countryside of Sabina near Rome with husband, Carlo, and daughters, Livia and Sabina, Nicole runs her own travel consulting business, Hidden Treasures of Italy, which organizes personalized group and individual itineraries. *www.htitaly.com.*

BARBARA MACLURCAN TAPP draws all of the delightful hotel sketches and illustrations in this guide. Barbara was raised in Sydney, Australia, where she studied interior design. Although she continues with architectural rendering and watercolor painting, she devotes much of her time to illustrating the Karen Brown guides. Barbara lives in Kensington, California, with her husband, Richard, and is Mum to Jono, Alex and Georgia. For more information about her work visit *www.barbaratapp.com.*

JANN POLLARD, the artist of the all the beautiful cover paintings in the Karen Brown series, has studied art since childhood and is well known for her outstanding impressionistic-style watercolors. Jann has received numerous achievment awards and her works are in private and corporate collections internationally. She is also a popular workshop teacher in the United States, Mexico and Europe. *www.jannpollard.com.* Fine art giclée prints of her paintings are available at *www.karenbrown.com.*

Notes

Karen Brown's World of Travel

A FREE KAREN BROWN WEBSITE MEMBERSHIP
IS INCLUDED WITH THE PURCHASE OF THIS GUIDE

$20 Value – Equal to the cover price of this book!

In appreciation for purchasing our guide, we offer a free membership that includes:

- The ability to custom plan and build unlimited itineraries
- 15% discount on all purchases made in the Karen Brown website store
- One free downloadable Karen Brown Itinerary from over 100 choices
- Karen Brown's World of Travel Newsletter—includes special offers & updates
Membership valid through December 31, 2010

To take advantage of this free offer go to the Karen Brown website shown below and create a login profile so we can recognize you as a Preferred Customer; then you can utilize the unrestricted trip planning and take advantage of the 15% store discount. Once you set up an account you will receive by email a coupon code to order the free itinerary.

Go to *www.karenbrown.com/preferred.php* to create your profile!